THE TWILIGHT'S LAST GLEAMING

On Your Own In America

Nathan L. Combs

WILL YOU SURVIVE?

First published by Dog Ear Publishing
4010 W. 86th Street, Ste H
Indianapolis, IN 46268
www.dogearpublishing.net

ISBN: 978-145750-348-1

This book is printed on acid-free paper.

Printed in the United States of America

For my children: Chris, Beckee, Randy & Jody; for my grandchildren, Nate, Shayne, Tyler, Hunter, Chyna, and Troy; for Faith and Adam … and for my fellow Americans; wherever they may be.

CONTENTS

INTRODUCTION

AT 6:30 AM ON 13 September, 1814, during the Battle of Baltimore in the War of 1812, Francis Scott Key stood on the deck of the British ship HMS Tonnant and watched the opening salvos on Fort McHenry. An involuntary "guest" of the British, Key watched as the bombardment continued non-stop the entire day. As darkness approached, and "at the twilight's last gleaming" Key could still see the American battle flag flying proudly over the fort. The bombardment continued unabated that entire night, and Key observed that "the rockets' red glare" and "the bombs bursting in air" gave proof through the night that our flag was still there.

As dawn broke on the fog-shrouded morning of the 14th, Key nervously waited to see if the tattered American battle flag was still flying high or if it had been replaced by the British Union Jack. When the fog finally cleared, Key was elated to see a huge 30 ft x 42 ft American flag flying over Fort McHenry. Moved by what he had observed, on his back to Washington, Key penned the poem that was destined to become our National Anthem.

Flash forward 196 years. America is under attack once more. This time the enemy comes from within. This time we're facing the *Grim Reaper* cleverly disguised as American citizens and cloaked in the protective cocoon of the constitution. The phrase "The Twilight's Last Gleaming" is relevant once more. The question that must be answered today is the same question that Key asked himself during that night so long ago. When the "new dawn" breaks and the fog clears from this battle, will "Old Glory" still be flying high and proud "O'er the Land of the Free and the Home of the Brave?"

CHAPTER 1

PREPARE TO SURVIVE or PREPARE TO DIE

I'M NOT GOING TO WASTE your time telling you how ridiculous American politics are or how worthless the current Congress is. I'm not going to bad-mouth President Obama, and I'm not going to lay the blame for the current state of the Union on George Bush. Nor will I insult you by telling you how perilous the situation in the Country actually is. The dangers are readily visible. If you refuse to recognize the warning signs you're either blind, brain-dead, or you buy into the BS that comes out of Washington. From a survival perspective, who's to blame is irrelevant. Whether you're a far-left Liberal or a far-right Conservative is also irrelevant. The Grim Reaper isn't political.

There are so many things that *could* go wrong it's almost inconceivable at least one of them won't happen in the near future. People are concerned. And rightly so. Many are preparing to survive whatever's coming. The bottom line is, if a national catastrophe does happen, and *you're not prepared to survive . . . you should be prepared to die.*

A lot of people will likely find that statement to be harsh. The truth usually is. Like any other "truth", you either decide it's an absolute, it has some merit, or it's all BS.

What is the truth? It doesn't matter where you look, you're not going to find it. In addition, if you did stumble across it, how would you determine it was true? The bombardment of disinformation from television, the Internet, radio, newspapers, and magazines is relentless. We're forced to listen to or read "facts" as presented by a host of "experts" who are usually paid to give an opinion that coincides with the agenda of the host. Everyone with a venue is an expert, and everyone has an opinion. They're like pop-ups. You can't escape them.

What's that old saying about opinions? Oh yeah, they're like assholes. Everyone has one.

It's almost impossible to believe anything anyone says today. Part of the problem stems from the fact that most Americans believe whatever they read or whatever they're told. "No, really, Clarice, it's true, pigs *can* fly, bears *are* Catholic, and the Pope *does* crap in the woods— it's on the Internet for crying out loud."

The news? It's usually distorted in some way to support a pre-determined conclusion or to justify an agenda. Too many people are influenced by the opinions of those from Hollywood, the music industry, and the world of sports. We've become a population with zero ability to form our own opinions. We simply adopt someone else's. Unfortunately, there are very few hard, cold facts when it comes to the news. On the plus side, most of us do know that pigs can't really fly, that *most* bears aren't Catholic, and that the Pope (probably) does not take a dump in the woods.

I think it was last Spring, perhaps early summer, when Glenn Beck was telling his listeners the only logical way to get our country back was through the ballot box. And from a logical perspective he's right. But logic has a way of disappearing when you're broke, can't find a job, and can't feed your family.

Does anyone think the average American citizen has the patience to sit around waiting to vote every two or four years in an effort to improve the situation? Do you really believe Americans will put up with this type of government for the next couple of election cycles? Furthermore, does anyone believe that electing an entirely new Congress will instantly restore our freedoms, traditions and way of life? If you do, you'd better think again.

I'm not advocating violence in any way, shape, or form. Nevertheless "shit happens," as the old saying goes, and since the country has been pushed to the brink, it's simply a matter of time until a catastrophic event of some sort initiates an open revolt against the federal government or until some hothead or radical group decides to take matters into their own hands. I don't want that to happen; you don't want that to happen, yet with each passing day the odds increase that you're going to be *On Your Own In America* sooner, rather than later.

It could happen tomorrow, it could be years from now. However, unless something dramatic occurs to prevent it, "*it*" is coming! If you want to survive whatever "*it*" is, you'd better get off your butt and make some plans. Not tomorrow either, you need to start today.

Other than voting, what can the average American citizen do to change the course the Country's on? Should we become politically active? Continue to trust those who've proven beyond any doubt they can't be trusted? Should we do nothing and hope for the best?

I can't speak for you, but where I come from hope is for losers. If you'd rather be a trusting little federal sheep and do nothing, go for it. Sit there and take what's coming. Don't make any preparations or think for yourself. Just continue to believe the rhetoric and the BS you're being fed, and eat it with the little federal spoon you've been issued.

Assuming you're still capable of thinking for yourself, doesn't it make sense to prepare to survive a worst case scenario? You can still hope for a miracle if it makes you feel better, but if there's no divine intervention, and there won't be, at least you'll have a chance.

How many people could die in a major national catastrophe? It depends on the type of disaster, of course. Yet it seems reasonable to me that as many as half of the people who read this book could be dead within the first thirty days following the inception of a major national disaster. My youngest daughter said, "But, Dad, what if only 1000 people read the book? That's only 500 people!" I wanted to tell her that if only 1000 people read the book, then the book probably sucked. However, I tactfully informed her that, while her statement was true, half is still half. Which half would you rather be a part of? What if one million people read the book? That would mean 500,000 people could be dead in the first thirty days.

Someone's bound to ask how I came up with such a high casualty figure. Simple! The same way a weatherman tells you with a straight face there's a 50% chance of rain. Maybe it will, maybe it won't. Either way, he's right. Besides, 50% is a very safe figure when you're looking for numbers to throw around. It's also a nice way of saying "I have absolutely no clue." But I like being right, so 50% it is. Use 25% or even 10% if it makes the potential casualty figures more palatable to you. Just don't tell those who might be in your version of the casualty figures that only 10% of them are going to die.

CHAPTER 2

WHAT IF?

SOMETIME IN THE NEAR FUTURE, outside a small town somewhere in Wisconsin, a man sat in his garage writing a letter similar to this?

To whoever finds this:

My name is Bill Chambers. I don't write very good and I really don't know what to say. But I'm writing this so there is a record of what happened to us. It don't look like Heather and me and the girls are going to make it. If you find this maybe you can get it to our family's if they made it through. I appreciate it very much.

My neighbor Danny Clark was really nervous when the rioting in the big cities started a couple of months ago. He has been stocking up on food and stuff for years because of all the problems with the economy and all of that. He wanted us to go with him to his cabin up by Eagle River in the North Woods but I told him Heather and Me and the girls were staying put, and that if something bad happened here the National Guard would come to take care of things. So they left.

That was about a month ago. I don't know exactly what happened but the power has been out for over 3 weeks and our food is almost gone. We have one can of beans left. I been listening to the emergency radio but it's hard to hear with all the static, and the batteries are almost dead anyway. The guy on the radio said there was riots everywhere and it wasn't safe anyplace. As far as I can tell, the entire power grid failed. And some kind of nuclear attack happened in Washington, New York and some other cities too. Anyway, I biked into town last week to see if I could find anything out and to try and get some food and medicine because the girls are really sick.

I couldn't drive because the snow is too deep and the roads haven't been plowed. Anyway when I got close I could see a lot of smoke and when I got closer it looked like half the town was burned to the ground. I saw some guys I didn't know walking around with guns and 2 of them were beating up old Ken Swartz.

I couldn't really do anything and I was scared so I came back here.

It's 2 below right now and it's starting to snow. It's freezing here in the garage too except in the shop area by the little wood stove. That's where we have been sleeping. Heather and the girls are there sleeping right now. I have to cut pine branches from the trees with a butcher knife for heat because the axe handle broke and I worry about the smoke because of those guys in town with the guns. I don't even own a gun. I never believed in them. I always believed in the government you know?

We can't make it much longer and I have to get some help somehow. But if I go into town I might not get back. And if I take Heather and the girls with me I'm afraid of what those guys will do to them. If I don't go we're all going to die here. I feel so stupid and helpless. I even tried praying. I wish I had listened to Danny Clark but I didn't. I know the National Guard isn't coming now. So I have to make a decision by tomorrow morning and I just don't know what to do. I've failed my family and I'm scared. I'm scared real bad.

Sincerely,
Bill Chambers

NORMALCY BIAS

Poor Bill Chambers! He purchased every type of insurance he thought was necessary to protect his property and his family in case something happened. He had homeowners insurance, car insurance, health insurance, and life insurance. He even had insurance on his dog. But he neglected to provide the most important insurance policy of all because he couldn't buy it. He couldn't purchase it because it's not for sale, and in any event he didn't believe it was necessary. I call it *Disaster Insurance*. If Bill would have protected his family with a simple disaster insurance policy in the form of survival supplies, his family might still be alive. Furthermore, he could have provided them with that protection at a fraction of the cost of his regular insurance polices.

Most people aren't prepared to survive any type of disaster. Well, maybe for a day or two, but that's probably about it. Most Americans are like Bill Chambers. Because a national disaster has never occurred in their lifetime, they simply refuse to believe, or they choose to ignore that a true national disaster is not only possible, it's probable. It's called a "*Normalcy Bias.*" In other words, they're biased towards their lives always being normal. In a way, I suppose you can't blame them. After all, this is the U. S. of A where generally speaking, a "bad thing" is when your team loses big over the weekend, and a "really bad thing" is when you find out your mother-in-law is coming for a two-week visit.

Until recently, most of us have placed a loose trust in the federal government to take care of the details during an emergency and to provide us with protection and accurate information. Unfortunately, that thought process is no longer valid. Today, a significant segment of American society no longer believes the government is capable of doing anything other than screwing things up. The government will take care of it? Don't make me laugh.

Unfortunately there are a lot of Bill Chambers' residing in the USA, and for all intents and purposes most are likely to end up the same way Bill Chambers and his family did if something really bad does happen. For the rest of you, at least for those who think a major catastrophe (either natural or man-made) is possible in the near future, and who think it might be a good idea to do something, the questions then become, what do you do and how do you do it? Where do you start, and can you afford to spend the money and allot the time necessary to provide a viable survival solution for you and your family? *Can you afford not to?*

If you can look in the mirror and honestly say you don't think anything bad can happen in America, but that if it does, you're positive the government can and will provide your family with 100% of the food, water, shelter, and other items you're going to need to survive, *welcome to Bill Chambers-land*, and good-luck to you and your family.

Let's assume for a moment you've come to the conclusion that some sort of survival preparation is necessary, but your knowledge of the subject is limited. You have a lot of work to do! The best place to begin is by gaining survival knowledge. The easiest way to accomplish that is with a survival book that can provide information you can actually use.

Before I go any further, I want you to know I'm not going to suggest you become a full-fledged survivalist or that you give up your job, move to the "boonies," stockpile tons of supplies, and hunker down to await whatever may (or may not) be coming our way. Even if you wanted to indulge yourself, the cost would be prohibitive. Besides, how many people can pack up and leave everything behind because something *might* happen?

I'm not even telling you something is definitely going to occur, since my crystal ball doesn't function any better than yours. What I am telling you is, given the sad and deteriorating state of the country, a wise man will develop some sort of survival plan to protect his family in the event the unthinkable becomes reality.

Back to survival books. There are tons of them available. Some are good to excellent, and some are, for the most part, useless. Personally, I have one problem with every survival book I've ever read. They all tend to cater to those with a *survival mentality*, and they assume the reader has rudimentary survival skills and knowledge. In addition, I haven't found one that offers information that's going to be of much help to the average person living an average life.

The info most survival books provide won't help that young single mom with two kids who lives in a one-bedroom flat in Chicago, waits tables, and can't quite make ends meet. There isn't any useful information for that nice old retired couple living in a trailer park in Ft. Myers either. If the kaka hits the fan, how do they survive? Where do they go? How do they get there? What do they do when they do get there?

Furthermore, what about the millions (maybe tens of millions by now) of people who aren't financially capable of making survival preparations of any kind? In addition, there are millions of other Americans who don't know anything about firearms, how to protect themselves, or even how to light a fire. How are all of those people going to survive without some form of massive governmental assistance during a true national emergency? Additionally, survival books tend to provide information predicated upon a pre-determined set of circumstances. If this happens, do that, if that happens do this sort of thing.

Here's the problem with that type of survival information. Every family is going to require a unique survival solution since they themselves are unique. There are simply too many factors to take into consideration to attempt to come up with a viable one-size-fits-all survival plan and/or kit. Location, weather and temperature, health concerns, age, disabilities etc. will all play a huge role in the type of survival plan you're going to need, as well as the type of gear you're going to require.

A one-size-fits-all survival plan is not only foolish, it could be dangerous as well.

We're going to start at the beginning. I'll assume you have zero survival knowledge and no skills. I'll recommend skills you should have. It will be up to you to acquire them. For example, there's no sense wasting a tree attempting to tell you how to build a fire since that type of information is readily available on both the Internet and in books. A word of caution is in order here. Reading about how to start a fire, for example, is not the same as actually doing it. Especially if you're going to be doing it for the first time under stressful and unfavorable conditions.

The Twilight's last Gleaming won't tell you exactly *what* to do, but rather, will show you *how* to develop a survival plan and survival kit tailored for your specific needs, and to point you in the right direction to learn the skills you'll need to survive.

Do you remember what I said earlier about experts? Well, the information and opinions you'll be marveling at in this book makes me one of those distasteful experts with an opinion. Do I qualify as a survival expert? That's a matter of opinion, too. (I survived two divorces; does that count?)

Regardless, when your survival plan is formulated and your survival kit is packed, you'll have a disaster insurance policy that Bill Chambers would have given anything to have had. In addition, you'll have gained the peace of mind that comes from knowing you did what you could to protect your family, and the knowledge you gained from learning new survival skills will allow you to confidently implement your plan if, and when, it becomes necessary.

You won't be able to prepare for every possible disaster or every possible contingency, but eliminating the Normalcy Bias, opening your eyes and your mind, and making a genuine effort to survive is a great place to start.

CHAPTER 3

ANAYLSIS

MILITARY COMMANDERS AND SPORTS COACHES have a lot in common. They both learn everything they can about their enemies and opponents. They constantly research and analyze strengths, weaknesses, vulnerabilities, capabilities, and tendencies, and if possible they learn about the character, background, and personalities of the opposing commanders and coaches. When they gather as much intelligence or information as they can, they formulate a battle or game plan. The troops and the athletes then practice that plan prior to the initiation of hostilities, or the start of the game. Knowledge, in this case, is power.

So rather than throw a rusty old knife, a jug of water, some ammo, and a couple of granola bars into a closet and call it survival preparations, we're going to gather as much information as we can, and we're going to formulate a game plan for survival based on the information we gathered.

People have been predicting the end of the world forever. Yet the world's still here. So are the predictions. In fact, if you watch the *History Channel* you'll see continuous cataclysmic documentaries based upon ancient prophecies, newly released scientific data, and recently discovered stone tablets. ..."Hey John, did you see that the earth is gonna be struck by a giant asteroid next week?"

"Oh yeah?"... "Hey man who won the game last night?"

Now don't get me wrong. I watch the *History Channel*, too, and I enjoy those programs just as much as you do. Disaster predictions from the Internet, television, newspapers, magazines, and let's not forget Hollywood, just keep on coming. Even that old coot down the street who dresses funny and carries that big sign saying "repent the end is near" has an arcane message to deliver. We simply don't take any of it seriously due to disaster overload, and because not one of those predictions has ever come true. It's all become entertainment.

But what if it's not just entertainment? Is it possible that so many diverse sources, all predicting the same basic event, could be 100% wrong? Could the world as we know it really come to a calamitous end? Should we actually be concerned? Let's take a look.

There are two methods used to determine how close the world is to a cataclysmic ending. The oldest and best known is the Doomsday Clock. Scientists developed the Doomsday Clock in 1947. It takes into account both the good and bad events that shape our world.

The Doomsday Clock is simply a symbolic clock face with a minute hand attached. Depending on the event, the scientists move the minute hand either towards or away from midnight. If the minute hand hits midnight, it's the end of civilization, or Doomsday. The minute hand currently reads six (6) minutes to midnight.

Survivalists use the second method. Teotwawki (tee-ought-walk-ee.) It means the end of civilization as we know it. Teotwawki uses a numerical system from 0-100 with zero being total tranquility and 100 being Teotwawki. There 's no official measurement for Teotwawki.

Additionally, both measuring systems are purely subjective; I mention them to make you aware that some highly respected people believe that at some point in the future, society or the world as we know it will end

Some of the following disasters, listed in no particular order, could definitely bring about the end of the world

Climate change (Global warming)	Asteroid impact	Gulfstream shutdown
Polar/glacier ice-melt/sea level rise	Meteorite impact	Ice age
Plant and animal extinctions	Comet impact	Solar flares
Extreme heat waves	Tsunami	Sunspots
Extreme drought	Volcanic eruptions	Pole shift
Super volcanic eruption	Gamma ray burst	Gas hydrates
Water shortages	Severe flooding	Earthquakes
Increased forest fire activity	Severe winter storms	Plague
Increased hurricane activity	Peak Oil	Gas rationing
Gas shortages	Food shortages	Socialism
Economic collapse	Extended power outages	Nuclear war
Extended periods of extreme cold	Nuclear plant accident	Chemical warfare
Depression	Nuclear terrorism	Terrorism
Biological warfare	Biological terrorism	Marxist Communism
Race war	Civil war	Riots
Martial law	Curfews	Coup d'état
Constitutional by-pass	Succession	Governmental collapse

Increased thunderstorm activity: (hail, tornados, lightning, straight-line winds, heavy rain)

That's a lengthy and intimidating list, and right now you're probably looking at it and asking yourself how anyone, much less anyone on a budget, could possibly prepare for and survive that many potential disasters. Well, that *is* a problem. Would it be helpful if we had a realistic idea of which were most likely to happen, and where and when they might occur? Of course it would. If we can figure that out, we'll have a much better idea of how to formulate a survival plan, so let's take a closer look.

Many of these disasters are indigenous to a specific region. For the most part their impact will be local or regional, although some will have the ability to affect the entire nation within a short time, depending upon what the impacted area provided in the way of goods or services for the rest of the country. Hurricane Katrina is a good example. If you lived in Montana, you were high and dry, but you paid more for gas shortly thereafter because Katrina destroyed oil platforms and refineries. Of course, the knowledge that a disaster's local or regional doesn't help the people who live in the impacted area. If you live in Los Angeles and there's a major earthquake, it's not very comforting to know that people living the good life in Virginia aren't going to be immediately impacted.

The good news, such as it is, is that a local or regional disaster isn't a Doomsday type event, even though it probably feels like one to the people stuck in the middle of it. In addition, if a local or regional disaster does happen, you won't be on your own for long. Help will arrive in a relatively short period. The preparations and supplies needed to survive a local or regional disaster are pretty much the same. If you don't already have a list of the recommended supplies, you can get one from your local Emergency Management Agency, or from the FEMA website.

While critical to those who are affected by them, local disasters don't constitute a survival event such as we're going to prepare for, so let's take the liberty of removing the events that are local or regional and put them into a category of their own. We'll call that category SHORT- TERM SURVIVAL EVENTS.

Removal of the following eighteen local/regional disasters reduces the number of disasters we need to prepare for. Look closely. There's not a single area of the country that can rule out every one of those potential disasters. In addition, nearly all are weather-related and happen on a regular or seasonal basis, which makes *everyone* susceptible to at least one of them. So regardless of where you live, it makes good sense to prepare a short-term survival kit ASAP even if you never intend to prepare for long-term survival. A nice aside to preparing a short- term survival kit is that the items you put into it will automatically become part of your long-term survival kit. Besides, if your mother-in-law does come for that two week visit, you can stay in the tent in the back yard under the guise of checking out your equipment.

Volcanic eruptions	Extreme heat waves	Extreme cold
Tsunami	Extreme drought	Ice storms
Increased forest fire activity	Water shortages	Severe winter storms
Earthquakes	Severe flooding	Food shortages
Severe thunderstorms	Gas shortages	Gas rationing Extended
power outages	Nuclear plant accident	

Now let's take a closer look at the remaining events, shorten the list further, and through the process of elimination, figure out which disaster or event is *most likely* to cause you to be "On Your Own in America."

Climate change due to *global warming* is creating a lot of controversy. Is the planet warming or isn't it? If it is warming, is man the cause, or is it a natural cycle of the earth? For our purposes, if it is happening, the reason *why* it's happening is totally irrelevant. We're concerned about the effects, not the cause.

Global warming could be responsible for every event we put on the short-term disaster list, plus sea level rise via glacier melt.

(The seas can't rise from *polar ice-cap* melt since the ice is floating on the ocean.) It's the same as putting ice cubes in a glass of water. When the ice melts, the amount of water in the glass is the same as it was when the ice was present. Global Warming may also be responsible for plant and animal extinctions, severe food shortages and plague, as well as a contributing factor to riots and even war.

From an immediate threat perspective, global warming is not an instantaneous cataclysmic event. We'll feel the effects of global warming a little at a time over a long period. Therefore, while it makes sense to keep a long-term eye on the effects of global warming, it's not something that's going to threaten our immediate survival. We're going to put global warming on ice for now and let it cool off.

Without going into a lot of scientific detail about *gulfstream-shutdown*, suffice it to say it's a "river of warmer water" within the ocean that helps keep the global climate stable. If the gulfstream were to shutdown, or radically alter its directional flow, it could bring about a mini ice age. There's zero evidence that a shutdown of the gulfstream is imminent, so it makes no sense to concern ourselves right now with the gulfstream.

If an *asteroid*, large *meteorite*, or *comet* (which is an asteroid) impacted the Earth, it would certainly have dire consequences for all living things, and it could very well be the end of the human race. Fortunately, none of those "planet killers" is on the immediate radar. It simply wouldn't make sense to be concerned with any of them until scientists tell us an impact is imminent and Jim Cantori of *The Weather Channel* is broadcasting from the projected impact site. Let's take all three of them off our list.

A *pole shift* (Earth rotates on its axis up to 180 degrees; (North Pole becomes the South Pole and the South Pole becomes the North Pole) is conceivably the ultimate disaster and probably *would* cause the extinction of the human race. Both the Mayans and Nostradamus predict a pole shift on 12-21-12 due to astrological alignments. If a pole shift happens, it won't be as enjoyable as watching the movie 2012, although the special effects will probably be more realistic. Is a pole shift possible? Your guess is as good as mine, but if it does happen, there's nothing we can do to prevent it, so it makes no sense to spend the next few years worrying about it. Shift it on out of here.

Solar flares and *sunspots* are cyclic and occur periodically. The effects aren't generally noticeable to the average person because they're limited to communication disruptions and an increase in solar radiation. The possibility does exist for the eruption of an intense solar storm that could take out sections of the "grid" for long periods of time, which would wreak extreme havoc on our high-tech society. Additionally, a big solar flare could cause worldwide crop failures.

It's important to note that sun spots and solar flares have more impact on our climate than *any other single event!* Again, there's nothing anyone can do about the sun and its cycles, so let's snuff out the solar flares and sunspots, and remove them from our list.

Peak oil is the term used to describe the time when the world's available oil supply begins to decline, while the consumption of oil continues to rise. This would likely cause a dramatic increase in the cost of oil and gas and could result in severe supply shortages, which in turn might result in gas rationing. Peak oil doesn't qualify as a disaster, but it's definitely a potential problem somewhere in time. While it's conceivable the USA could go to war over oil in the future, it also appears that peak oil is years away, so let's slide it off our list.

Polar and *glacier ice melt*, *sea level rise*, and *plant* and *animal extinctions* are more or less related to global warming, and although they may occur down the line, they're not a cause for immediate concern.

An *ice age*, while related to global warming, can also be caused by sun spots and solar flares. A "mini ice-age" is a distinct possibility and could cause severe problems worldwide in a short time.

Not too many people are aware of *gas hydrates*, which are pockets of methane gas buried in the ocean floor and produced in the deep by decaying bacteria. Most of the methane is trapped in ice and is often referred to as "the ice that burns." The worst-case theoretical danger from methane hydrates is that pure methane is lighter than air, but methane loaded with water droplets is heavier than air. A disturbance, maybe an earthquake, forces the water-laden methane closer to the surface where, under reduced pressure, the gas starts to bubble out. Moving quickly upward, it leaves the water, entering the atmosphere in one big "burp." (It's estimated that the methane contained in just 1% of ocean volume can contain 10,000 times more explosive power than the combined nuclear arsenals of the entire world!)

Since the escaped methane is loaded with water droplets and is heavier than the air, it spreads across the land until it encounters, perhaps, a bolt of lightning, or maybe your Cousin Vinnie's "Bic," where it explodes with the afore-mentioned power. TEOTWAWKI! The fact is, the methane exists. The scenario you just read, however, is the most extreme of all the methane theories. Other theories range from tremendous regional explosions to gigantic underwater mudslides, and an abrupt increase in air temperature due to huge amounts of suddenly released methane. The latter event would contribute significantly to global warming, a possible gulfstream-shutdown, and a mini ice-age, and the list goes on. Can any of it happen tomorrow? Maybe, but if it does, there's nothing we can do about it, so let's leave the methane with Sponge Bob in Bikini Bottom and take it off our list.

A *super volcanic eruption*, such as Yellowstone, according to the experts, would probably push man to the edge of extinction. There are seven known super volcanoes in the world, three of which are located in the United States. A super volcanic eruption would *not* be fun. There's some evidence that, in geological terms, the Yellowstone Super Volcano is going to erupt sometime soon. In fact, there've been a series of minor quakes in Yellowstone as recently as last year.

Will it erupt in our lifetime? The experts say no, so let's go ahead and park Yellowstone and the other six (6) super volcanoes.

A *gamma ray burst* from an exploding star that's close enough to Earth, and assuming the directional path of the explosion is focused on the Earth could definitely be the end of mankind. The extreme theory of a GRB is that we won't know the star exploded until the gamma rays hit us with zero warning. That's it! End of story. Other theories state that a close and focused GRB would deplete the ozone layer contributing to a mass extinction.

Again, why worry about something that no-one can do anything about, or that we'll never know happened? Gamma ray burst is busted.

So just like that, we've eliminated another fifteen plus potential catastrophes as not having immediate relevancy to our long-range survival preparations or that no one can do anything about. However, we still have twenty (20) "titles" that are just cause for concern.

When you look closely at the remaining categories, it's apparent a lot of them are similar or would have similar consequences, so let's condense as many as we can. Let's put economic collapse and depression in a category of their own and call it *Economics*. Simple!

We can combine civil war, race war, riots, governmental collapse, coup d'état, martial law, curfews, socialism, Marxist communism, succession, and constitutional by-pass under one category since they're all civil related. Let's call that category *Civil Unrest*.

We can also place nuclear, biological and chemical warfare under the title of *War*, and we can label terrorism, whether it's conventional, nuclear, or biological as just *Terrorism*.

Finally, let's quarantine *Plague*, since it's a definite "wild card" and place it in a category by itself.

The catastrophe will likely come from one of the following categories:

Civil unrest
Economics
War
Terrorism
Plague.

By preparing to survive the threats in these five categories, we're automatically preparing for every event in the short-term disasters category. Additionally, if any of the disasters occurred that we could do nothing about, or that we removed as having no immediate relevancy (except for the visit from your mother-in-law,) you might be able to survive some of them, too.

If you look more closely at every event we removed, with the exception of gas shortages, gas rationing, nuclear plant accident, and peak oil, every one of them are courtesy of dear old Mother Nature, and theoretically, she could be responsible for those four events too.

Now look at our final five categories. Interesting, isn't it? With the exception of plague, every one of them is the direct result of that most dangerous of all animals, man!

We've now reduced our list to twenty (20) potential disastrous events in five (5) categories. But we're on a roll, so let's narrow the list more and see if we can find out which of the remaining events is most likely to happen.

Let's take a look at the *war* category first.

A nuclear war, like the one that didn't happen with the former Soviet Union, seems unlikely at this time.

It's hard to conceive of a nation with nuclear capability that would even think about attacking the United States, although it would be folly to say a nuclear exchange with Russia is impossible. Between us, we have enough nuclear weapons to destroy the world many times over. The possibility of an accident, a miscalculation, or a simple mistake on either side could easily start WWIII. The same logic would apply to chemical or biological warfare with another country, although the likelihood of either happening is almost non-existent.

However, it's not at all difficult to conceive of some kind of attack by Iran on Israel and, as I'm sure you know by now, Ahmadinejad has repeatedly made comments that Israel should be wiped off the face of the Earth.

Because of the Iranian threat to the existence of Israel, it's not difficult to imagine a pre-emptive nuclear strike by Israel on the Iranian nuclear facilities. The result of such an attack would have far-reaching consequences indeed.

Iran would undoubtedly retaliate with an attack on Israel and, although a plausible response from President Obama would be to "scold" the Iranians, the United States, like it or not, would be involved in a retaliatory response. It's a given that Iran would consider the United States to be jointly responsible for the attack, and they might retaliate by attacking the USA through their terrorist organization, *Hezbollah*. In addition, Iran may already have "the bomb," and may actually have that weapon on location somewhere in the United States.

The assumption that Iran possesses a nuclear weapon isn't that far-fetched since the (former) Soviet Union is missing over 100 suitcase nukes. It doesn't require a leap of faith to figure out where at least one of them ended up. The ultimate Iranian response might be that, through *Hezbollah*, they detonate that weapon, or weapon(s) in New York, and/or in Washington DC.

Pakistan is a nuclear country. India also has the bomb. Pakistan and India apparently don't like each other very much, and a nuclear exchange between those two countries will remain a possibility with far-reaching consequences. Moreover, Pakistan has serious internal problems with Muslim extremists, who are attempting to procure nuclear weapons to attack the United States.

In addition to harboring Al Qaeda, Pakistan has the Taliban to deal with. Pakistan could end up as a major terrorist state with nuclear capabilities! A very troubling thought indeed.

That brings us to the nuclear loose canon of North Korea. They're held in check reasonably well by China, and they're more bark than bite, but they're unpredictable and, from the American perspective, they're highly irrational. We can only hope they're not stupid, too.

Although China is nuclear capable, they would be foolish to get into a shooting war with the USA for any reason, since their economy is just now emerging. Besides, why attempt to take over a country militarily when it can be done much more efficiently economically. Like it or not, nuclear detonations should be near the top of our list, but as a direct result of terrorism, or from a war between other countries, not as a direct result of a nuclear exchange between the United States and an unnamed enemy. Chemical and biological warfare between the USA and another country is also highly unlikely. Let's go ahead and remove all three of the war categories from our preparations list.

Plague will always be a possibility. The threat of emerging viruses increases every year, and certain strains of bacteria have become increasingly resistant to antibiotics. Fortunately, many variables must come together before a virus can be termed a global threat. *If* it mutates and can pass from animal to man, *if* it becomes airborne and can pass between humans, and *if* it hitches a ride on a commercial jet and is free to spread in a large metropolitan population, then it could become a pandemic.

The flu is the first thought that comes to mind when the word pandemic is used, and for good reason. A major flu pandemic has historic potential. In the event a serious flu pandemic takes place, it would almost certainly crush the world economy due to fear, business closures, etc.

Moreover, if the world economy is already in a shaky position when the pandemic "hit" it could be the coup de grace for many nations, including our own. However, those are a lot of ifs, and while we can't absolutely rule out the possibility of all of them coming together, it doesn't appear it will occur tomorrow.

Unfortunately, it's no longer a question of *if* it's going to happen, but of *when*. For the time being, though, let's take plague off the final list and assign it wild-card status. We'll keep a close eye on plague.

As an aside, you should be aware that normal, everyday disease(s) and sickness can be devastating during a disaster situation. The likelihood of contracting a contagious, life-threatening disease will increase dramatically. (A section containing definitive information on infectious disease is located toward the end of the book.)

Now let's examine the remaining categories.

Some form of *civil unrest* may be just over the horizon, but it won't happen unless something dramatic pushes us in that direction. Of the possibilities we listed under civil unrest, some are highly *unlikely* to happen. It's difficult to envision a full-fledged nationwide race war, and I think we can safely eliminate that as a possibility, although the threat of local race-riots will still be possible.

There's currently a lot of anti-Muslim sentiment in the United States, and it appears to be growing. It's not outside the realm of possibility to imagine some sort of conflict along religious lines.

We can be reasonably confident that a Coup d'état, or overthrow of the government by military means, isn't on the table, and Marxist Communism is also unlikely to occur in the United States anytime soon.

Constitutional by-pass is the term I use to describe the apparent efforts by the President and Congress to ignore, or at least to circumvent the articles of the Constitution of the United States. Because of these outrageous actions, constitutional by-pass is already happening. In the process, you and your family are losing your freedoms, and the country is racing towards a form of socialism. (Incidentally, the term "Democratic Socialism" is defined as: left wing, supporting a fully socialist system, but seeking to establish that system by *gradually* reforming capitalism from within.)

It's obvious that circumventing of the Constitution and the theft of our freedoms doesn't qualify as a disaster to those in power, but I assure you it does to millions of other Americans.

As such, it's not outside the realm of possibility that some of those citizens will resort to violence at some point in time. Regardless, the act of constitutional by-pass lends credibility to the very real possibility of *major rioting* in the near future.

Another *civil war*, while not impossible, is also unlikely to happen. It's difficult to imagine another "North vs. South" type of war, unless that war was borne from attempts at secession. If things get worse, attempts at secession by some states is a possibility. In fact, the Governor of Texas mentioned secession in a speech last year. What does that mean? It means people are thinking about it, and they're discussing it in private. By the way, we're not talking about a few rednecks in the back of some remote country bar either. Every revolt begins with people talking in private. It's how our own struggle for independence from England started. Concerned citizens met in private and had private conversations, which ultimately led to a revolt against unjust taxes. Well guess what? In reality, it's likely that an attempt at *secession* by any state would result in instant and forceful Federal intervention, which could actually light the fuse to many of the civil situations that we've listed. While serious talk of secession isn't impossible, an actual attempt at secession is, like civil war, not likely to happen.

So, like it or not, even though it's not a pretty picture, a *collapse of the Federal Government* isn't outside the realm of possibility, especially if there's an event which would exacerbate and accelerate the collapse.

As for the economy, is it really worth discussing here? If you're don't know how bad things are you're looking the other way. The actual economic situation is much much worse than we're being told. Don't be surprised if you see unemployment at record levels in 2011 and 2012. The Federal Government is either incapable of doing anything constructive to alleviate the situation, or worse, they're indifferent. Without jobs, there will be no recovery, and if there's no recovery, it's likely the current recession will become a full-fledged *depression* sometime in the near future.

Finally, let's take a look at *terrorism.* Islamic terrorism is as real as the sunrise, even though many people have conveniently forgotten the message they delivered to us via air on 9-11-01. An Overseas Contingency Operation (OCC) is nothing more than a naive and childish response to a genuine threat. Calling the War on Terror something that sounds less ominous won't change the fact that Muslim extremists are never going to stop trying to kill us.

Most terrorism experts agree that the odds of a terrorist "slipping through a crack" are tremendous, and the odds of successful attacks increase daily.

Ultimately, one or a combination of the following events will likely be the cause of the catastrophe that we're going to plan to survive:

CIVIL UNREST	*ECONOMICS*	*TERRORISM*	*PLAGUE*
Riots	Total economic collapse	Nuclear	Flu pandemic
Martial law	Depression	Biological	

Before we head off to chapter two and examine these four categories more closely, let's take a quick look at two survival wildcards.

DISASTER WILDCARDS

Plague

We've ascertained that a severe flu pandemic has the potential to devastate the world. A virulent pandemic is undoubtedly the most difficult event for us to prepare to survive. You can't see it, hear it, taste it, smell it, or touch it. In fact, until you're sick, you're unaware you've been exposed. Likewise, you can't tell if others are infected until it's obvious, which is too late for preventive measures.

There are enough "virus" or "plague" type movies out there to scare the crap out of anyone. How realistic are they? My guess is they're a lot closer to reality than disaster movies such as those depicting asteroid impacts. I don't know about you but a truly nasty plague makes me nervous.

As the population of the world increases, the potential for new and previously undocumented virus' have the potential to devastate the unsuspecting world. It's happened before. It will probably happen again. Using masks and waterless wash won't do any harm, although the jury is out as to their actual effectiveness. In the end, common sense will probably be your most effective defense against any strain of flu or other life-threatening virus.

Weather

Normal weather is likely to cause you more grief, additional survival hardships, and threats to your safety than anything else you encounter on a daily basis. Why?

Well pilgrim, because you won't be able to watch *The Weather Channel* anymore to find out if that gentle breeze that's picking up (depending upon the time of year and where you're surviving at) is going to turn into a Category Five hurricane, a violent thunderstorm with hail and damaging winds, or a raging blizzard. You won't know if there's a heat wave or a severe cold snap on the way, whether it's going to rain, snow, or if there's an extended drought in your immediate future. Weather has a huge impact on our daily lives under normal circumstances, and that impact will increase dramatically in a survival situation. Weather has the potential to affect *every* aspect of your survival life.

CHAPTER 4

DECISIONS

BEFORE EXAMINING THE REMAINING DISASTER categories, there are a couple of survival details that need to be addressed. People are always talking. Talk, talk, talk, and as the old saying goes, talk's cheap. However, when it comes to the topic of survival, talking about preparing a survival plan won't be accomplished by talking about it. There's also a tremendous difference between the instinct to survive an immediate *known threat* and the determination to survive a *threat* that *might* take place. In the former, humans are programmed to survive anything considered an immediate threat to our well being. Our bodies produce a rush of adrenaline, a response called "fight or flight" kicks in, and we take the (hopefully) appropriate action without actually thinking about it. It's totally instinctive.

Becoming determined to survive something that *might* happen is a bit more complicated. You have to have, or you have to develop a will to survive. Some people are apparently born with the will to survive and have the mentality to do whatever it takes to accomplish the task. For others, it's not so easy. You can't go to Wal-Mart and shop for a five pound box of willpower in the motivational aisle. At least not yet. So if you don't have it, how do you get it?

The first question you should ask yourself is, *do you really want to survive?* That question isn't as dumb as it sounds. Some people would prefer being at ground zero rather than to be a survivor in a post nuclear world. If you have a family, which most of you undoubtedly do, then wanting to survive shouldn't be a part of the equation.

Ask yourself *why* you want to survive. It can be because you want to protect your family, your friends, your girlfriend, your dog, your country, for revenge, or simply because you have some work to do before you have the big meeting with St. Pete. It doesn't matter what it is, as long as you have a *reason.* Once you've determined what your reason for wanting to survive is, you have to determine exactly how important that reason is to you. If survival is extremely important to you, then gaining the will to survive is as simple as making a decision that you're going to survive, no matter what it takes. The problem most people encounter is in maintaining the determination to do whatever it takes to survive before the desire to survive becomes a necessity.

It's the same thing as starting a New Year's resolution to quit smoking or to lose weight. Most people start-off with a rush of newfound desire, but fall by the wayside after a short period and revert to whatever it was they were doing before they went temporarily insane. In this instance, falling by the wayside and going back to their old ways may mean death to their family. Therefore, you have to find the motivation and develope the determination to prepare to survive. If that sounds simple, it's not. I can't help you with determination. If you don't have the will to survive or you're not willing to make the effort to gain it, you might as well sit with that moron at ground zero. As I mentioned earlier, if your survival knowledge and skills are lacking, and you're serious about surviving, there's a lot of work to do.

I'm going to make a suggestion. It's not necessary to get uptight about any of this. You don't need to lose sleep over it or develop an ulcer. Go on with your life just as you planned. Simply incorporate your survival preparations into your life. *Don't allow survival preparations to become your life.*

A low-key sense of urgency should be more than adequate. Preparing a survival plan and kit, learning new skills, and gaining new and useful information doesn't have to be a drag. It can and should be enjoyable, as well as challenging. Proper preparations will require a bit of research, which translates into time, and time, unfortunately, is one of the problems we'll all be facing in the coming months.

Here are a few simple things you can to do jumpstart your survival plan. Almost anyone can set aside an hour a day to further their survival knowledge and can allot twenty bucks a week to purchase extra food and/or supplies. If you're a smoker, for crying out loud, quit! You can use that cigarette money for supplies. If your diet sucks, start eating healthy. If you're a couch potato, get your fat ass off the couch. If you're out of shape, start exercising. Believe me when I tell you, you're going to need your health and stamina. Besides, how much of a disaster would it be if you got healthy and in shape, and nothing happened?

And now, the moment you've been waiting for. It's time to look at our remaining categories and determine which disaster is *most likely to happen.*

If you remember, we eliminated, or decided the following events are unlikely (in and of themselves) to be the cause of a national catastrophe: *communism*, *race war*, *biological warfare*, *chemical warfare*, *nuclear war*, *civil war*, *succession*, and *coup d'état.*

In addition, we quarantined *plague* and gave it wildcard status. We also decided that *Constitutional by-pass* and *socialism* could be contributing factors, but on their own wouldn't cause a catastrophe. We're left with the following list as the most likely candidates:

Terrorism
Riots, Martial law, Curfews
Economic collapse
Depression
Governmental collapse

Attempting to pin down which of these events is most likely to happen is a real toss-up, although it's probably safe to say that riots, martial law, and curfews, by themselves, are highly unlikely to be the cause of a national disaster. Although a major terrorist attack, economic collapse, a depression, and a collapse of the federal government could cause all three, we're going to remove riots, martial law, and curfews from the list of probable causes. That leaves us with four potential candidates

AND THE WINNER IS

While it's possible an act of terrorism could help bring about economic collapse and an ensuing depression, it would require a horrific attack to have that kind of impact. Even though it's within the realm of possibility, an act of terrorism by itself is also an unlikely candidate. On the other hand, economic collapse is looking more and more probable with each passing day, and there's no question a collapse of the economy would result in a *depression.*

Unfortunately, it's not that simple, and it doesn't end there either. While a depression may be the initial survival event on the menu, it's merely the tip of the iceberg. This is where it get's dicey, and potentially nasty, too

While the economy and a depression are inseparable, and although riots, martial law, and curfews are virtually inevitable at some point in time during a depression, a collapse of the federal government isn't quite as simple to pinpoint. Unfortunately, the stability of the federal government isn't sacrosanct.

There are realistic scenarios that could cause the federal government to crumble or to partially collapse.

Let's suppose for a moment the economy does collapse, followed by a severe depression.

Let's further assume there's major rioting, and that martial law and curfews have been imposed in certain areas. Enter terrorism. I don't pretend to have any idea how a Muslim terrorist thinks, and it's perfectly obvious that the people from sand-land have no clue how an infidel thinks either. Regardless, I can't conceive of flying a plane into a building in the name of God, Allah, Buddha, or any other deity. It just doesn't compute.

But it makes perfect sense, at least to my deranged western mind, that economic collapse, and an ensuing depression in the USA, would create an ideal opportunity for Muslim terrorists to wreak havoc with a series of coordinated attacks, or maybe one or two big ones. Namely, a nuclear and/or biological attack against anything called New York. Would that administer the coup de grace to the Federal Government?

A brief message to those of you who take exception to the phrase Muslim terrorist, (you know who you are). If a terrorist is a Muslim, and he (or she) is committing Jihad in the name of Allah *and* the Muslim religion, then he (or she) is, by definition, a Muslim terrorist.

All right, it's time, may I have the envelope please? And the winner is: *ECONOMIC COLLAPSE* with an ensuing *DEPRESSION* resulting in rioting, martial law and curfews. Additionally, *ANARCHY* could ultimately occur with a total or partial collapse of the federal government due to the depression and a possible major terrorist attack.

Since knowing your enemy is the first step to victory, and in this case to survival, let's take the time to get to know what a "new depression" might look like, and while we're at it we might as well take a similar look at anarchy too.

The Great Depression of the 30's was, by any account, depressing. A statistically similar depression today would surely make the Great Depression look like the proverbial walk in the park. A new depression would be more than a mere depression; it would be a *Super Depression*. Here's why.

It goes without saying a lot has changed since the Great Depression. After all, it ended approximately seventy years ago when the country was, by today's standards, little more than a third world country.

It also means few of us alive today recall anything about the Great Depression of the 1930's. Let's look at some major differences between the Great Depression and a Super Depression of the early 21st Century.

Let's examine the most obvious difference first. During the Great Depression, the country was rural in nature, and for the most part people were self-sufficient. Many households grew their own food, and they had the equipment and the knowledge to preserve that food. Raising animals for meat was the rule rather than the exception, and baking bread, and heating and cooking with wood or coal was commonplace. In addition, many homes didn't have electricity, but depended on oil lamps as a light source. Indoor plumbing was generally available only in the big cities, but there were many neighborhoods within those cities that, like the people living in rural areas, depended on the good old outhouse and on wells with hand-pumps for their sewer and water needs.

Incidentally, the "weekly bath" normally consisted of heating water on a stove, then pouring it into a tub where the bather had the luxury of sitting in his or her own "dirt" to get clean.

Additionally, the vast majority of Americans were God fearing, hard working, and independent people. They depended upon themselves and their neighbors, not the government, for the things they needed. Hard work was the order of the day, not a dirty word to be avoided at all costs.

If you wanted to eat, you had to work. If you wanted to stay warm, you had to work. If you wanted a new pair of shoes, you had to work to get the money to buy them. Period!

In addition, the average American citizen of the 1930's possessed firm conservative values with genuine and honorable convictions, their lives weren't overly-regulated by a bloated, worthless bureaucracy, and compared to 2010, violent crime was non-existent.

Fast forward to today. Our economy is inexorably intertwined with the economy of the rest of the world, and most countries are in the same boat we're drifting around in. The average person has little or no knowledge of how to plant and grow food, or if they do, they don't have the space necessary to grow it on. The majority of the food we eat today is prepackaged and grown or raised in foreign countries. If you can follow the simple directions on the box, you're a cook.

We're no longer a rural country. In the urban America of today, raising animals for food is doubtless against some ordinance, all of which means that the average American citizen is totally dependent upon the supermarket for virtually every last bite of food and relies almost exclusively on public utilities for heat, electricity, and water. With the exception of a few rural homes, harvesting, heating, and cooking with wood is a lost art in the 21st century

For the most part, today's Americans don't know who their neighbors are, what they do, or where they're from. We just wave at them if we see them in their yard or perhaps have a polite conversation with them every now and then. "Hey, how's it going?"

"Sue, what the hell's that guy's name again?"

Can you imagine asking one of your neighbors to help you do something like building a barn? For nothing? Can you even imagine neighbors, on their own initiative, volunteering to help you do anything, then have the audacity to bring along buckets of food?

Hard work was no stranger to people in 1930. But what constitutes a hard day's work in 2010? Yep, you sat at a desk or stood behind a counter for eight hours a day.

Moreover, the modern definition of a hardship means you weren't able to secure that four star hotel for the weekend getaway. "Hey, Herb, how was the weekend?"

"It sucked man; our motel didn't even have a swimming pool!"

During a Super Depression it seems likely that crime would be off the charts. Do you really think the criminals of today, the thieves, burglars, muggers, child molesters, rapists, drug-addicts, gang members, killers, and politicians (oops) will worry about the law or worry about apprehension if they're hungry and you have food or something they want?

They don't worry about being apprehended now. In addition, they would likely look at the situation as an *opportunity* rather than a problem. It's certain they wouldn't get their hands dirty working on some sort of Obamanized New Deal II to get food. It would be simpler and easier to take yours.

Immigration during the Great Depression was an honor. Immigrants flocked to this country for the opportunities the country offered. Today they come for the handouts. They don't care about American history, values, or customs, and they have little interest in learning our language. America today is overly obsessed with political correctness and of feeding and caring for the millions of illegal immigrants who annually drain billions from our economy.

Where do you think all of those illegal immigrants will go during a Super Depression? What do you think they're going to do to survive? They'll either go home, compete with you for crumbs, or join the ranks of the criminally employed.

The last time I looked, I didn't see a single "hitching post" on Main Street USA. However, I've seen plenty of modern day hitching posts in the guise of parking meters. Those money gobbling sentinels stand as mute testimony to the highly mobile and hi-tech society we've become.

Americans depend almost exclusively on the automobile to get to work, for shopping, recreation, and to visit family and friends. In addition, we think nothing of driving fifty miles round-trip to get to work or of driving ten minutes to the local convenience store for a gallon of milk.

What will happen during a Super Depression if you don't have a job and you're not eligible for governmental assistance, food stamps, or unemployment benefits? No job means no money. No money means no gas, no gas means no shopping, and, of course, no shopping means no—and the list of no's goes on. On the other hand, what if you're lucky enough to have a job, but gas becomes so ridiculously expensive you can't afford it?

No gas means no ride, and no ride means you can't get to work, which means no job, which also means, of course, no money. It's the same song by a different vocalist.

If you're unable to secure transportation for any reason, will the government provide transportation for you and the millions like you who need it? Will they feed the hungry? If they do feed you, what will they feed you, and how long will they be able to provide that food?

Compared to the America of 2010, the America of the 1930's looks positively backwards. Nevertheless, that backward America of the Great Depression was much more capable of taking care of herself than the America of today will ever be.

To say the conditions I just mentioned would be unpleasant would be facetious since any of them would be extremely unpleasant. None, however, can hold a candle (no pun intended) to the biggest problem Americans will face during a Super Depression.

THE LACK OF ELECTRICITY!

We take electricity for granted. We flip switches, push buttons, and use electricity in hundreds of different ways every day without ever giving it a thought. There are only two times when we actually think about electricity. One is when we pay the bill and the other is when we flip the switch and nothing happens. Boy, we notice electricity then!

"Holy crap, a $350 electric bill!", Or,

"Herb, the power's out. Do somethin', I'm gonna miss Idol."

Imagine for a moment your electricity was shut off because you had no money to pay the bill, and you had no chance of coming up with the money (not to mention the deposit) to get it turned back on. Would the government subsidize your electricity? Would they provide power to millions of people free of charge who were in the same boat as you?

If so, how long would they pay for it? Where is all of that money coming from? By increasing taxes on the few citizens who could still be considered rich? By increasing the tax burden on those who were fortunate enough to have retained their job?

"You have a job, therefore it's your duty as a citizen of the United Socialist States of America to pay extra taxes to help subsidize the electric needs of those less fortunate than yourself."

"I am so sorry your Worship, please forgive me for being so selfish."

Can you imagine what it would actually feel like to have your power turned off because you couldn't pay the bill, and that there was absolutely no way for you to come up with the money to have it turned back on? While you're busy fantasizing, imagine it was during the heat of a Florida summer or the cold of a Wisconsin winter. Imagine also that the government was unable or unwilling to provide you with assistance. Would you expect the power companies to provide you with power for nothing? They're a business. Why would anyone expect a business to provide millions of people with millions of dollars worth of electricity every month free of charge?

So, what would happen? Would the government declare a state of emergency and take over the power companies to provide electricity to a huge segment of the population? If they did that, how long would it take them to get a program of that magnitude up and running? A bigger question, though, is how long could you go without power?

If the government did nationalize the utility companies and did manage to get the "juice" flowing again, do you think it would happen in two or three days? Or even two or three weeks?

There's no way you could live normally without power for that long. Furthermore, if a governmental program *was* instituted, do you think they'd allow you unlimited use of free power? Of course not! They'd ration the power. You'd get X number of hours of electricity per day, or X number of kilowatt-hours per day. And you can bet it wouldn't be rationed equitably either.

Have you ever experienced a power outage of three or four days? If you have, I know you remember what a pain in the butt that was. I experienced Hurricane Charley in 2004, and the people who were without power for two weeks thought it was the end of the world. So, how long would you be able to function without electricity? You'd be in the dark. No lights, no television, no Internet, no cell phone, and no landline either. In addition, you couldn't use your microwave or range, wash and dry your clothes, use the garbage disposal, use your fridge or freezer, use your air conditioner or heat your home if it's winter. Almost every device in an American home operates on electricity, which means virtually everything we take for granted, but that we need to live the life we've become accustomed to would be gone. Perhaps permanently!

If that were to happen, millions upon millions would have no choice but to abandon their homes and relocate to some sort of government center, probably consisting of tent cities with soup kitchens.

Everything you know, or thought you knew, your perceived independence, your freedoms, your entire way of life would disappear into the gaping maw of massive governmental controls.

I know you're thinking, that simply can't happen here in America. It just can't. You're probably right, too. The same way it couldn't happen in Germany or Russia, in the 20th century!

How long would a Super Depression last? Well, the Great Depression lasted about twelve years, and I think it's safe to assume that a Super Depression would last at least as long, and quite possibly a lot longer. Or, a Super Depression could be the end of the United States as we know it, since anything that even comes close to approximating those types of hardships could easily beget violence on the part of a disillusioned and angry populace. After all, who are they going to blame for the nasty turn their lives have taken? George Bush?

They'd blame the current government, of course, and they'd be justified in doing so, too. If major rioting ensued, the Super Depression would likely end relatively quickly and would be replaced by the "disaster of the day," partial or total anarchy.

If anarchy ensues, terror will reign supreme and the law of the jungle will replace the law of the land.

As mentioned previously, *those who aren't prepared to survive should be prepared to die!*

For better or worse, we've answered the questions of *why* we want to survive, and *why* and *how* the catastrophe happened. We also know *what* the most likely event will be. However, it's difficult to pinpoint *when* it'll happen, although since it's already started, we'll have the answer to that question pretty soon. *Where* it happens and *who's* to blame should be obvious. Both the President and the Congress will be responsible, and it will begin where those who "rule" reign. In Washington DC.

Suppose, just for a moment, that a small portion of what I just described comes true. Would you be comfortable living in a government "tent city" and eating the "free food" they'll graciously bestow upon you and yours? Would you be comfortable depending upon the government for your very existence? Like a slave?

And in a nightmare scenario for those who failed to prepare , what if there are no tent cities, handouts aren't available, and no government exists?

An old saying states: "We're 9 meals away from anarchy." That's how much food the average household in the United States has on hand. Most experts recommend a six month food reserve, but that's a lot of food, and let's face it, not everyone will be able to buy and store a six month food supply. I recommend a *minimum* of ninety (90) days worth of food and supplies. That will give you three months to make a reasonably informed decision about the situation. In addition, during that time the problem could be alleviated, or even ended. At the very least, ninety days will give you the opportunity to plant a garden, form a co-op with neighbors, relocate, or perhaps receive some sort of assistance from any governmental agency that might still be in existence. Unfortunately, a lot of you aren't going to be able to accumulate ninety days worth of food either.

If you're one of those people, the *absolute minimum* you should have on hand is a thirty day supply. That amount of extra food is attainable by (almost) everyone. More on food and food amounts later on in the book.

For now though there's one last question to answer, and one more decision to make before you begin actual survival preparations. *Where* will you and yours be spending your time during these festivities?

Location, location, location

This section deals with the most crucial and arguably the most important aspect of disaster survival. There's no doubt what so ever that *where* you live during a catastrophe will have more impact on your survival chances than any other cause.

Let's cut right to the chase. If you live in a ghetto, or any other "bad" neighborhood, you're probably not going to survive. In any event, it doesn't matter what the area you live in is called. If it's not safe under normal circumstances you have to find another location to use during a disaster survival situation.

Finding a suitable *primary survival location* or *safe area* is your first order of business. Not only is a safe area the most important aspect of survival preparations, for most of you it will likely prove the most difficult to achieve. Bear in mind all the survival food and supplies in the world won't do you any good if you can't keep them long enough to use them. If you're going to attempt to survive in an area that's not safe, you're not only going to lose your food and supplies, you'll probably lose your life, too.

So, what constitutes a safe area? There are seven *basic* features to look for during the selection process. They are:

1. Safety
2. Distance (to)
3. Water and food (availability)
4. Fuel (availability)
5. Defensible
6. Waste disposal
7. Escape routes

Let's examine each of them.

Safety covers a lot of territory but in this particular instance, we're mostly concerned with scumbags and other vermin. The bad guys! Obviously, you don't want to be anywhere near them, and you'd prefer a location they couldn't easily find. But where's that? Hard to say these days, but any rural setting would be preferable to an urban one since their numbers will probably be fewer than when they're in their natural habitat of concrete and asphalt.

But as the new saying goes, safe from one kind of vermin, probably exposed to another. Unfortunately, unless you can relocate to a remote area, like the North Pole, you're going to have to accept the fact there will be some bad guys in your future. (We'll cover that later.)

At any rate, when looking for a safe location, the overriding factor in your decision should be the residents of the area (or neighborhood) you're thinking about. It comes down to your assessment of their character. Would you feel comfortable, and reasonably secure living among or near those people under survival circumstances?

Escape, in this instance, refers to a route, a method, or a plan to get out of Dodge if the bad guys locate you and you're forced to make a strategic withdrawal.

Defense means just what it says. The area, house, neighborhood, section, whatever, has to be reasonably defensible from the bad guys, regardless if that defense is a neighborhood collaboration or a solo effort on your behalf. If the area you select requires the use of an M1A1 Abrams tank to defend it, you should consider that position indefensible. (More on that subject later too, and wood, and water.)

Fuel, in most areas of the country, will consist of wood, and more specifically, trees. While there are a few areas that could use coal, the most readily available fuel source for cooking and heating will be wood. That wood supply should be accessible after a ten or fifteen minute walk, and preferably a lot closer.

Water is critical for survival. It's unlikely municipal water will be available, so the survival location has to be in reasonable proximity to a water source, namely a creek, (crick if you're from Iowa) river, pond, or lake. The ideal distance will be short, but shouldn't be more than a thirty minute walk from where you'll be hanging your hat. The area should also have a potential food source nearby. (Fish, game, or a future garden site.)

Waste, often referred to as shit, can't just be dumped in the yard, or on the patio. If you don't dispose of it properly, you could expose yourself to disease. Besides, the odor of eau de kaka tickling your nostrils when the wind's right, not to mention the flies that will be drawn to the waste like ... well, like flies, is another thing you can do without. It won't require a huge amount of space, but you're going to have to either bury, burn, or carry the waste away from your shelter.

Distance is a bit trickier than the other requirements. Distance, in this instance, is referring to the distance from your residence to the safe area. That distance shouldn't be too extreme, and in fact, the shorter the distance the better. The question is, how far is too far? That's hard to say. Driving to your safe area after the fact may be difficult, or even impossible. Unless you're able to ascertain a disaster is imminent and are able to get to the safe area prior to the inception, the chances are you'll end up walking to it. *The safe area has to be close.* How far can you walk carrying a bug-out bag loaded with supplies and carrying children who are too young to walk?

Selecting a safe area that's too far away creates problems which may prove insurmountable. A rule of thumb is, if you think you can drive to the safe area, keep the distance around 100 miles. If you have to walk, it should be no more than 25 miles. There are state parks within a reasonable distance from almost any location in the United States. Being stuck in a tent in a state park would beat the hell out of being stuck in the city.

As you can see, finding a safe area within a reasonable distance, then making the determination of how and when to go will require a bit of research.

A safe area consisting of a cabin in the woods or the mountains is a better choice than an inner city high rise. That's obvious. Here are a few comparison locations to give you a better understanding of what to look for.

A small home in rural Colorado would probably be a better choice than an apartment in Des Moines, while a brownstone in Philadelphia may or may not be a better location than a three bedroom home in Atlanta. That choice would undoubtedly come down to the neighborhood and surrounding area. Suppose you live in a bad neighborhood in Milwaukee and relocate to a duplex fifteen miles away in Brookfield. Your chances of survival have probably increased significantly. Conversely, if you live in that same duplex in Brookfield and can relocate to a farm in the hills south of Baraboo, your survival chances are likely to increase dramatically. For the most part, *any* improvement in location should increase your chances of survival.

All right, relax. I'm not telling you to pack up and move next week or even next year. However, you do need to select a safe area where you can go before things get out of control.

Some of you will have it made and won't have to worry about relocation since the area and residence you're in will be sufficient.

However, most people don't live in an area that meets the minimum requirements and will have to relocate to survive. Here are a few suggestions on how to locate a good safe area.

The first and best option available is to contact relatives or close friends living in an area that's a better choice for a safe area than where you are now. A rural area upstate would probably be preferable to Brooklyn, and a three bedroom home in a suburb of Harrisburg would likely be a better choice than Philly.

Contact family and friends living in other areas and enlist their assistance. If you don't have family, or if no one likes your ass and you don't have friends, contact co-workers and/or neighbors. You might be surprised how many share your concerns. It's possible you can devise a workable co-op plan.

After you've made plans for a safe area, pay close attention to what's going on in the nation and the world. If Homeland Security raises the threat level, it's a good indication there's credible information a terrorist attack is possible soon. If you live in NYC, it might be a good idea to pay an immediate visit to your *safe area,* if only until the threat is eliminated. Anything that sounds bad or creates an undue amount of apprehension would be cause for you to consider beginning your move.

Some of you undoubtedly have the skills, tools, and survival mentality necessary to go solo. If that's your game plan, I hope your spouse is as qualified and as capable as you are, since it's possible you'll be removed from the picture and she'll have to "carry the mail" alone. For the rest of you, there's definitely safety in numbers, and the chances of the survival of your family in the event you were disabled or killed will increase dramatically by taking on a partner(s), or by joining a group.

There are many positives to having a survival partnership. Sharing the expenses and pooling your knowledge and skills are invaluable. Having companionship and the extra workers to share the workload isn't a bad idea either. Nevertheless, you should be aware there are downsides to a survival partnership. Disagreements, power struggles, and perhaps jealousy are just a few, so you should know your survival partner(s) well, trust them, and be confident they'll have your back.

Survival groups have existed in America for a long time. I'm not talking about cults; I'm referring to genuine survival groups; like-minded people who pool their knowledge, expertise, and money to survive the very thing that you're preparing for. In the coming months, if the situation in the country continues to deteriorate, it's likely new survival groups will form.

For entry into most of the older established groups, sponsorship by an existing member is usually required or the applicant must bring a special skill set to the group. If you're a doctor or a nurse, have a law enforcement or military background for example, you might be considered for acceptance into an established group. If you're a pencil pusher, or a car salesman, not so much. Newly formed groups are more likely to be looking for members first and an area of expertise second, so your chances of hooking up with a newly formed survival group are probably better than they'd be with an established group.

If you choose to join a survival group, you should proceed with extreme caution, especially if you're a single female or a single mom. Use your head and check out the group to the best of your ability. Pay special attention to the leader. If you can't verify who they are of if they refuse to give you any information about themselves, move on. You're going to be entrusting your life and the lives of your family to their honor, integrity, and expertise. Know who they are, and ensure the leader knows what he (or she) is doing before you decide to throw in with them.

CHAPTER 5

REALITY CHECK

EVERYONE REALIZES A STRUCTURE HAS to be built on a solid foundation if it's going to last. Your survival preparations are no different. If your preparations aren't built on a foundation that allows them to be effective, they won't work. At least they won't work as good as they should. You now have enough information to prepare a solid foundation, and you're going to begin building your survival structure shortly

First, though, it's time for a reality check!

Right this second all across the country, calls are coming in to the 911 service. When you call 911, you can be confident help will arrive within minutes. Whether it's for police, fire, or ambulance, you call, they respond. Guaranteed!

A major disaster, however, is likely to provide a different ending. If the service is available at all, the chances are good that the system will be overwhelmed with calls for help. In addition, since the number of available responders is limited, you could end up waiting for assistance a long time. You should also consider the possibility the service will be permanently unavailable.

Let's pretend for a moment the only thing you ever watched on TV was re-runs of *I Love Lucy*, and that you can't even spell *breaking news*. Let's further pretend rioting broke out in your neighborhood, and that a group of rioters was just blocks away. The first thing you'd probably do would be to turn on the TV to see what the hell was going on, but, oops, no TV signal. Yelling "holy shit" or something equally profound, you'd probably dial 911. Beep, beep, beep, beep, out of service.

Continuing with our imaginary skit, you can see the rioters torching houses and overturning cars. "I'll try the landline Martha," beep, beep, beep, beep.

"Herb, they're 3 houses away!"

What now? Do you hide and hope they don't burn down your house? Do you attempt to defend your home? (Oh, you don't have a gun?) Guess you'd better run then. Don't know where you're going to run, or what you'll do when you get there, but "beatin' feet" beats dead.

Yeah, I know the scenario was a bit lame. However, if it *was* real and you didn't know what to do immediately, you'd have a problem.

Unfortunately, most people experiencing something similar would be clueless, and because they didn't know what to do, someone close to them would probably die, or at least be seriously injured. The message? *Don't count on calling 911 for help that may never arrive!*_

In addition, if the 911 service is down, you should assume assistance from every other governmental agency is also unavailable, including the National Guard. Units from the Guard may ultimately make it into your area, but you'd be wise not counting on them for assistance.

Let's head over to Hollywood. Pick a movie, any movie, any genre. Action, adventure, horror, drama, romance, or comedy, it won't matter because they all have one thing in common. None of them has any resemblance to the life of a normal person. In addition, few of them are realistic.

In fact, Hollywood (and television) is probably responsible for more misconceptions about life, liberty and the pursuit of happiness than any other source in the history of man. Look at your average Hollywood hero in almost every action movie. Is he (or she) anything like you or even like anyone you know? The hero is handsome, and the heroine is devastatingly beautiful. I mean, she doesn't even have a freckle for crying out loud. The hero is incredibly clever, witty, a 32nd degree black belt in every form of martial arts, highly intelligent, almost invulnerable, and can hit a dime at 200 yards with a handgun just seconds after running a marathon.

The bad guys? They're either totally inept or they're positively brilliant, but toward the end of the movie they screw up and do something incredibly stupid. The bad guys can't shoot straight either, unless they're shooting at the supporting cast. They hardly ever miss the supporting cast.

Fortunately, with the exception of a few lost souls, the vast majority of us know there's not much attached to Hollywood that represents real life, even if that acknowledgement comes at a sub-conscious level. Yet real life, in the case of a movie, is irrelevant because if the movie was good, and a lot of them are, we go home entertained and happy. We watched the hero kick some major league booty, we got out of the house, and we were ecstatic to spend fifty or sixty bucks on theatre popcorn and watered down Coke to help the economy.

The actors, who are just overpaid people pretending to be someone else, the producers, directors, and the hundreds of other people who were responsible for the creation of the movie, pocket a fat paycheck and they go home happy, too. A good movie makes everyone happy. But as far as reality in a Hollywood goes? That's a stretch.

I'm being too harsh. There have been some good ones. *Saving Private Ryan* was one, and I'm sure you recall the landing on Omaha Beach. That was about as intense and realistic as any war movie you're ever likely to see. Yet it was only a movie. Hollywood hasn't figured out a way (yet) for viewers to experience the fear of the soldiers, to smell the body odor, the feces and urine, or the blood and guts of the wounded and dying. There's no way to duplicate the feeling of the water, the sun, or the sand grinding into your skin, the cacophony of noise and confusion, or to allow the viewer to hear a real bullet buzz angrily past their head. And no movie could ever replicate the horror of watching a buddy killed while you lie helplessly nearby.

I mention this to reinforce in your mind that the situation(s) you're likely to encounter when your life is actually at stake will be real. You won't be experiencing a Hollywood movie. It will *not* be exciting, and it definitely *won't* be entertaining. If you take a Hollywood "round" to the shoulder, you won't be returning to action later in the day. In fact, there's a good chance you'll die from that shoulder wound unless someone's capable of treating it quickly. In real life, the bad guys you'll run into will probably be much worse than a Hollywood bad guy, since a Hollywood bad guy needs to have some sort of redeeming quality to make the movie palatable to the viewer.

Your bad guys are likely to be as smart as you, but they'll be much more cunning, more street-wise, and much more ruthless than you could imagine. Besides, as you can tell by that shoulder wound, some of them use the proper shooting stance and can actually shoot.

In a real life survival situation, where it'll be survival of the fittest and where the law of the jungle applies, the things that you're likely to see, the odors that you smell and the sounds that you hear won't be pretty, but they'll be real.

That's it for Hollywood. Let's head on over to the news media, which won't be much of a journey, since the lines between Hollywood fantasy and professional journalism have blurred so much over the years they're now nearly identical.

The *creation* of the news using sound bytes is commonplace, and anyone can be "made" to have said anything, other than what was actually said. In addition, when a reporter twists the words, changes the meaning of a sentence or of a story, then uses that story as a platform to advance a personal or political agenda, that piece of work loses its journalistic legitimacy. It's more like a Hollywood script.

The bottom line on newscasts is: don't arbitrarily believe everything you hear or read. Learn to do your listening or reading between the lines and realize there's probably a personal or political bias to whatever the article or the news item is about. The story may resemble the truth. It might even be partially truthful, but sadly, it's unlikely to be the whole truth and nothing but the truth.

The news today is about the ratings or furthering a political agenda. It's about winning a Pulitzer, of securing advancement, or of stroking the reporter's ego. It's about a lot of things, but it's seldom about the truthful, unbiased reporting of the news.

Furthermore, good news is generally boring and not very interesting. On the other hand, bad news draws far more viewers or listeners. ("If it bleeds, it leads.") Therefore, a network is more likely to report on "bad news" than "good news" since the bad news broadcast draws a far larger audience. If a network can increase its viewing or listening base, they can charge more money to advertisers, which in turn means the network will make more money. Networks are a business, and they're in business to make money, not to provide a public service.

"I'll take strange words for $100 Alex."

"And the answer is *Poligion*.".

"What is the mixing of politics and religion?"

"Yes, that is correct for $100".

Who said politics and religion don't mix? I don't know. I suppose I could look it up, but I really don't care. It's an outdated statement. Politics and religion do mix, or at least they interact in a very big way on today's stage. Just in case you haven't been paying attention, politicians are painfully aware of the religious right, especially around election time when they need the religious vote to get elected or to remain in office.

Politicians are also keenly aware of a vocal, but minority Muslim religion and acquiesce to their outrageous religious demands out of . . . fear? (The United States is a Christian nation. If talk of God or open displays of Christianity is offensive to you, you're free to leave the country!)

Religious leaders don't get a free ride either since they pander to the politicians to gain favor for their own religious agendas

Additionally, the Federal Government and the judiciary have been meddling with religion in America for a long time. By removing prayer from schools, by striking down the words In God We Trust, and by removing Christmas decorations depicting Jesus, politics has inserted itself into Christianity in a big way. The bottom line is that politics and religion do mix, and they interact dramatically.

So, what does religion have to do with survival? Under *normal* circumstances, most religions are a positive influence in the daily lives of those who practice their faith. However, at the onset of "hostilities," religion could conceivably cost you your life.

Let's suppose you're a devout Christian, and shortly after the disaster begins you come in contact with a group of people who're equally devout atheists. These people are experiencing a tremendous amount of stress, and they're pretty angry. Not because their entire world came crashing down or because they just witnessed some of their loved ones die or anything like that. They're just surly. Do you think this might be an opportune time to attempt to save their souls? Alternatively, as an atheist, you come across that same group of Christians who also lost everything, including loved ones. Do you think it would be wise to tell them their concept of God was all BS, while simultaneously asking for their assistance?

The wise thing to do would be to go on worshipping as you always have, either within your own group or within yourself, until the situation stabilizes. In addition, unless you know the person or the people with whom you want to discuss religion, it might be safer for you to wait before attempting to initiate any discussion about religion.

On the other hand, a major catastrophe will create a mass migration toward religion, since people will have a need to believe in something. Religion fits that need. It always has. It always will. However, during the first few days or weeks following the inception of a major national catastrophe, you'd be wise to keep your religion to yourself.

I'd like to share with you one unique aspect of human nature and religion that I've observed over the years.

Atheists, agnostics, non-believers, or those who have strayed and who say they don't believe in God will, when they think they're going to die, invariably begin to pray or to beg God's forgiveness. Therefore, it appears the majority of disclaimers of God are nothing more than a psychological method of avoiding the will of God. In other words, when the jig is up, their chips go down.

Let's take a quick look at *prejudice*.

During a major national disaster, prejudice is likely to be rampant. People are going to be afraid, paranoid, and angry. All ethnic groups will be susceptible. It could be because you're White, Black, Hispanic, Asian, or American Indian, depending upon where you're at. It could be against anything, anybody, or any concept, including religion and sexual orientation. A life-threatening situation frequently brings out the best in people, but it just as often brings out the worst.

One thing's for certain; if the disaster is the result of a Muslim terrorist attack, and you're a Muslim, I wouldn't advise telling anyone your name is Mohammed, and I wouldn't recommend wearing anything that even resembled a turban or a hijab. If you're a Sikh, you shouldn't wear your turban either, since most Americans don't know the difference between a Muslim turban and a Sikh turban.

The bottom line on prejudice is to be aware, stay alert, be smart, use common sense, and stay alive.

CHAPTER 6

TIME KEEPS ON TICKING

TIME IS OF THE ESSENCE. It's time to lay the foundation for your survival preparations. Take a break, consider your options and, if you haven't already done so, this would be the appropriate time to make the decision (and the commitment) to build a survival plan for yourself and your family. If you've already made the decision, don't procrastinate, the clock *is* ticking, and no one has any idea when the disaster might occur. Whatever you do, *don't become a Bill Chambers.* Furthermore, once you begin preparations, don't stop if the situation in the country improves. It could all go south again in a heartbeat.

Begin your preparations by developing a functional plan. All of the supplies, knowledge, and commitment in the world are worthless without a workable plan. Putting a lot of thought into its development is essential if your plan's going to work. To help you as you progress through each stage, remember this acronym: KISS. (*keep it simple stupid*). A long, complicated plan is certainly doomed to failure. Your wife, older child, or whoever should understand the plan and be able to implement it if you're incapacitated or unavailable. There won't be a dress rehearsal, so you won't know if the plan you've developed will be effective until after the fact. With that in mind, ensure your plan is *flexible.* A plan that depends on events, sequences, and specific time lines won't work. In addition, you should devise both a primary and secondary plan.

The following questions are an example of just a few of the *type* of questions that you're going to have to attempt to answer. Where are you *likely* to be when the disaster begins? Will it start in the middle of the afternoon, late at night, on a weekday or the weekend? Are your mate and kids likely to be at work or school, on a field trip, or will they be at grandma and grandpas? If the family gets separated, how does everyone get to a rendezvous point or the safe area?

Obviously it's impossible to answer any of those questions since we don't have an exact time and date to work with. However, you can (and should) examine multiple scenarios that take those (and many more) situations under consideration.

Don't forget that at least initially, different disasters are likely to require different (*initial*) preparations. Start with the most likely and work your way down. Most of the scenarios will have the same basic answers.

Remember this is going to be your plan, and one size doesn't fit all. You have to develop a plan that will work for you and your family.

I don't claim to have all the answers to surviving a catastrophe of this nature. Who does? The evaluations, conclusions, responses, and suggestions that I've offered are based on my concept of common sense, and I know they'll work for me. Are they the only possibilities that can work for you? Of course not! Use what you can, adjust as necessary, change as you see fit, and come up with new concepts or ideas of your own. At the very least, you have a starting point. Just remember *time keeps on ticking*!

Recap chapters 1-6

1. A disaster insurance policy should be part of your family structure.
2. You should prepare a short-term disaster kit ASAP. The short-term disaster kit will become part of your long-term survival kit.
3. The most likely disaster that you'll be preparing to survive is an economic collapse followed by a Super Depression and ensuing civil unrest. A major terrorist attack and a potential collapse of the Federal Government are also possible.
4. You must make a decision to survive and to develop a survival mentality through commitment and increased knowledge through study.
5. Don't alter your current lifestyle to incorporate a survival plan into it; rather, incorporate the survival plan into your life.
6. Get healthy and in shape.
7. Prepare for 30-90 days without assistance from outside sources.
8. Analyze your current residence and, if necessary, find an alternate location or safe area.
9. Check with relatives or friends who would be interested in forming a survival group. As an alternative, you can join an existing group.
10. Don't count on any assistance from 911, the National Guard, FEMA or any other governmental agency.
11. Remember that the situation you find yourself in is real. It's not a movie.
12. Avoid religious discussions with people you don't know.
13. Be aware of extreme prejudices and hostility toward virtually anything and anybody.

14. Create a simple, flexible plan (KISS.)
15. Remember, there's not a "best" way to accomplish the goal of building a viable survival plan and kit. You have to figure out what you need and what will work for you.
16. Time is of the essence.

CHAPTER 7

BASICS

Bare Necessities

TO SURVIVE AS A SPECIES the Human Race requires *food*, *water*, and *shelter*.

Castles, condos' and tents

Regardless of where you live right now, whether it's an actual castle, a condo, a tent, a VW bus, or a cardboard box, makes no difference; there's simply no place like home. I doubt many people have ever considered their home to be a sanctuary, but it is. Most of us are more comfortable in our own home than anywhere else.

What're the chances you'll be forced to give up your current home to survive? For the majority of you, it's almost a certainty. In addition, it's possible you'll be forced to move locations, and therefore "homes," several times before the situation stabilizes. To make that transition as painless as possible you should consider *any* residence, including your primary survival residence, to be expendable once the disaster begins. Since shelter is one of the three basic requirements for human survival, it would be psychologically advantageous for you to think of your home, and all future homes, as a shelter rather than a residence.

It's obvious the human race can't survive without food, water & shelter. But that's pretty vanilla, and the statement is so stone-age. So before we go any further, I think an up-grade is in order. After all, this is the 21st century. Let's take a few liberties and make some additions to the list, and let's create a new statement while we're at it, too.

Let's say, while the human race requires food, water, and shelter to survive, it needs *food, water, shelter, fire, light, tools, medical care, communications*, and *clothing* to *survive* and *thrive*. That looks better. Ah, what the hell, it's free, so let's add a few more. We can add *sanitation, hygiene, fuel* and uh, let's see, one more. Okay, I Got it. The Weather Channel.

Well of course TWC isn't realistic, but even without it, the updated list is a bit less prehistoric. Kinda like a remodeled Motel 6.

Here's our updated basic human requirements list.

Shelter
Food
Water
Fire
Light
Clothing
Communications
Sanitation
Hygiene
Medical care
Tools
Fuel

Let's take a closer look at shelter. A house, by virtue of its construction, will provide you with many of the new basic requirements, including shelter, (of course), a place to cook and bathe, and depending upon the location of the shelter, you'll have access to water, fuel, a sanitation/sewage area and, if you can plant a garden, hunt or fish, you'll have food.

Nevertheless, many different scenarios could cause you to abandon your shelter and everything in it within minutes. An obvious example would be a threat to your shelter caused by the disaster.

However, for this example we're going to use a hypothetical attack on your shelter by forces that are more powerful than your own. It won't matter how prepared you are to defend your shelter, since an attack by a larger force with superior fire-power means you'll stand little chance of successfully repelling the attack. In addition, there's a good possibility that you, or someone close to you, will be seriously injured or killed during the defense.

In this type of situation, an attacking force has options you don't have, and since your goal is to survive, not to be a hero, a strategic withdrawal would be in order. Remember, this ain't Hollywood. So use your shelter for as long as it's safe, but if and when the time comes to abandon it, don't hesitate to get out of there. We'll be examining the actual defense of your shelter later on in this chapter.

Let's assume you had to leave your shelter in a hurry, and in the process you were forced to abandon the majority of your supplies. But you're alive, and that's all that matters. So, what do you do now?

Since you were driven out of the shelter you were in, it wouldn't make a lot of sense to find an abandoned home in the same area since it'd be a matter of time until you were forced to leave that one, also. It might work for a night or two, but that's probably it. This predicament is the main reason God invented tents and tarps. A good backpacking tent would be a huge upgrade over a tarp, and if your budget will handle it, you should definitely consider purchasing one. However, if your budget is extremely tight then you should purchase a tarp, which is a piece of reinforced, rectangular nylon. You can buy a good, inexpensive, lightweight tarp (with grommets) online or at almost any good sporting goods or camping supplies store.

To make a tent out of a 10'x12'tarp, start by tying a 3/16" or ¼" nylon support rope between two trees that are 16'-20' apart. Tie the rope to the trees about 4' off the ground, making sure the rope is taunt. Center the tarp over the rope with the 12 ft sides hanging down. Tie an 18" long nylon cord (parachute cord is excellent) to each grommet on the 12 ft sides of the tarp. (Burn the ends of the nylon cords and the support rope with a lighter to melt the tips so they don't unravel.)

Using the *metal* tent stakes you purchased when you bought the tarp, tie the loose end of the 18" parachute cord to each stake. Wrap the excess cord around the stake, leaving about 2" between the stake and the tent grommet. Now pound one of the stakes into the ground with the point of the stake angled back toward the tarp. If you're looking at the tarp from the front, it would look like ½ of the letter A. Duplicate this process around the entire perimeter of the tarp. When you're finished you'll have an "A" shaped tent that's open at both ends, about 6' wide by 10' long.

If you purchased a 6' x 8' ground cloth, put it inside your improvised tent as a floor. If the ground cloth has grommets, you can use a tent stake to secure the floor to the ground by placing the hooked end of a tent stake into the grommet and driving the stake into the ground. You can place pine branches or similar material over the ends of your new tarp shelter to provide further protection from the elements, or if you have a couple of ponchos in your pack, you can rig them up to cover the ends. It's not the Ritz, but it'll work just fine as a temporary shelter.

You can construct a shelter from just about anything, including ice and snow. Books pertaining to this subject are in the appendix.

The bottom line on shelter BTC (before the catastrophe) is that your house was your home, your home is now a shelter, and your shelter just might be a tarp. Whatever it is, and wherever it is, you'll be spending a lot of time in it, so choose your shelter wisely.

Survival Kit Essentials

1. Heavy duty reinforced nylon tarp with grommets, minimum size 10'x12'.
2. Heavy duty 6'x8' tarp with grommets for use as a ground cloth.
3. 12 metal tent stakes.
4. 100' of 3/16" nylon rope for shelter construction and *clothesline*.
5. 50' to 100' of HD nylon cord or parachute cord.

Water, water everywhere but . . .

A human being can live for weeks without food, but only (about) three days without water. Put water at the very top of your list since it's the most important of the original three basic requirements for survival. Without water, you *will* die!

City water is not a reliable source. It's almost a certainty that power will be unavailable to run the pumps. In addition, the water could be contaminated or poisoned, or the water plant may be destroyed. Besides, it's unlikely the plant workers will be showing up to treat the water anyway.

As a rule of thumb, the average person needs one gallon of water per day for drinking and three gallons per day for minimal cooking and personal hygiene. Therefore, if my math is correct, a family of four, consisting of two adults and two smaller children, needs a minimum of sixteen (16) gallons of water per day. However, you don't have to bathe every day, so you can reduce that total to three gallons per person per day, and you don't have to "flush," so let's take off another gallon. Then, just because we can, let's subtract one more gallon per person per day on the assumption that you'll use your available water for drinking and cooking only. That's still a total of four (4) gallons per day for a family of four. Furthermore, that's an average. If you're surviving in a hot, arid environment, performing strenuous tasks etc. you're likely to require a lot more water than one gallon per person per day.

But using 1 gallon per person per day as a minimum, that's still a grand total of *120 gallons* per month, and although you won't die from dehydration, you're going to be really "ripe" at the end of those thirty days. Now, if you're having a difficult time envisioning what 120 gallons of water looks like, picture twelve (12) gallons of milk in ten (10) rows. Bear in mind that's a minimum amount!

If you drink milk, you can use gallon milk jugs to provide your family with an emergency store of water. Using milk jugs for emergency water storage is both cheap and effective. If your family consumes three gallons of milk per week, that means in ten months you'll have a thirty (30) day supply of emergency water.

Wait, that won't work. You're gonna have to drink more milk. How about ten (10) gallons of milk a week instead of three? That reduces the time to get your 30 days worth of water to four (4) months.

Not going to work, is it? I hope that example shows you just how much water you're going to need.

Nevertheless, the milk jugs *can* take the edge off, and any water you store is better than no water at all. To use the milk jugs, wash them before you fill them, mark the fill date on the cap with a magic marker, number them one thru whatever, and rotate the water every few months beginning with number one. Some of them will leak so be careful of where you store them.

"Hey Marge, do you have any water?"

"Yeah, look under the bed. Oh, and I think there's some in the oven, too."

Storage might become a problem, but it's doable if you have the space.

If your shelter is near a natural body of water like a river, stream, creek, lake, pond, slough, or a natural spring, then you have access to water. Okay, that's a valid question. How far is near? The answer depends on your ability to transport the water. If you're adjacent to the source, then you're good to go. If you have to walk miles to access it, you're too far away. Consider that a half hour walk to get water, carrying two 5-gallon water containers, plus the return trip, will take the average person about an hour and a half to complete. Not only that, but trust me, those two containers will get heavy before you get back to camp.

That means for a family of four, one person would have to make one trip a day totaling six hours. That's a lot of work to provide *minimum* water requirements, not to mention the drain on your time.

Your choices are to deal with it, find a way to cut down on the number of trips by carrying more water per trip, or move closer to the water source. Obviously, if you have enough containers, two people can make the trip and double the supply.

A note of caution is in order. You won't be the only one using the water source, so be careful when making your approach.

If you have a well on your property or you know where one's located, you can get the water out of the well, even though there's no electricity to run the pump. The well casing is the vertical pipe, usually located in the back yard that's about a foot high. Drilled residential well casings vary in size from 4" to 6". A drilled well has a submersible pump attached to the end of a hose and is located near the bottom of the casing/pipe. The casing may also be a 2" driven well with a "sand point" attached to a pipe at the bottom of the well. The pump for a driven well will be located somewhere near the well casing, in a small shed, a pit, or in a protected area of some sort.

There's a big difference between a driven well and a drilled well. When the cap is removed from the well casing, if there's a smaller metal pipe inside the casing, it's a driven well with a sand point attached to the bottom of the small inner pipe. It will be necessary to remove that inner pipe from the well casing to access the water.

To remove the inner pipe, you have to turn the gaskets on the sand point. It won't be easy to do, but once you've turned the gaskets by pulling the inner pipe up about 6" or so, the inner pipe can then be pulled out of the well casing. If you don't have a tripod and a chain hoist, eat a lot of Cheerios before you begin, because it's a real bitch.

If the well casing is 4" or more in diameter it's almost certainty a drilled well. A drilled well has electrical cables and a flexible water hose inside the casing that runs down to a submersible pump.

Removing the hose and cables from a drilled well is simple. Just pull the cables, hose and pump out of the well casing. Once you've removed the inner pipe from a driven well, or the cables, hose, and submersible pump from a drilled well, you can access the water at the bottom of the well.

Here's how: You'll need a slim container of some sort with an open end (top off) that'll fit inside the well casing. You'll also need to tie a rope to the container to lower it into the well casing. Place a weight at the bottom of the container so that it sinks once it enters the water. As an option, you can make a few small holes in the bottom of the container so it fills with water and sinks more readily. When the container is full, pull it up. If you punched or drilled holes in it, pull it up quickly since water will be leaking out of it.

You can purchase a device made specifically for this purpose. It's called a well bucket, but they don't work on a 2" driven well since the bucket is about 3" in diameter and about 4' long. The well bucket also has an eye at the top to attach a rope and a valve at the bottom. Lowering the bucket into the water will open the valve filling the bucket with water. It holds about one gallon. I highly recommend this device for those of you who have a drilled well or for anyone who lives in an area where drilled wells are common. Look in the hard to locate items section of the appendix for information on purchasing a well bucket.

If you know where a natural spring is, or you just stumble upon one, you've just hit the mother lode. You *know* spring water is good since you probably spend $50 a month buying treated tap water marketed as Natural Spring Water.

Other ways to provide water is by making a solar still, catching rainwater, melting ice and snow, and if you're really desperate, I suppose you could perform a rain dance.

So, now you have access to water, but is it safe to drink? Probably not!

If there's any question regarding the safety of the water, it has to be treated.

Methods of treating water can be cheap and effective or moderately expensive and highly effective.

A good hand-held water filter will provide great tasting water even if that water came from a mud puddle. While a top of the line microfilter, such as the Katadyn Pocket Filter, isn't cheap, it's worth every penny and will treat roughly 13,000 gallons of water.

However, there are other effective and cheaper ways to treat water for human consumption.

One simple method is to add chlorine bleach to the water. First, strain the water through a coffee filter or clean cloth to remove any large particles suspended in the water. Then add sixteen (16) drops of *unscented chlorine bleach* per gallon, stir to mix and let stand for about five minutes. Smell the water. If it smells like chlorine, it's safe to drink. If it doesn't, repeat the process until there's a faint odor of chlorine. Sulfur and other minerals can cause some water to smell like rotten eggs.

The water's safe to drink; it just smells. Removing the odor requires aeration. To aerate the water simply pour it back and forth between two containers. Adding air to the water will eliminate most, if not all, of the odor.

Other methods of purifying water include exposure to sunlight. If there are pathogens in the water, exposure to sunlight will kill most of them. Filter the water through a cloth and let it stand in direct sunlight for the day. It's not as effective as adding bleach, but in an emergency it beats dying of dehydration.

Boiling the water is one of the easiest methods of all to make water safe for consumption. Pathogens in the water will be killed off long before the water reaches the boiling point, but as long as fuel isn't a consideration, bringing the water to a full boil certainly won't do any harm. Allow the water to stand until it cools. Strain the water if you need to, and aerate it if it smells.

You can filter the water through sand, but this method will require some engineering on your part. Punch or cut holes in the bottom of a bucket and fill the bottom of the bucket with small pebbles, rocks etc, 2-3" deep. On top of the rocks, add, washed sand. Simply pour the water onto the sand and catch it in another container when it comes through the holes in the bottom of the bucket.

Water purification tablets are reasonably effective for treating small quantities of water for emergency purposes. Katadyn water purification tablets work well for treating small quantities of water.

Making your water safe to drink is *critical*! If the water is unsafe for human consumption, you're opening yourself up to a host of illnesses, the most likely of which will be horrible diarrhea, which in turn could easily lead to dehydration and death.

The following procedure will make almost any water safe to drink:

1. Filter the water through a clean cloth to remove large particles.
2. Boil the water and let it cool.
3. Add bleach to the water as described.
4. Aerate the water.

Whichever method of water treatment you use, allow the treated water to stand for several hours in direct sunlight (If possible.) If the water still has particulates suspended in it after it's been strained, allow the water to stand long enough for the particles to settle to the bottom of the container. You can then siphon the water off the top of the container using a piece of plastic tubing.

Survival Kit Essentials

1. Unscented chlorine bleach (Bleach is bleach. The best bleach is the cheapest bleach).
2. Clean cloth for filtering water. (Cheesecloth is excellent).
3. Eyedropper or measuring spoon. (1/2 teaspoon = about sixteen drops)
4. One five-gallon collapsible water container. (two if possible)
5. Bucket or other container (for aeration and other uses)
6. 6' length of 1/8" inside diameter plastic tubing. (Can also be used to siphon gas).
7. If you're cooking over an open fire (likely), you can use a heavy-duty steel pot with a bail handle as a bucket as well as for cooking. You can also use a Dutch Oven for boiling water, baking and cooking.

What's for dinner?

Food is the third and final "old basic" need for human survival, but it'll probably be the most difficult to secure. While it may not be the Ritz, shelter is going to be the easiest of the three original basics to provide, and although water may be more difficult to provide than shelter, it's in abundance almost everywhere in the country. Water just has to be made safe to drink. Food is a different story. When the store shelves are empty and there's no government to provide for you, when game is non-existent or scarce, and when you can't catch fish or harvest grains or vegetables, the survival stakes will have been raised dramatically. In other words, if you don't have a supply of food to rely on, you and your family are going to *starve to death!*

In fact, in a genuine catastrophe, starvation is likely to be responsible for more deaths than any other cause. Most people in this country have never experienced genuine hunger in their lifetimes since there's really no reason for anyone to have done so.

"Man, I'm starving," and "I haven't eaten anything in over two weeks" isn't the same kind of hunger. One is a craving; the other is genuine.

Will a thirty day supply of food be enough? Probably not, but it's a good starting point, and at least you'll have thirty days to figure out what to do next. In addition, stockpiling enough food to last for thirty days is well within the reach of everyone reading this book.

So what types of foods can you purchase that'll be economical, nutritious, and have a good shelf life? Fortunately, there are a lot of them.

Uncooked brown rice is available almost everywhere in 25 lb bags. Brown rice is high in nutrition, goes a long way, and will store for about a year. Moreover, it's inexpensive. White rice? Don't bother.

"But I don't like rice." Too bad! You don't have to like it; you just have to eat it.

You can purchase canned goods by the case and store them for years. (If the can has a bulge on the top, the contents are spoiled. Get rid of it.)

Other foods that last a long time are pastas such as macaroni, cereals, dry milk, dried fruit, syrup, etc. The expiration, or best if used by date on the package or can, doesn't mean the food's spoiled after that date. It simply means the food might begin to lose nutritional value after that date.

Dried beans or peas will store for about a year. Flour, pancake mix, soup stocks, bouillon, and just about anything else that's canned or packaged will actually last for quite awhile. Salt, which you'll need a lot of, and sugar, which you won't, will both last forever. One of the best survival foods you can store is honey. Honey literally lasts forever. If it crystallizes, simply warm it up to reconstitute it. Honey will provide a nutritious alternative to sugar and should definitely be a part of your survival food.

Other super-market foods that make sense are fully cooked microwavable meals, such as those from Hormel. Even though you won't be able to microwave them, you can empty the contents into a pan and heat them. They're a viable alternative to MRE's when you need a quick ready to eat meal and, although they aren't as tasty and the serving's aren't as large as an MRE, they can come in handy.

Adding a few extra items, such as a bag of rice or a jar of honey to your shopping cart each time you go to the store will allow you to build up a thirty day supply of food in a short period. Purchasing extra foods from the supermarket (if you're strapped for cash) is your first line of defense against future food shortages

How much food do you need for thirty days? Well, that depends, but it's definitely not as much as you might think. Your baby brother

"Beef," who normally consumes six or eight half pound burgers at the monthly barbecue's going to have to cut back, and you might have to consume a bit less too, but the actual amount of food you'll require will depend on your activity level.

If you're performing strenuous tasks that you weren't doing before the disaster happened, you'll be expending more energy, which in turn means you'll require more food. You'll also need more food in cold weather than you will in hot weather. In the end, everyone's requirements will differ, but regardless, you're likely to eat less food then than you do now since, for most Americans, eating is more a habit than a necessity.

If you doubt the veracity of that statement, sit on a bench, in any mall, in any city in America, and count the Twinkie eating fat asses waddling past.

Let's take a look at dehydrated foods, freeze-dried foods, and MRE's. All three types of long-life foods are extremely convenient, nutritious, and have exceptionally long shelf lives.

Dehydrated foods are simply foods that have the water removed. To reconstitute dehydrated foods, just put the water back. Nearly every type of food imaginable is available in dehydrated form, including butter, margarine, eggs, and, of course, milk. In addition, nearly every vegetable and fruit, plus desserts such as puddings, can also be purchased in dehydrated form. Dehydrated foods come in #10 cans (approximately 1-gallon), and in 5-gallon buckets, which is approximately 4.5 gallons.

If your budget will stand the strain, I whole-heartedly recommend that you purchase some of these foods. The hard red or white winter wheat in particular can become a life-sustaining staple. You can grind the wheat by using an inexpensive modern wheat grinder, or you can pound it the old-fashioned way with mortar and pestle. Either way, the bread you bake from using freshly ground wheat will be nothing like the bread you buy at the supermarket. It's the real deal, and you can live a long time on real bread. Depending on the specific type, dehydrated foods have a shelf life of five years to indefinitely. Note: If any of your food has weevils in it, don't worry about them. They won't hurt you. Consider them bonus protein.

Freeze-dried food also has the moisture removed, but the method of removal is different. Freeze-dried food is tasty, but they're also more expensive than dehydrated foods.

Freeze-dried foods come in #10 cans and can also be purchased in single-serving and family serving packages. To the best of my knowledge, they're not available in 5-gallon buckets. The main difference between dehydrated and freeze-dried foods is in the type of meal. Dehydrated foods generally consist of one type of food per container, such as green beans, while freeze-dried foods are usually one-dish meals, such as Mountain Chili. Some survival foods offer a combination of both. When you're using foods from a #10 can, it's not necessary to use the entire can all at once, as they come with a plastic lid to re-seal the can. Good thing, too. Who wants to eat a gallon of green beans at one sitting? The down side to the #10 can is, once opened, the contents begin to lose their nutritional value quickly. For that reason, you should attempt to consume opened cans within a reasonable amount of time.

Ultimately, freeze-dried foods should have a place in your long-term survival food supply. They'll be great for special occasions such as birthdays or simply as a moral booster. Freeze dried foods have an effective shelf life of five to seven years.

MRE's are foods issued to the troops in the field and can be purchased by the packet or by the case. They're precooked, tasty, high in nutrition, and can be eaten cold if necessary. MRE's have a shelf life of about seven years. When buying MRE's make certain they were packed within the last year. Some unscrupulous vendors will sell you MRE's that are due to expire within a year or that have already expired.

A vendors list for all three long-life storable foods is available in the appendix. (I've purchased from all of them and can vouch for the quality of the foods and the services they provide.)

The stated shelf life for all of these foods is an estimate, but if they're stored in a cool, dry location, the indicated shelf life will be fairly accurate

Now, having said that, I stored (out of necessity) about 100 #10 cans of various types of dehydrated foods and a couple of cases of MRE's that I purchased in 1997 in an outdoor, non air-conditioned storage unit in Florida for two years. When I removed them from storage in 2008, I checked several cans that had expired in 2003. They were perfectly fine and tasted as good as the day they were packed. How much nutritional value they provided, I don't know, but they were still edible.

Foraging for wild edible plants, nuts, berries, insects, grubs, catching fish, and hunting wild game will also be on your menu at some point in the future. We'll be covering them in Chapter nine.

Rather than attempt to tell you how to cook the food that you have, I'm going to focus on the type of cookware and utensils that you're going to need.

For the short term, the cookware and utensils you currently have in your kitchen will work. For the long-term, however, most of them won't hold up to the heavy usage you'll be giving them every day over an open fire. But if it's all you have and they're all that you can afford, you'll have to make them work. Of necessity, all camping items should be heavy duty, since they should last as long as possible.

If you can have only one piece of open-fire cookware, you can't go wrong with a cast iron Dutch oven. Cast iron is virtually indestructible, heats and cooks evenly, won't scratch, and unlike other types of cookware, you don't wash cast iron, you simply wipe it out. With the proper care, cast iron cookware will last for generations and gets better with each use.

While cast iron is heavy, its usefulness more than offsets its weight. You can use a cast iron Dutch oven to bake bread, as a pot, or as a frying pan, which makes it the most versatile piece of outdoor cookware you can own. In addition, you should consider a cast iron frying pan, a good set of grilling tools, and a heavy grill or grate to set the cookware on while you're cooking.

A potholder or towel will be necessary to move the cookware (it'll be hot,) and good aluminum or stainless steel dishes, bowls, cups, and cutlery will also come in handy. Throw in a pan of some sort to wash the dishes in, and before you forget, put a dishrag and dishtowel in, too. If you'll be packing your cooking gear in a bug-out bag, you can forget about cast iron. It's simply too bulky and heavy. Bug-out bag cookware should consist of a lightweight nesting cooking set. Look for a set made from anodized aluminum or stainless steel.

An indispensable (and inexpensive) cooking item is a large roll of the heaviest aluminum foil you can find. You can cook just about anything with aluminum foil by wrapping food in the foil and placing it on or near the coals of the fire.

Since you won't have refrigeration and, depending on the time of year, storing leftover foods will be a problem. Therefore, it makes sense not to prepare more food than you can consume in one sitting. Nevertheless, your days of throwing leftovers away are history. If it's hot, you can place leftovers in zip-lock storage bags and keep them edible by digging a hole and burying the baggie in the cooler soil. It won't last long, but it'll keep the food from going bad for a day.

Attempting to tell you how to cook over an open fire would be a book unto itself, and since there are, many, many books on the subject, you'd be wise to visit the library or go online to find information about campfire cooking. Suffice it to say, however, that a lot of the cooking you'll be doing, if you've never done it before, will be a trial and error affair. Learning outdoor cooking skills from a book has limitations.

In conclusion, if your budget won't allow you to purchase long term storable food, you'll be limited to the store bought foods you stock. A food supply that will last for thirty to ninety days isn't much when compared to a disaster that could last a year, five years, or more, but it's better than the old "stick in the eye."

The short answer to the food problem is a garden. We'll be covering gardening in Chapter Nine, Nature's Market. Having the ability to provide your own fruits and vegetables is the real key to ensuring your long-term survival.

I'm not going to recommend any essentials for food other than to urge you to consider the following minimal suggestions:

1. 12 #10 cans of hard red winter wheat
2. Wheat grinder
3. 10 lbs of *iodized* salt (because you wouldn't look good in a goiter)
4. At least 2 quarts of honey
5. Powered milk (enough to make at least ten gallons)
6. Some of your favorite spices

Survival Kit Recommendations

1. 10-12 quart cast iron Dutch oven, (not for the average bug-out bag)
2. 12"-14" cast iron fry pan (not for the average bug-out bag)
3. 10-12 quart HD steel or aluminum pot with bail handle (not for the average bug-out bag)
4. Cooking grill or grate
5. Plastic dishwashing pan
6. Dish towel and cloth (two ea.)
7. 200' roll HD aluminum foil
8. HD dishes, bowls, cups
9. HD cutlery
10. Grilling tools, spatula and tongs
11. Large serving spoon and soup ladle
12. Anodized aluminum or stainless steel nesting cookware set if using a bug-out bag. (Replaces items 1-2-3)

Light my fire

Fire is arguably the greatest discovery of all time. It changed everything. The well-appointed cave could be heated, you could see your mate at night (which might not have been a good thing), and you had a degree of protection against marauding animals. Fire also allowed ancient man to begin the long journey toward civilization.

Yeah, fire was definitely a big deal to prehistoric man. It's going to be just as big a deal for you, too.

Imagine that you live in the north and it's winter. There're plenty of trees around for fuel, but you don't have a way to harvest them. You don't have an axe, a saw, or a knife. There're plenty of pine needles and twigs you can burn, but you don't have any way to light them, which means you won't be cooking the fish you just caught. But it's not all bad. You *can* eat the fish raw, so even though you're faced with the prospect of a long, cold, dark night, you'll have some food in your belly.

How ridiculous is that? The answer is, it's not ridiculous at all. The ability to create a fire is going to rank right up there with water on your list of necessities. Without fire, you're going to be living in the stone age, or whatever age it was when man discovered sushi before discovering fire.

A heat, light, and cooking source that you probably never gave a second thought to now becomes a life-saving necessity. If you had fire on the night described above, you would have considered it an absolute luxury. But you get the point. Fire, or rather the ability to make a fire, will be one of your top priorities.

One nice thing about technology is that we don't have to wait around for a lightning strike, make a fire-bow, or attempt to use a flint to create a fire. Providing a flame today is as easy as striking a match or flicking your Bic.

We're going to look at fire from a heating and cooking perspective even though fire does produce a degree of light.

Some of you probably have a 500-gallon LP bomb in your back yard and you probably use it for heating, and maybe for cooking. If you do, you won't be able to use that gas for heating anymore, since there won't be any electricity.

However, if you have a gas range, you can use the oven to heat a small area, and you can still use the stove for cooking until the gas is gone. If you're going to use the oven as a source of heat, remember to provide adequate ventilation. Crack windows on opposite sides of the room even if it's below zero outside. Waking up warm, but dead, would be a sorry ending to your survival efforts. Along those same lines, *under no circumstances* use a barbeque grill indoors.

Okay, where were we? Oh, yeah, fire.

To produce heat from a fire, or to cook food, you have to have fuel. Fortunately, you can use many things. Wood is the obvious choice, although if you live in coal-country you might opt for coal. Woods, such as dry oak, hickory, maple, and birch are all hardwoods and produce more BTU's (heat) than softwoods such as aspen or evergreens. Nevertheless, dry aspen, for example, will produce more heat than wet oak since the majority of the energy in the oak is expended driving the moisture from the wood. To burn efficiently, wood has to be dry, which means that the moisture present in the tree when it was alive needs time to evaporate. The process of curing (drying) the wood is done by splitting the wood and exposing it to the air. Curing green (live) wood can take months or even years if the tree was large enough and the wood hasn't been cut, split, and stacked. Unfortunately, you don't have the luxury of waiting for green wood to cure.

Green wood of any kind will burn, but it's hard to ignite and to keep it burning. It also won't produce a lot of heat. It *will* generate a lot of smoke. Woods from different trees burn differently and produce different types of coal beds. You'll use the coal bed for cooking purposes, so a good bed of coals is essential. To keep it simple, remember this: If the wood you're going to burn is from an evergreen tree (think Xmas tree) or, the bark of the tree is light grey or smooth, it's probably a softwood. Softwoods will generally have low heating values, burn quickly, and produce little or no coals. If the tree has leaves, or no leaves in the winter, and the bark is rough, it's probably a hardwood. If there are acorns on the ground under the tree, it's an oak. Hardwoods such as oak and hickory are excellent heat producers when dry, provide outstanding coal beds, and they burn slowly. In addition, some variant of oak grows in almost every state.

So hardwood trees are preferable to softwood trees for heating and cooking, but the wood has to be reasonably dry to burn efficiently. Since you can't wait for green wood to cure, try to locate standing deadwood, which is a tree that's dead, but is still standing. Depending upon how long ago the tree died and how large it is, at least some of the moisture will have evaporated, leaving some (or all) of the wood burnable. The smaller the diameter of the tree, the better the chance that the wood is cured. If the tree's too large for you to cut down, you can lop (cut) off some of the branches and cut them into smaller, usable pieces. On the other hand, you can look for deadfalls, which are dead trees that have fallen down. Deadfalls may have stood dead for years before finally falling, but the deadfall could also be the result of a lightning strike six months ago, in which case the wood will still be green. If the tree's been dead for years but has been laying on the ground, the part that's in contact with the ground is going to be wet. In any case, the branches that are sticking up will be reasonably dry, and they're your best bet for burnable wood from that tree.

Remember this: The smaller in diameter the dead wood is, the drier it's likely to be.

If you're going to harvest trees for firewood, you'll need some tools to cut them down with. For larger trees, you'll need two felling wedges, an axe or a saw, and preferably both. For branches, you can use a hatchet, a small saw, or even a machete.

Experienced woodcutters know that felling large trees, whether dead or alive, can be *extremely dangerous*. Therefore, I would suggest you read up on how to cut down trees in a safe manner. You'd look pretty silly lying there with a couple of tons of oak sitting on your head.

All right, you've located some dry wood and you've gathered enough to last for awhile. However, you can't light a log and expect it to burn easily. You have to have some tinder. Tinder can be small dry twigs, dried grass, moss, paper, or a commercially available fire starter. You'll also need matches or a lighter to ignite the tinder. If you have a magnifying glass in your pack, it'll work okay on a bright sunny day but it's best used as an emergency back-up.

There are many ways to build a fire, and you can learn about them at your leisure. However, a simple way to start a fire is: Choose an area that's sheltered from the wind, or that will be if it gets windy, and clear the area where you're going to build the fire by scraping away the leaves etc.

Prior to starting the fire make certain it's located far enough away from anything that can ignite, including your tent and the branches of trees that are directly above the area where the fire will be located. Let's say you've located some dead, dry grass. Place the grass in the center of the scraped area and arrange the twigs in a "teepee" over the grass. Light the grass, and when the twigs begin to burn, patiently place proportionately larger twigs on the burning pile. Continue to place progressively larger pieces of wood on the fire until you have a decent blaze going. When the fire is big enough, put a small log on and continue adding larger logs as necessary.

If the fire you're going to build will be permanent or semi-permanent, you can dig a "fire-pit" prior to starting the fire. Simply dig a hole about 10" deep and perhaps 24" long by 18" wide; the size doesn't make much difference. If you need a large fire, dig a larger pit. Line the pit with *heavy* stones, such as granite. (Some stones will explode when heated and are dangerous, so avoid light-weight rocks such as sandstone.) Start the fire in the pit. After the fire is going, the rocks will get hot and hold the heat, and the coal bed will last long after the fire itself has burned out. If it's cold, you'll appreciate the stored heat the rocks will slowly give off during the course of the night. In the morning simply put more wood on the remaining coals to rekindle the fire.

Other fuels can be cardboard boxes, rolled up magazines or newspaper, peat, dried sod, corncobs, dead bushes, grass, pine needles, and leaves. In fact, you can burn any plant for fuel. You can also break up furniture, benches, flooring etc. but be aware that any wood that's been treated, which includes painted wood, will produce a toxic gas. Make sure you don't breathe the smoke, and don't use this type of wood for cooking until it's burned down to the coals.

Consider this section to be a starter course since there's certainly more you can learn.

To make your own tinder, tear or cut newspaper into strips about 1" wide and compress them into one gallon zip-lock freezer bags. Two bags is a good start. Be cognizant of the fact that moisture can ruin your survival supplies. Critical items should be double-bagged in zip-lock HD freezer bags. Since you're only getting one shot at this, the last thing you need is to have your supplies ruined by water.

Survival Kit Essentials

1. A camping saw with an extra blade
2. A cruiser axe (3/4 sized)
3. A hatchet (optional; will double as a hammer)
4. Two boxes of large "farmer" matches (definitely double bag these)
5. Two disposable lighters
6. Folding entrenching tool (shovel; make sure it's a good one)
7. Tinder
8. 10" single mill bastard file with a slip on handle. (Yeah that's what it's called. Probably refers to the offspring of two unmarried files or maybe an adjective used to describe the word

that's uttered when it slips during use.) You'll use the file to keep your axe and hatchet sharp.

Who turned out the lights?

We now have shelter, food, water, fire and now, light. Not quite a Holiday Inn but we're getting closer. A fire will produce *some* light, of course, but only enough to chase away the darkness. However, there may be times at night when you won't want a continuous light from a fire for security reasons. In addition, if you're sitting next to the fire, you won't be able to see anything on the other side of the fire, but anyone just outside the lighted perimeter will be able to see *you* just fine.

Other reasons why you might not want to depend on fire as a light source are: fire produces heat, because the weather, (be it high winds or monsoon rains,) may preclude you from getting one started, and because it's difficult to do any intricate work by the light of a fire. In addition, fire isn't portable, unless you make a torch, and last but by no means least, burning a fire in your kitchen as a light source probably wouldn't be one of your better ideas.

A dependable light source will do wonders for your overall comfort and security. It'll push back the darkness, allow you to read, write, do necessary intricate work, and you can luxuriate in all of the emotional benefits the light will provide for you. If you've never sat in total darkness in a house or in the woods for an extended period of time, take my word for it, it won't be high up on the list of things you'll want to experience before you go to that big campsite in the sky.

When selecting items for your survival kit, you'll have thousands of options to choose from for your lighting choices. However, let the buyer beware, not all flashlights, for example, are created equally. It's the job of any marketing company to create an effective advertisement that will help sell as many flashlights as possible. I guarantee that you won't find an ad anywhere like this.

"Hey, we're well aware this flashlight is a cheap piece of junk, but we need to pay the rent and buy some beer, so please try one."

In fact, it probably *is* a piece of junk, only works the first time you turn it on, shatters into several pieces when dropped, corrodes even when sealed in a vacuum, and is probably made in China. However, the ad says something like this.

"This is the last flashlight you'll ever have to buy." It functions flawlessly, first time, every time, and in an emergency, when seconds count, it can be used as a defibrillator."

In the old days, before the disaster, you'd simply toss it or take it back and attempt to get a refund. You can't do either now.

Every item you put in your survival kit has to work the first time, everytime. NO EXCEPTIONS! Every item you have has to be able to take abuse, too. They all have to last, and they have to be dependable. They should also be economical.

So regardless of how effectively the product is hyped, don't believe every ad that you read. If I personally recommend an item by name, it's because I know from personal experience that particular item will fit the criteria I just mentioned, or the product was recommended to me by someone whose experience, expertise, and word I would bet my life on. Recommended products, as well as reliable vendors, are in the appendix.

You can produce light in a variety of ways. One of the earliest methods and one that's still in use today is the candle. No moving parts, nothing to break, and they're relatively inexpensive. Any candle will work, but like everything else in life, some work better than others. The only real shortcoming to the candle is that it's expendable. If the candle is going to be your only light source, when it's used up the fat lady sang her song and you're in the dark.

Soy candles, while more expensive than paraffin candles, burn longer and don't give off toxins since they're produced from soy, which is a bean. In addition, they also don't have lead in the wicks.

Paraffin wax candles are made from petroleum products, do give off toxic fumes and don't burn as long. Paraffin candles, however, are much more readily available than soy candles and they're quite a bit cheaper, too. As far as toxicity is concerned, it shouldn't be a big deal, since it's doubtful the Green Police will be bursting into your shelter to haul you off to jail for burning a disgusting, earth-destroying paraffin wax candle. If they do show up, you don't need any advice from me on how to handle those morons.

So, do you choose soy or paraffin? If you can afford it, the soy candles will last longer, but you can purchase several equal-sized paraffin candles for the price of one soy candle. Then too, there are so many different types, shapes, sizes, and aromas to choose from that making a final decision could take years.

Therefore, I suggest you buy unscented pillar candles about four inches tall and maybe two or three inches in diameter. Does it really matter if your tent smells like "chocolate-strawberry rhapsody surprise" as opposed to old wet socks?

In the event you'll be temporarily residing in a tent, a handy little item is a backpacking candle lantern. They're spectacular little lights using small styrene candles, come with a nifty little glass chimney, and can be hung from the center loop of a tent.

Don't forget that a lighted candle is capable of igniting something above it. Be careful where you place your burning candles, especially in a tent!

If you have a Coleman-style lantern, it will definitely produce light. You'll need extra lantern fuel and some spare mantels. They're great for outdoors use, but they can't be used indoors. *Ever!* They also produce quite a bit of heat. When the fuel's used up, you can use it as a boat anchor or maybe a minnow trap.

For indoor use, I've never found anything that compares to the Aladdin lamp. I have several of them, and they're the closest thing to an electric light you're ever going to find. They burn clean and are extremely reliable. The downside is they're not cheap. In fact, they're expensive. If you purchase one of these little beauties, you'll need to get some spare parts such as mantels, wicks, and maybe an extra chimney and a burner unit.

A special paraffin based fuel is available for the Aladdin, but it functions just as well on kerosene. As an aside, the Aladdin is quite decorative so even if you never use it in a survival situation, it'll fit nicely into a lot of decors.

Other types of lights are Hurricane lamps, which are relatively inexpensive, run on kerosene, and can be used indoors, and battery operated lamps. You can purchase a small, lightweight solar panel with an AA/AAA battery charger and rechargeable batteries for those devises that use batteries of that size.

The flashlight should be near the top of your list. You should have one flashlight per person and perhaps a spare. Purchase one made from quality heavy duty aluminum or other tough metal. It should be an LED type with no bulb to break or burnout, and it should take AA batteries. Large, D battery flashlights do throw a lot of light, but for survival purposes they're not as useful as a AA light.

The most critical part of a flashlight is the only part that moves, which is the switch. Cheap flashlights have cheap switches! Purchase a flashlight that has a tail-cap switch, which is a push button switch built into the bottom of the light. This type of flashlight will allow you to use momentary on/off, or even send signals. I recently purchased a little

2-cell AA LED flashlight that was on sale for about fifty bucks. It throws a focused beam out to about 100 yards, and it's almost as good as some of my other lights that cost four times as much.

You can expect to spend anywhere from $40 to $100 plus for a high quality LED flashlight. Whatever flashlight you ultimately choose, make certain you purchase a good one.

Another type of flashlight that's useful is a self-generating one. They require no batteries, but generate their own power by either shaking the light vigorously for about twenty seconds, by squeezing the handle built into the light, or by turning a crank. They're inexpensive, but most of them do have bulbs that can break. (Several companies make an emergency LED crank light.)

A glow stick, or snap-light, is a special glass tube with a chemical inside that's activated when the glass is snapped. They're great emergency or marker lights and come in several variants. Two of the most useful are the yellow light that lasts about twenty minutes, and the high intensity white light that lasts about five minutes. They're inexpensive and well worth your consideration.

One other type of light I'll mention briefly is the 250 trillion candle-power, hand-held spotlight. Not a mandatory survival item by any stretch, but if you're bored, you can amuse yourself by shooting down any satellites that remain in orbit or by blinding any critter (or person) that looks at the beam.

I recommend that all of your battery-operated devices use the same AA battery. It eliminates the need to purchase different size batteries and, in the event relocation is necessary, they weigh less and take up less space. In addition, if you're in a hurry, you don't have to hunt around for different sized batteries.

Although alkaline batteries are yesterdays technology and can leak, they're still useful. If at all possible, rechargeable Nickel-cadmium (NICAD) batteries are a much better choice. NICAD batteries can be recharged many, many times, so their initially high price, compared to alkaline batteries, makes them cheaper in the long run.

The small solar battery charger I mentioned earlier will recharge the NICAD batteries, and will even put a small charge back in dead alkaline batteries. A good solar battery charger won't require direct, bright sunlight to function properly. Get one. You won't regret it.

Batteries don't last long in cold weather. The colder it is, the less efficient they'll be, thus it's important to keep your batteries as warm as possible. In extreme cold you can put them next to your body to keep them warm.

Before we go any further into the book, I'd like to point out it's extremely important to make every effort not to draw attention to yourself or to your shelter. That statement applies to every aspect of everything you'll be reading about from this moment on.

It's likely the local citizenry will be much more dangerous than the environment. Therefore, it would be wise to remember there are going to be people willing to take whatever you have, using whatever means they deem appropriate, including killing and raping you and yours.

With that in mind, you should make every effort to make your shelter appear unoccupied, or at least as though you have nothing worth taking. The bottom line is, *don't draw attention to yourself.* Eliminate noise and visible interior light at night. (We'll cover this topic in more depth shortly.)

Survival Kit Essentials

1. LED flashlight with tail-cap switch and AA batteries
2. At least one set of batteries for each device that you have
3. Candles. The quantity and quality is up to you but at least two or three medium size pillar candles.

Sticks, stones and shotguns

Sticks and stones may break your bones, but a shotgun will definitely kill ya!

Since you have to be able to defend what you have, sticks and stones are off the table. Yeah, you could provide some sort of defense with a branch and a rock, but it would be short-lived against a bad guy with a gun. Will the bad guys have guns? Does it snow at the North Pole? There‘s absolutely no question you have to be armed. Not necessarily to the teeth, mind you, but you do have to be able to defend yourself.

If you ask a hundred knowledgeable people what the optimal survival weapon would be for this type of situation you'd get a lot of different answers. For the most part, anyone with firearms experience will have a personal preference. However, we're not interested in personal preferences; we're concerned about *the very best choice for a survival weapon.* The weapon you're going to need should be chosen for it's *defensive* capabilities above all else. If at all possible, *you should avoid any situation requiring an offensive weapon.* (More on that topic later.) Additionally, when referring to a weapon, we're not talking about a sword, bow & arrow, a main battle tank, or your mother-in-law's sharp tongue; we're talking about a firearm.

For practical purposes, there are three types of firearms to consider. They are rifles, shotguns, and handguns. Those categories can be broken down into different sections. A rifle choice comes down to a bolt-action or a semi-automatic, a shotgun to either an automatic or a pump-action, and a handgun should be either a semi-automatic or a revolver. There are other considerations too such as caliber and gauges, and after selecting the caliber and/or the gauge, there's the cartridge and shot size.

If that sounds complicated or confusing, relax, I'll simplify it for you.

Let's assume there can be only one best survival weapon. What criteria should be used in determining which one that will be? Let's take a look.

1. The firearm should be easy to use and maintain, and has to be reliable.
2. It shouldn't be necessary to spend hours of practice with the firearm to be a good enough shot to have a chance of hitting what you're shooting at.
3. As a defensive weapon, it should provide adequate stopping power and protection.
4. The weapon should have offensive capability.
5. The weapon should be versatile and allow you to hunt birds and small game as well as medium sized big game.
6. Ammunition for the weapon should be available from a wide variety of sources.
7. The weapon shouldn't cost an arm and a leg.

The only firearm in the world that comes close to meeting those criteria is a .12 Ga. shotgun

A person who knows absolutely nothing about guns can be proficient with a .12 Ga. in a short time. In addition, using a shotgun doesn't require hours of practice to become a good shot. Extreme accuracy isn't necessary; you just have to get close. The .12 Ga. is also simple to use and easy to maintain. In close quarters, a .12 Ga. shotgun will provide you with devastating stopping power, as well as limited, but effective offensive firepower if the need should arise.

The .12 Ga. is effective for hunting any type of bird or small game, and is adequate on certain types of big game. And, as far as ammunition availability goes, the .12 Ga. is used by both the military, all branches of law enforcement, and is far and away the most popular shotgun gauge in use today, which means you'll have an excellent chance of securing additional ammo if you run low.

Last but not least, a good .12 Ga. pump action shotgun won't require a 2nd mortgage on the farm.

There's no question that a .12 Ga. shotgun, and more specifically a .12 Ga. pump-action shotgun, should be your number one choice as a disaster-survival weapon.

Let's examine the .12 Ga. more closely. Are there any disadvantages? Of course there are. Two areas that make the .12 Ga. a bit less than perfect are the size and weight of the ammo and the effective range. However, you can eliminate range as a factor since the last thing you should consider is a gun battle with a bad guy at a distance of more than fifty yards. The ammo, while bulky and heavy, offers a degree of compensation by allowing the shooter to use less ammo to hit the intended target. For our purposes, the disadvantages are negligible.

On the plus side of the ledger, I assure you a bad guy who's hit with a load of .12 Ga. #00 buck isn't going anywhere but down. And quickly too. Depending on the load you're using, every time you pull the trigger from 9 to 15 .30 caliber pellets will be heading toward the bad guy.

In short, he's going down and you're getting away. A good barrel length for a defensive shotgun is 26"- 28," with the optimum being a 26" barrel with an improved cylinder choke. A 28" barrel with a modified choke is the only other logical combination to consider. An open-choked barrel (no choke at all) reduces the effective range too dramatically, while a 30" full-choked barrel, although increasing the effective range, is less effective in close quarters.

A .12 Ga. pump action shotgun with a 26" Improved Cylinder barrel loaded with 2-3/4" or 3" #00 buckshot will give you a world-class close quarters weapon at a very reasonable price.

A parting thought on the .12 Ga. pump. If you're ever involved in a fire-fight, your adrenalin will be off the charts. Under those conditions, if you're not experienced, it's easy to forget to "rack a round" (pump) after each shot. *Not good*! Spend adequate time dry firing and pumping the shotgun. (Use a Snap Cap to protect the firing pin.)

Realistically, a back-up weapon to a .12 Ga. shotgun should be a revolver or a semi-automatic handgun. The criteria for selecting a survival handgun is quite different from choosing a main line defensive weapon such as the shotgun. While a revolver is easier to use and maintain than a semi-automatic, maintenance and use of the auto isn't rocket science by any means.

Whatever handgun you choose will require a good deal of practice, which translates into time and ammo to become a good shot. That's reality. In addition, most handgun cartridges will *not* put a bad guy down with one shot. Or even two or three, contrary to what you see in the movies. Hunting with a handgun chambered for a center fire cartridge isn't a good idea for the average person since it requires a great deal of skill, and in any event most calibers are either too big for small game or too small for big game. That doesn't mean a handgun shouldn't be considered. To the contrary, a handgun is the obvious and logical choice as a backup to the shotgun.

What type and what caliber should you choose? There are two. Unfortunately, although I hate to admit it, since I'm not a big fan of the cartridge, the logical choice is the 9mm. That means a semi-automatic. Now I have no problem with the semi-auto; in fact I recommend the auto over the revolver. My problem is with the 9mm cartridge. Is it a man stopper? No, it's not. Even with a properly constructed bullet, the 9mm is marginal, especially when compared to the .45 Auto or the .40 S&W.

So why do I recommend the 9mm over all other calibers? With the proper bullet, and proper bullet placement, the nine is adequate. It's the availability of the cartridge that sends it straight to the top of the charts. All branches of the military and the majority of law enforcement organizations use the 9mm. The nine is also a NATO cartridge, and like the .12 GA., if you run low on ammo, the chances of finding some are good. In addition, 9mm ammo is reasonably lightweight (which means you can carry more of it) and practice ammo is cheap.

Furthermore, the recoil of the nine is light, and there are more handguns chambered for the 9mm than for any other round.

The 9mm is one of the two best choices for a disaster-survival handgun cartridge.

The other is the .22LR. The .22LR isn't a defensive cartridge. In fact, a bad guy smelling blood and pumped full of adrenaline may not even know he's been shot with a .22LR until later on. Can the .22 kill someone? Of course it can. Put it won't put them down, or stop them. With a head shot, maybe. But don't count on it. The .22LR is simply not a defensive or an offensive round. As a survival round, however, the .22LR is superb. It's the most popular caliber of all time, it's small and lightweight, inexpensive, and it's available almost everywhere. The .22LR is also a great small game cartridge and has no recoil. If you can swing a 9mm and a .22LR, do so.

The last viable survival firearm option is a rifle. A rifle chambered for the .22LR makes sense if you can carry both the rifle and a shotgun, but we're in the market for a center-fire rifle that can be used for hunting as well as defensive and offensive purposes. Lot's of choices here.

Most people who are preparing to survive are stocking thousands of 5.56 (.223 Rem.) rounds for their assault rifles. That's okay if you think you're going to need suppressing firepower, or you're looking for offensive capabilities. However, if you can only pick one rifle cartridge to use in a disaster-survival situation, there are certainly better and more versatile choices available.

What should you look for in a center fire rifle cartridge, and what type of gun should you select? We're looking for a weapon chambered for a cartridge that will allow us to provide defense, to take game, and perhaps offer a limited long-range offensive capability. We want the cartridge to be reasonably small, yet powerful enough to have enough energy at long distances to affect a kill. The cartridge should also be popular and readily available from a wide variety of sources. In addition, it should be available in a rifle that's reliable and easy to maintain.

Without doubt, you should choose a bolt-action rifle over a semi-automatic. They're easier to maintain, highly accurate, and extremely reliable. They won't provide the fire-power an assault rifle brings to the table, but for survival purposes, the bolt-action is a better choice. The cartridge I whole-heartedly endorse is the .308 Win. (7.62 NATO.) The .308 is used by the military and by the majority of law enforcement agencies. It's a popular commercial cartridge as well, and every manufacturer offers a rifle chambered for the .308 Win. Additionally the cartridge is short, meaning you can carry more of them, is much more powerful than the 5.56, is extremely accurate, and makes a superb sniper round. It also has a much longer effective range than the 5.56 and is capable of taking any animal in the lower 48. A bolt-action rifle in .308 Win. is the best survival rifle choice.

A collection of those four firearms will provide you with the most used, and arguably the most useful calibers in America. In addition, your chances of finding ammunition for all of them are good to excellent.

Survival Kit Essentials

.12 Ga. Pump-action shotgun with 26" barrel and Improved cylinder choke

1 box (24 rounds minimum) .12 Ga. #00 buckshot

9mm semi-automatic
1 box (50 rounds minimum) JHP 9mm cartridges

Optional

.22LR semi-auto pistol, revolver or rifle
.22LR Hi-Velocity cartridges (100 rounds minimum)
Bolt-action rifle (scoped) .308 Win. Caliber
1 box (20 rounds minimum) .308 Win. Cartridges, 180 Gr. Soft Point

Stop or I'll shoot!

When I told a liberal friend what this section was about, she informed me I'd be upsetting a lot of people if I wrote the chapter the way I planned to. She's probably right. Some people just don't like hearing the truth, especially if that truth doesn't fit into their perception of reality. However, changing how the truth is worded to make it more palatable means it's no longer the truth.

If a worst-case scenario unfolds and *you're* personally involved in a *genuine life or death situation*, the chances of your survival will be limited if you don't adjust your thought processes.

Do you actually think those gang-bangers coming towards you want to sit in a circle and sing 60's love songs or have a dialogue about global warming? If you do, you're going to be dead. Or God forbid, there *are* things worse than death.

When someone actually attempts to kill you or your family, when it's happening to you, and not to someone you saw on the news, or read about on the Internet, your thought processes will change instantly and dramatically.

But, I digress. If you honestly don't believe anything remotely resembling the situations in this book could possibly happen in this country, or to you personally, good luck. You're going to need it!

Ok, we're off.

Stop or I'll shoot means exactly what it says. *You* should mean *exactly* what you say too.

If you're not willing, or are emotionally incapable of pulling the trigger, then don't issue the command. The phrase *stop or I'll shoot* means you're telling someone to stop coming toward you, to stop doing whatever they're doing that makes you uncomfortable, that feels threatening to you, or that simply doesn't look right.

Don't make the mistake of running off at the mouth like a woodpecker with diarrhea "Take one more step and I'll blow your fricken head off" or "who are you and what do you want" may not be understood for a variety of reasons. They're also not commands. You have to issue *commands*. Those commands should be made in a *loud, clear, calm voice*, and they should be *short*. *Stop! Don't Move*, and *Drop the Gun* are all proper *initial* commands.

But I'm getting ahead of myself, so let's back up a bit. You've put in a lot of time, effort, and a significant amount of your hard earned money into the preparation of your survival kit and plan. You've gathered all the necessary survival supplies, and you've spent countless hours studying different survival applications. You've even prepared a safe area, and you're good to go. Then, suddenly, "it" happens. Within a matter of weeks, maybe days, society has descended into anarchy and your world has become a *very* dangerous place indeed.

The sun is setting and it's getting dark. You've been spending a lot of time watching the street in front of your shelter (house), which is what you're doing now. Fortunately, there's still enough light to see the two armed men walking slowly down the middle of the street. They stop directly in front of your shelter, turn, and look in your direction. Suddenly and, without warning they head straight toward your front door. Alarm bells should have been going off in your head the instant you saw them. If they weren't, they'd better be going off now.

Under normal circumstances, the image I just described would cause any sane person to question the motives of the two approaching men. Well, here's a news flash! *This is a normal circumstance*. Normality has simply taken on a different meaning due to the situation.

What might have happened under the "old" normal circumstances? The two men might have knocked on your door and, given the fact they were armed, you probably would have been reluctant to open it. Instead, you might have asked (through the door) what they wanted as your spouse feverishly dialed 911. The answer could have been that they just saw a man shoot someone a couple of blocks away and that the shooter ran in this direction. Asking if you saw anyone and telling you that the cops were on the way, they suggest you lock your door as they head back down the street.

It was probably true, too, which means all is well, and you have an exciting tale to tell the next day at work.

However, these are the "new" normal circumstances and those "new" normal circumstances are likely to change daily, perhaps hourly, for the near future. There's no 911 to call, and the two men coming toward your house are more than likely after whatever they think you have. It could be your food, your supplies, your wife, your daughter, or it could be they're simply criminals released from the constraints of society.

So if you *assume* they're not dangerous, you're going to suffer the consequences of that assumption. Unfortunately, the consequences are unlikely to be pretty.

Okay, should you shoot first and ask questions later? Do you hope they knock on the door and, getting no response, move on to the next house? Should you step out with gun in hand and ask what they want? Should you flee? You don't have too many options here, but the decision you make will have to be made quickly and will depend on your experiences since everything went to hell, any information that you were able to gather, and probably whatever your "gut" is telling you to do. *Your priority is to stay alive, and you should do whatever it takes to ensure that your priorities take precedence over everything else!*

I can't tell you what to do. Every town, every neighborhood, every house, and every circumstance will be different.

Perhaps the most difficult aspect of making a decision will be to acknowledge that the "old" normal circumstances no longer exist, and that the game and the players have changed. Dramatically!

A logical progression with the above scenario might be, as the men approach your shelter, and from behind cover, you command them (in a loud, clear, calm voice) to STOP! If they obey, you might ask them what they want. Their actions will tell you what your next move should be.

These guys could be a diversion, and others may be advancing on your rear. With that in mind, make sure someone has your back. They could also have a sniper covering their approach in the event you're stupid enough to expose yourself. Whatever their response is, you do the talking; they'll provide the answers. Under no circumstances answer any questions they ask until you're absolutely positive their intentions are benign.

If you're unable to conclude they're harmless to you, tell them to move off your property. If they hesitate or flat out refuse, then your response becomes more obvious. Let's assume they ignored the command to move off of your property, and they slowly begin moving apart while bringing their weapons, which had been held by their sides, up to waist level. What would that tell you? It *should* tell you they're getting ready to attack, because they are. Should you shoot? Under the "old" normal circumstances, few people would have opened fire. The Rules of Engagement (ROE) here are simple. There are none. It's every man for himself.

If you want to stay alive, which of course, you do, you have three viable choices: allow them to initiate hostilities, take them out, or flee. In addition, that decision will have to be made *instantaneously*! If you decide to shoot, make sure you get them both, which is a hell of a lot harder to do than it sounds. If you shoot and don't get both of them, you might as well exercise your last option and get out, because the one you missed will doubtless be coming back with reinforcements.

If you have to make a strategic withdrawal, don't hesitate. Do it *immediately*. By this time you should realize you can't afford to be injured or killed. Living to fight another day is the choice of an intelligent person who's putting their family's welfare first.

Alright, what if the two guys didn't speak English, and didn't understand what you were saying? Well, that could happen, couldn't it? If they don't understand English, that's not your problem. It's their responsibility to learn the language of the country they're living in. If they didn't take the time, or didn't care enough to learn our language, they'll have to suffer the consequences. That's just the way it is. If you assume, even for a second, that they might not have understood you because they didn't speak English, you could end up dead.

Don't misunderstand me, I'm not advocating that you shoot and kill anyone. What I'm advocating is that you do whatever you have to do to protect your family.

Right now I suspect there are readers who are absolutely appalled by this chapter. "But they're human beings, and they have rights, you can't just shoot them." The hell you can't! If you're offended by those words, I hope to God you're never involved in a situation of this type because the odds are you and your innocent family are going to die.

Remember that society, at least as we knew it, no longer exists. *It's gone*! Along with the police and the laws we lived by. *Gone!* For the near future, you're going to be alone with scumbags who'll kill you and take what you have. The phrases "it's a jungle out there" and "survival of the fittest" will be the operative words you'll be living with for quite awhile.

It's pretty easy to guess why a criminal, and I use that term lightly, would attack you, but it's difficult to determine how many there might be, where the attack will come from, the time that it'll take place, or how it will be conducted.

And because there're so many variables involved in a shoot/don't shoot situation, it's impossible to give you an example that could help you decide what to do if you're ever forced to make the decision to shoot. Your goal, no, let's change that, your mandate is to stay alive and to protect your family.

With all of that in mind, my advice is to attempt to find a happy medium between "shoot first and ask questions later" and "shoot as a last resort!" In the end, *use your head and listen to your gut.* Is it better to be wrong and alive or to have been right but dead? You decide.

If you're confronted with an attacking force that's larger than yours or that has more firepower than you do, it doesn't make a lot of sense to involve yourself in a firefight. You'll lose and you'll be dead. I know a lot of you will defend what's yours to the bitter end, and personally, I'm okay with that as long as you're prepared to conduct a capable defense. I can relate. It's not in my nature to head out the back door and abandon everything I have either. However, if the bad guys have a tank and all I have is a .12 Ga., adios. I'm not that stupid.

Since the odds are that you're going to have to withdraw at some point in time to stay alive, everyone should have a packed bug-out bag readily available, and your escape plan should be implemented the second your instincts tell you it's time to leave. (Much more on bug-out bags later on.)

All right, let's re-visit the two bad guys who were approaching your shelter. What caused them to stop, turn, and look at your house? They were walking down the street, then looked in your direction and stopped. Right? You forgot not to draw attention to yourself, didn't you? What was it? It could've been a noise, a visible light, cooking odors, or maybe the dog barking. Or perhaps your shelter just had that lived in look.

Unfortunately there's no way to occupy a shelter and eliminate every telltale sign of occupancy, especially cooking odors and the smoke from your fire. So if you can't realistically eliminate the signs that tell the world that someone lives here, what *can* you do? You can take two approaches.

You can make your house look as though it's already been vandalized, and that everything of value has been taken. Break an unimportant window, litter the lawn, and hope any bad guys cruising through the neighborhood pass you by. This method won't be effective for long, but it could buy you the time to get out safely.

The best long-term methods are much more dependable and effective. First, begin by doing your best to curtail any obvious signs of occupancy, such as noise, a light visible from the outside, or the dog barking. Second, if you ended up with a partner you'll have more "eyes" and be in better shape to repel an attack launched against you. Last, but not least, you can provide yourself with an early warning system that'll give you some notice of an intruder or of an impending attack. Here's how to utilize those extra eyes and build an early warning system.

To begin with, an assault on your home will almost certainly occur during the nighttime hours. If you have survival partners, you should take turns standing watch (24/7 if need be,) with not more than four hours on watch at a time. That means the watch will be looking out the front door and/or the back door of the shelter to ensure your first indication of trouble isn't when the door comes crashing in or gunfire erupts in the kitchen. An attacker may have scouted you out in advance, so it's possible when an attack comes it will be a planned assault.

However, it's more likely to be totally unscripted, and the attackers are much more likely to be criminals, not professionals. Kind of like, I see something I want, and I'm gonna take it now, which means they'll probably come straight in from the front. However, you can't count on them doing that, since they may have learned from previous assaults that those types of decisions can be detrimental to the probability of having their next beer.

Ultimately, you can assume nothing. They could just as easily come in the back or attempt entry through a side window. The point is that, while the front and the rear should receive the majority of the attention from the watch, you can't ignore the other possible points of entry. It's also imperative that the watch remains concealed. If the bad guys see the watch before the watch sees them, they'll either attempt to take the watch out, or they'll devise a more effective attack plan.

You can easily rig an effective early alert system in conjunction with standing watch. If possible, you can pile brush or "junk" around the perimeter of the shelter, leaving small openings where an attacker could easily get through. This can work to your advantage by allowing you to focus the majority of your attention on the openings, since it's a natural human tendency to take the easy path through or around debris, rather than attempt to climb over it.

If you've created easy access into your compound, that's where the attackers will most likely make their initial probe, making them relatively easy targets.

You can also create obstacles the attacker would have to walk around or climb over to gain access. Again, most people will walk around it rather than climb over it, which gives you another opportunity to focus your attention on a specific area of the perimeter. If the attackers do climb over the obstacles, you'll likely hear them if you rig some sort of device to create a noise, such as trip wires with bells or tin cans with a handful of small pebbles inside.

Be aware that the mere presence of a barrier around your shelter is going to be the same as hanging a neon sign on your shelter flashing *occupied.*

You can also set properly concealed trip wires rigged with bells (or something similar) at strategic locations at the outer edges of your property. Humans aren't the only ones capable of setting off a trip though, and you probably won't be able to differentiate between a trip set off by a human or one set off by a 4 legged animal, which means you could encounter a lot of false alarms. Going into combat mode every time a hungry dachshund trips your alarm will quickly become annoying. The problem's similar to the boy who cried wolf. After several false alarms, it's easy to become complacent when the alarm goes of again.

"Man I'm gonna nail that little bastar, bang, bang, bang, . . . oops.

If you have enough manpower, and someone in the group has the expertise, you can send out neighborhood patrols. If you elect to send out patrols, make certain they don't fall into any type of pattern or make their rounds at specific times. If they're predictable they'll be ambushed.

While none of these methods are foolproof and won't guarantee you'll be safe, they *can* provide you with advance warning. Whether your plan is to repel attackers or to gain advance notice so you can withdraw, the precious seconds gained by taking precautions could be the difference between life and death.

Put a band-aid on it!

Relax, I'm not going to tell you that you can't afford to be injured or killed since I'm sure you're painfully aware of that fact by now. Instead, I'll tell you that minor scrapes and cuts are one thing, as long as they don't become infected, but gunshot wounds or other serious injuries are something else. Under the "new" normal circumstances, any injury that would require a hospital visit or surgery would be a devastating blow to you and your family. With that in mind, it's imperative you have medical supplies available, and in sufficient quantity to deal with whatever might happen. You'll definitely need more than you kept in your medicine cabinet before the disaster started.

I don't think it's necessary to explain how to put a band-aid on a cut, but it might be wise for me to remind you to make certain the wound, no matter how slight, is thoroughly cleaned, and that you put an antibiotic ointment, like Neosporin, on the wound prior to applying the band-aid. I'm also reasonably certain most of you know how to treat and care for bruises, sprains, and other minor injuries. But what if something more serious happened, such as a broken bone, or possible internal injuries, an appendicitis attack, a tooth that required extraction, an injury to the eye, a drowning, frostbite, or a heart attack? In addition, what if someone in your family did suffer a gunshot wound? If your spouse or child suffered a serious injury and you were their only hope of surviving, would you have any idea of what to do, or would you watch helplessly as their life slipped away? That's a harsh vision, to say the least, but nevertheless it's also one that could become reality if you don't make an effort to prepare for it.

Even if I were qualified to do so, it'd be impossible to explain how to go about treating the myriad injuries and emergencies that will confront you. It's also next to impossible for you to learn how to treat every possible serious illness or injury. If you knew how to do that, you'd be House, and you could afford to build a bunker.

Please remember that knowledge is not only power, it's also confidence. If you take a basic first-aid course, and learn CPR, (both of which every parent should do regardless) you'll have the knowledge to provide effective, initial treatment to an injury.

You can purchase supplies that go well beyond basic first aid at any medical supply outlet, at most good drug stores, or online. You can buy splints, pressure cuffs, and stethoscopes, clamps, hemostats, and any number of other types of equipment. There are also many excellent books on basic first aid and quite a few that go well beyond the basics. A reference book I highly recommend (in the event that you had to perform surgery) is *Emergency War Surgery*. It's listed in the appendix. Prepare for the worst and, if it doesn't happen, no harm, no foul.

Here's a given. You *will* suffer from aches and pains from using muscles you aren't accustomed to using, including backaches, and you're definitely going to suffer minor injuries such as bumps, bruises, cuts, and scrapes. If you're forced to do a lot of walking, which is a distinct possibility, you're almost certainly going to get blisters on your feet. If you've never had bad blisters, I can tell you from personal experience they can effectively cripple you and will put any relocation efforts you might be involved in on a long hold.

Mosquitoes, gnats, no-see-ums, black flies, sweat bees and the like can make your life a living hell if you're in the woods or by water. If you've never experienced swarms of these miserable pests, and if you haven't paid one bit of attention to anything I've said so far, for your own good, pay attention now. Protection from these insects is vital, and has to include *no-see-um head nets.* I'd get two head nets for everyone and some very light gloves too. You simply won't be able to walk in the woods or stand by a body of water at certain times of the year without them.

In addition to their already bloodthirsty and aggressive nature, the populations of these pests are likely to increase as the governmental controls currently used to keep their populations in check fall by the wayside. Other insects, like cockroaches, ticks, ants, spiders, and the common housefly will likely experience population increases as well. Some insects, such as ticks, are capable of carrying disease, and some, like the Black Widow or Brown Recluse spider can kill you, so it makes sense to protect yourself by utilizing your own controls.

If you're in tick country, check daily and treat any bug bites immediately. To keep bugs such as cockroaches and the common housefly at bay, keep your living quarters, specifically the cooking and dining areas, as clean as possible. Leave zero crumbs or dirty dishes anywhere in the shelter.

Other dangerous critters that you should be aware of are bees, (specifically the African Honey bee, wasps and hornets) fire ants, and snakes. If you live in poisonous snake country, a snake venom kit would be a worthwhile investment. Don't disturb bees nests that you come across, and stay away from fire-ant mounds. Anaphylactic shock is always a possibility for some people who are sensitive to, or have an allergic reaction to insect bites. Some of you might not be aware that you're allergic until after the fact. If your body overreacts now to insect bites, it would be worth your while to study up on anaphylactic shock, and/or to talk to your doctor about possible tests and, or treatment.

If someone in your family does become seriously ill or injured, the worst thing that you can do is to freak out. Making the ill or injured person think they're dying isn't the result you're looking for. Even if it's true, the last thing you should impress upon them, through your actions, is that they're going to die. Treatment of the illness or injury is entirely up to you, so use your head, remain calm, and do the best you can.

If possible, everyone in the family should have updated vaccinations, especially a tetanus shot. Additionally, a fluoride treatment should be packed for young children.

Survival Kit Essentials

1. Assorted waterproof band-aids and 2"x2" patches
2. Large, sterile gauze pads
3. Kling bandages
4. Neosporin or equivalent
5. Mosquito repellent
6. Mosquito head nets
7. Benadryl
8. Isopropyl alcohol
9. Elastic bandage
10. Small scissors
11. Roll of medical tape
12. Band-aid sutures
13. Pack of various sized needles
14. Waterproof bag for your medical supplies
15. Fluoride treatment for children

(A more complete medical kit is listed in the next chapter.)

Communications

Man, we're going to miss our cell phones and the Internet. Communications has landed right alongside electricity as one more convenience we take for granted, but whose absence will cause a major change in our lifestyles. Cell phones, texting, landlines, AM/FM radio, the Internet, newspapers, satellite, cable, and broadcast television are all methods we use to communicate and to keep abreast of what's happening in the World.

Well say goodbye to information, and of having any knowledge of what's going on. Without some way of obtaining information, you're going to have a difficult time making an informed decision about your immediate plans or your long-range future.

Ultimately, the only form of communication that will probably work will be radio. Since the importance of information can't be overstated, it's absolutely essential for you to pack a small (not pocket-sized) battery operated AM/FM radio in your kit.

If anyone is broadcasting, you're more likely to receive a transmission via the AM band than you are the FM band, unless the FM station is reasonably close to you. Depending on the wattage output of an AM station, and under optimum conditions, you can receive AM transmissions during the nighttime hours from a distance of about a thousand miles. So if you don't hear anything on the FM band, switch to AM and check for broadcasts. If anyone's broadcasting at pre-selected times, midnight would seem to be a logical time. You'll also be able to hear stations from a greater distance between the hours of midnight to just before dawn. The AM band isn't as clear as the FM band and it's entirely possible that you'll receive a lot of static, as well as "fade," (the station that's broadcasting fades in and out.) but stick with it, you'll eventually get some info.

Another form of radio that will almost certainly be operable is shortwave.

Utilizing a shortwave with the proper antenna will allow you to receive broadcasts from countries as far away as Europe. At least some Ham radio operators should be operating in some locations, and they could become a valuable source of information. (Radio Shack sells a decent little shortwave (receiver) at a reasonable price.)

The problem with receiving information from any source, be it word of mouth or via the airwaves, is in knowing if the information is accurate and reliable. That's a tough one, and ultimately, you'll have to determine the reliability of any information you do receive.

For informational purposes only, since we're not really planning on a nuclear war as a possible scenario, a nuclear detonation high up in the atmosphere would create a devastating EMP, or electromagnetic pulse, which would render every piece of electronic equipment that wasn't shielded by lead or covered by many feet of earth, totally useless.

From an information viewpoint, communications will obviously be important to you, but there's also the aspect of interior communications to consider. Learning how to make and read smoke signals or how to send and receive Morse code might come in handy, but there are certainly more practical and efficient methods of communications available.

A 2-way radio is an effective and inexpensive method and has a range of approximately one to two miles under good conditions. A lot of them advertise a 25 mile range, but that's over water, with absolutely no obstructions and under optimal conditions. Nevertheless, a mile is more than adequate for your needs. If you decide to purchase a set of hand-held radios, consider the ear buds or headsets that are available as options, since you'll want to be able to communicate with members of your group without unfriendly ears hearing the conversation and pinpointing your location.

Another form of communication, and one you should definitely make use of, is hand signals. Both the military and law enforcement use hand signals effectively. It'd be a good idea to teach everyone in your family, including the youngest children, at least three basic hand signals.

They should all recognize and react instantly to your hand signal for *stop*, *down*, and *quiet*. You can use the military's or devise your own, as long as they're simple and easily understood. You should make it clear to the children that if you ever give them a hand signal, they're to comply instantly. Hand signals could one day save your life.

Survival Kit Essentials

1. Small AM/FM radio with AA batteries
2. Two extra sets of AA batteries

Animals

Americans love their pets. Dogs, cats, horses, fish, hamsters, reptiles, even spiders, (you people are sick) all have a place in our homes and in our hearts. In fact, it's safe to say that some people care more for their pet than they do their spouse. In some households it's probably justified, too. Nevertheless, during a disaster of the type we're preparing for, a pet is the last thing you can afford, unless the animal in question has other value, such as a horse or a well-trained and well-behaved dog. Now I know that someone is out there reading this and thinking something like,

"I will nevair give up my leetle Fluffy. Not evair! I would die first!"

Guess what lady, you probably will.

As long as you're able to remain in your shelter (home) and you have the ability to feed and care for the animal it *might* be okay to keep it. However, if you're forced to relocate, the animal should be left behind. The circumstances will dictate whether "should be left behind" becomes "definitely left behind". If it becomes necessary to give up your pet, you have to make a rational decision regarding its fate. That won't be an easy decision to reach and, for a lot of you, a rational decision won't be possible. Nevertheless, your pet, depending on the circumstances, could easily imperil your life and cause the death of you and your family. In addition, if your food supplies are running low, sharing an already diminished food supply with an animal and risking the lives of your family in the process isn't all that smart. On the other hand, if your food situation is nearing the desperation stage, the pet could become the food.

"You are absolutely disgusting, Monsieur, I would *nevair* consider eating my leetle Fluffy. I would starve first!"

And again, Madam, you probably will. – – Knock, knock, knock.

"Hey, Get the door for me will you Son?"

"Okay Dad."

"Who is it Boy?"

" It's PETA Dad."

Personally, I love animals just as much as the next person. However, I stop short of equating them to a human being.

If the choice is between your family and your pet, then that choice is simply no choice at all. So, what do you do if you have to evacuate and you can't take Old Shep along? Should you turn him loose so he has a chance?

This is the hard part, and the answer is no. In addition, it'll be up to you to dispatch the animal in a humane manner. The last thing you should do is turn the animal loose to fend_for itself. It'll either become a meal for a hungry predator or in the case of a dog, it'll likely turn feral. If your pet is a cat and it still has its front claws, there's a chance that it could survive, since cats will quickly revert to their natural instincts, which is to stalk and kill their food. If the animal doesn't have its front claws and you let it loose, it's a death sentence, and is actually quite selfish on your part.

A dog that has "gone feral" is a different story. Dogs are pack animals just like their ancestors, the wolf. So your beloved old shep, if he survives, will undoubtedly become a member of a feral dog pack. Because they don't have a wild animal's natural fear of humans, feral dogs are much more dangerous than the elusive wolf.

With that in mind, and given enough time, you could easily encounter a pack of feral dogs. Be careful! They might look like family pets, but they're not. If they look hungry, it's because they are, and they're looking at you the way you look at a choice steak at the meat market.

Given enough time, wild animal populations are all likely to increase due to decreased pressure on their natural habitat and because the animal control methods that are currently used to keep them in check will have ceased. Bears, wolves, coyotes, perhaps cougars, and in some states, alligator populations will all likely increase. Therefore, in some areas of some states, your odds of encountering a wild animal may be increased.

The good news is that, although these animals can be dangerous at any time, they're not likely to become any more dangerous in the future; just more numerous.

Recap chapter 7

1. To survive as a species, the Human Race needs food, water, and shelter.
2. We've added fire, light, defense, medical care, communications, fuel, personal hygiene, clothing, and sewage disposal to the list of Human necessities and we're calling it modern day basic human survival needs.
3. You should consider your home to be an expendable shelter.
4. Electric power will be out, which will eliminate all of the hi-tech comforts that you currently depend on.
5. Securing a water supply is essential to your survival.
6. You must have enough food to last a minimum of thirty days (preferably ninety.)
7. You must have a means to start a fire and to secure fuel.
8. Flashlights and candles are essential lighting sources.
9. You must be capable of defending yourself and your family.
10. You can't afford to be seriously injured or shot.
11. You shouldn't get involved in a fire-fight unless there's no alternative.
12. Basic medical supplies must be a part of your survival kit.
13. You should learn basic first aid and CPR.
14. It's imperative that you have a small, battery-operated AM/FM radio.
15. If you're forced to relocate, it's not a good idea to take your pet(s).

Chapter 8

IS THERE A DOCTOR IN THE HOUSE?

SINCE YOU'RE LIKELY TO BE on your own without professional medical care, it's important to make an effort to eliminate injuries or illnesses of any kind. No one ever plans to get sick or injured. I mean, you don't wake up one morning and say, okay, I think I'll break my arm today or maybe catch a cold. However, the majority of injuries that people sustain are the direct result of carelessness. Not staying focused on the job, using the wrong tool, and hurrying to get the job done are responsible for more accidents than any other reason. To a lesser extent, that same philosophy applies to sickness, since there are many things you can do to maintain your health. If health is important to you in real time, consider for a moment how important it'll be during a national disaster. I'm not certain who said "If you have your health, you have everything," but they knew what they were talking about. Your health, both physically and mentally, is going to be a huge factor in your survival.

Is there a doctor in your future? We could proceed with the assumption that you've joined a survival group which has a doctor or a nurse as active members. However, that's too easy. Let's assume you're either alone or that the group you've joined doesn't have anyone who knows anything more about the medical profession than you do and that any future medical care your family will need will have to be provided by you.

Mental health

Your kit is packed, your plan is formed, and you're ready to go if anything happens. However, planning for a catastrophe, and experiencing it, are at opposite ends of reality.

Nothing I could say would ever allow you to experience what the beginning of the catastrophe might be like. Nevertheless, it's important for everyone to remember why you're reading this book, so do your best to visualize the following event.

The disaster started on a Thursday afternoon in early November in the form of nationwide rioting due to X. You were able to avoid the worst of the local rioting, and even though you were prepared, you had a difficult time getting out of the city. Now, four hours after you left your house, you and your family stand greasy, soot covered, and exhausted on a hill overlooking the burning remnants of your hometown. The sun is setting, and a cold November rain has begun to fall. Through your binoculars, you watch as the rioters continue to loot, burn, and kill. You can hear the faint, distant cries of people begging for their lives, and you listen helplessly to the calls for help from the injured and the dying.

Even from this distance, the thick, acrid smoke assails your nostrils and hangs over the entire area like a shroud of death. You had friends and family down there but not one of them would listen to you. None of them believed this was possible. You look at your wife and children and realize they're crying. Shaking with rage and fear, you realize you're crying too. As you attempt to grasp the reality of the situation, your three-year-old daughter takes your hand, looks up at you and asks, "Daddy are we going to die?" That tearful, innocent question crystallizes your thoughts, and the reality of the situation hits you like a ton of bricks. *This is real! This is actually happening!*

If the guy in that scenario was you, one of your first thoughts might be because you're overwhelmed, exhausted, and emotionally drained, that depression would be a heartbeat away. The reality is depression requires *thought* about something; in this case, the event you just experienced. However, you can't take the time to think about it right now.

Later on, when your family's reasonably safe and you have the luxury of reflection, and when you've had time to digest everything, depression may be paying you a visit. Fortunately, it's not on the menu right now.

Some people are going to shrug this entire event off as though it never happened. They'll just accept things as they are and go ahead with the plan they developed. They're the lucky few, the mentally tough, cold-hearted SOB's you never liked. Most of you, however, because you're normal, will experience periods of despair. That's normal, too. After all, everything you ever worked for, everything you ever had, and people whom you loved, have disappeared as though they never existed.

So, if despair is normal for normal people, what should you do? Well, go ahead and cry. Grieve and do whatever else you need to do to come to grips with the reality of the situation. Because you don't have the time to sit around feeling sorry for yourself. Your family needs you, and it's up to you to protect them since they're still in danger. If you find yourself thinking there's no point in even trying to survive, that it's hopeless, and you can't shake it off, then you and your family are going to be in serious trouble. Yes, I know it's ten times worse than you ever imagined, and yes, I'm aware the entire situation is as scary as hell. Moreover, I'm also aware that it's probably going to get a lot worse. However, I also know, since you realize those things, too, you just might survive.

Fighting off bouts of despair is going to be one of the biggest personal problems you're going to encounter. Your emotions will run hot and cold; confident one minute, filled with doubt the next. Just remember, no one ever promised you life would be easy, and if they did, they lied. The bottom line is, as long as you're alive and can remain alive, you have a chance to rebuild your life. It won't be the same life you left, but it'll be a life, and it'll be yours.

Some people are probably wondering what's up with the pep talk. Well, partially because it's true and partially because everyone better get used to giving themselves a pep talk on a daily basis. If you mentally fold your tents your family will be doomed. Maintaining a healthy attitude won't be easy, even for the toughest of you, but it'll get easier as time goes by. All I can tell you is, do the best you can and fight off the bouts of despair you'll be experiencing. Do something that's familiar and comfortable. If you're religious, have family prayer sessions every night.

Just keep busy, and keep your mind occupied. Keep everyone in your family or group busy too. People who worked their butts off all day are prone to sleep the minute their heads hit the pillow. That doesn't allow a lot of time to think about what was.

In time, you'll develop a routine. Routines are familiar and comfortable to humans, and time is what you need. As long as you don't dwell on the past, you'll soon begin to accept the reality of the situation and start to regard it as temporary. The length of time necessary to arrive at that realization and to make plans to go forward will vary from person to person. It could be anything from ten minutes to a couple of days, or for some unlucky souls, perhaps never.

Most people have probably never considered mental health as a contributor toward the ability to survive a disaster, but if you're smart, and I know you are, you'll move mental health toward the top of the list. Remember, your family will be looking to you to provide the guidance and reassurance they'll need, and you should realize that they're probably much more frightened and confused than you are.

Physical health

From this point forward I'll be referring to the disaster, which is now a catastrophe, as *BTC* (before the catastrophe) and *ATC* (after the catastrophe.)

Your physical health is going to be more important to you ATC than it is now. Currently, you have access to professional medical care for everything from a runny nose to a heart attack and from a blister to a broken back. (At least you do until Obama Care kicks in.) None of those options will be available ATC. There will be no pharmacies to pick up prescription meds or cold and flu treatments, and no hospital ER's or doctors offices to visit for diagnosis or treatment. "An ounce of prevention is worth a pound of cure." I don't know who said that either, but it's a relevant statement.

Prevention will be your best defense against future illness. How many Americans today eat anything close to a balanced diet? I know I don't, and I suspect most of you don't either. Guess what? Our diets are likely to become healthier by default ATC, and our overall health is probably going to improve. Gone will be the days of grabbing a quick fat burger at the local drive-thru. No more junk food while we're staring at the mindless garbage on TV either.

If you're overweight and you're serious about getting rid of those extra pounds, here's a little secret *they* don't want you to know about. Losing weight does *not* require expensive special meals, pills, potions, hypnosis, or any other miracle BS. What it does require is willpower and a commitment. There's a biological law that reads: *If you burn more calories than you ingest, you will lose weight!*

Let's see, what other positives might we expect out of this disaster? How about tobacco? That won't be easy to come by unless you live in tobacco country. Booze won't be much of a problem either. Drugs? Are you kidding me? In addition, almost everyone will be getting more than their share of exercise and fresh air, so overall, strange as it might sound, and as ironic as it is, our general health is likely to improve. Bad by-products from the disaster could be toxins in the air or water, and bullets.

It wouldn't be the worst decision you ever made to stock up on some vitamins. A good multi-vitamin and some vitamin C certainly won't do any harm. However, make sure you check the expiration dates and select those that expire at least two years down the line. If you don't check, you'll discover too late that some of them are due to expire in a few months.

If you remember, we quarantined *plague* and eliminated it as a possible cause for the catastrophe, but we also agreed to keep a close eye on it. The flu could be a big problem ATC, although exposure to the virus will likely be limited by default. Nevertheless, (just in case) it wouldn't hurt to get vaccinated or to buy some Tami-flu tabs. You can buy them online without a prescription, or you can try to get some from your doctor.

As far as over the counter flu medications are concerned, it's up to you. I'd read the ingredients first and see how much you're actually paying for the few milligrams of Tylenol, expectorant, and cough suppressant that you're buying. (Here's another hint: you can buy all of the products individually for a much lower price per serving.)

By the way, aspirin is aspirin, which means the *best* aspirin you can buy is the *cheapest* aspirin that you can find. (That's right, *just like bleach*. You have been paying attention). Both aspirin and Tylenol should be in your survival kit.

In the United States, we're too stupid to know when we require an antibiotic. But in second world Mexico, where the citizens apparently all have medical degrees, antibiotics are available over the counter at every pharmacy in the country without a prescription, and at a price that would turn your pharmacists face a bright red.

To be fair, the price of antibiotics in the United States isn't really the fault of your pharmacist. Doctors and hospitals, pharmaceutical and insurance companies, as well as the FDA, are all responsible for your stupidity as well as for the ridiculously high prices you pay *after* you visit a doctor, and *after* you pay an exorbitant office fee so you can be told what you knew before you went. It's like paying a nutritionist $100 to tell you you're hungry before you can eat, then paying another $20 for the food. God, I hate being stupid!

Because of all the regulation, and because we're all stupid, you might have a problem obtaining the antibiotics you know you should be putting in your survival kit. It's not impossible though.

Penicillin is the original wonder drug (before all of the myacins,) and contrary to what you've been led to believe, penicillin still works perfectly fine today. It's not prescribed like it was years ago because it's cheap, and because bacteria have *allegedly* built up an immunity to it. How did I reach the conclusion that penicillin works perfectly fine today? Well, I've had a recurring problem with an abscessed tooth which is located in a portion of my mouth that, if it were to be extracted, would alter my appearance from,

"I wonder what happened to him," to

"Martha, get the kids in the house, NOW!"

So in order to obtain antibiotics when the infection flared up, I had to pay my $100 office fee at a walk-in clinic, and then pay the ridiculous fee for the current "myacin" wonder drug. Ten days later the infection would be history. That happened twice over a period of six months.

The third (and last) time the abscess came calling, I dutifully paid my visit to the walk-in clinic and was told by the cocky, young doctor on duty,

"You aren't getting any kind of myacin, old man. I'm giving you penicillin."

"But I'm allergic to penicillin," I told him.

"That's too bad; and stop whining. You old guys are all such candy asses."

Three days later, for less than 1/3 the price of the "wondermyacin," the infection was gone and hasn't returned.

So, am I telling you that penicillin works better than the latest, greatest, and most expensive wonder drug for a whole lot less money? No, but it worked just fine for me.

Okay, so you don't have an infection, and your doctor's a jerk. Where can you get antibiotics? Try your vet's office. Many of the antibiotics used in the treatment of animals are the same as those used in the treatment of humans. If you have a good relationship with your doctor or dentist, you can explain why you want them and ask him or her to prescribe some for you. They're certainly not illegal. On the other hand, you can try a Mexican or Canadian pharmacy online.

If you choose to order online, make certain the pharmacy is also a brick and mortar store, and that their license is on display at the website. Different antibiotics, as you probably know, treat different infections, but if the only antibiotic you can get is penicillin, you should be in good shape.

Place a moisture-absorbent packet, along with the pills, inside a zip-lock freezer bag and store them in a cool dry location. (Don't put them in the fridge or the freezer.) In addition, even though the expiration date printed on the container will read one year, they can still be effective for two years or more.

Purchase extra quantities of any other medicines that you use frequently, such as antacids, hay-fever meds, inhalers, feminine products, etc, and take the time to analyze what you've used in the past and project what you might need in the future. Be sure to take into consideration that your kids will require a few different types of medications as they grow.

Your new lifestyle, and the after-effects of the disaster will dramatically increase the risk of encountering one or more of the following diseases. *Cryptosporidium*, *Hepatitis A-B-C- & E*, *Pneumonia*, *Strep Throat*, *Typhoid*, *Lyme Disease*, *Rabies*, *West Nile Virus*, *Hantavirus*, *Rocky Mountain Spotted Fever*, and of course the *common cold* and *Seasonal Flu*. (A section containing in-depth information on these diseases is located in the back of the book.)

Staying warm and dry or cool and dry is also an important issue from both a health and comfort standpoint. It would be difficult to make recommendations about clothing selections since there are simply too many factors to take into consideration. You're going to need the appropriate clothing and good footwear to effectively deal with the weather and terrain that you'll encounter in your primary survival location. Those clothing needs could range from expedition outerwear and Pac-boots to sneakers and shorts, everything in between, or a combination of both. It's important to note it's much easier to survive in tropical heat and humidity without much clothing than it is to survive a winter in the north without the proper clothing.

Let's assume for one moment you'll be one of the fortunate survivors who are able to remain where you are, or that you've moved in with others who have adequate shelter. In all probability, the only contingency you'll need to prepare for is an emergency relocation. If that's the case, you can continue to use the bedding you've always used. For those of you who now live in a tent or under a tarp, your bedding will likely be a sleeping bag. The importance of a good nights rest shouldn't be overlooked. It's going to be difficult to stay alert and to do the physical chores that will be required of you if your bedding keeps you from sleeping comfortably.

If you don't own a good sleeping bag and sleeping bag pad, I highly recommend you purchase one. In the north, where temperatures can easily reach below zero, a quality winter bag might be required. In fact, if you're living in a tent, in the north, it'll be absolutely necessary.

There are many different types of insulations used in sleeping bags, ranging from premium goose down to the latest synthetics. The type of insulation as well as the "fill" amounts and design will ultimately determine the bag's temperature rating. Temperature ratings of sleeping bags are an approximation since different people sleep more comfortably at different temperatures. By that I mean, some people require several hundred pounds of blankets to stay warm whenever the temperature drops below seventy degrees, (you know who you are), while others kick off the covers if the temperature exceeds 35 degrees. Therefore, a bag rated at zero might keep some people comfortably warm while others might still be freezing.

Most of the synthetic insulation used in today's' sleeping bags approximates the insulating efficiency of premium goose down without the negatives of down insulation.

Synthetics will continue to insulate, even when wet. Down will not. Down can clump and synthetics won't. For those reasons, I recommend a quality synthetic over the goose down, although I personally own and enjoy both types. For survival purposes, the synthetic bag makes more sense.

If you live in a warm climate, such as Florida, there are always those few nights when the temperature falls into the twenty's or low thirty's, and in the panhandle, it's not uncommon to see occasional temps in the teens. A summer bag on those nights simply won't cut it, but a winter bag that you'll only use a few nights of the year doesn't make much sense.

For warm weather locations, you should purchase a bag rated somewhere around forty degrees. On those nights when it gets colder, you can use a blanket or sleep in the bag fully clothed, and on the warmer nights, you can either partially unzip the bag or sleep on top of it.

Purchasing bags that mate or zip together to create one large bag will allow a small child, or even two, to sleep between the parents to provide extra warmth through body heat. Zip-in liners are available on many models that will add five to ten degrees to the temperature rating of the bag. Thus a bag rated at forty degrees, becomes a 30-35 degree bag with the liner attached.

One item of clothing that everyone should have is raingear. For the budget conscious among you, a military poncho will work. You can use a poncho as a ground cloth for a tent or in a pinch as a small emergency shelter. Any Army-Navy store will have them in stock. However, there's nothing like modern rain gear to keep you dry and comfortable in wet weather. Old-fashioned raincoats will protect you from the rain, but your perspiration won't have anywhere to go. It can't evaporate, which means you're going to be chilled and clammy. Becoming chilled and shivering uncontrollably isn't much fun. If you've never experienced it, I can tell you it's not comfortable.

Modern raingear incorporates an inner membrane, which "wicks" the perspiration through the garment to the outer shell where it can evaporate. While quality raingear isn't cheap, there are models that work well for a reasonable price. Look for the Gore-Tex or similar label on any raingear you purchase. You don't have to have the pants, but the jacket with a hood should be on your purchasing radar.

Survival Kit Essentials

1. Aspirin
2. Tylenol
3. Military style poncho
4. Heavy blanket or sleeping bag (one per person)

Hygiene

Effective personal and shelter hygiene will be necessary to keep you healthy. No one should need advice on how to keep clean, even though some people live like animals. If you're one of those people and you're too lazy to keep yourself or your home clean BTC, I doubt that you'll put forth the effort to do so ATC. However, you might want to consider cleaning up your act, even if you don't clean your home since your poor hygiene habits might be the death of you.

For the rest of you, a little common sense should suffice. Don't leave dirty dishes or half eaten food around, and keep your food prep and cooking areas as clean as possible. Don't forget grease that might have spilled onto the ground. Ants and other bugs love grease.

If you're a total neat freak, you're going to have to learn to change your mentality. If you don't, you'll go crazy.

Everyone knows what a sponge bath is, but when's the last time you took one? What's that? The next one you take will be the first one? Get used to it! For those of you who just have to have that shower, you can purchase a camping shower, which is simply a HD black vinyl bag with a hose and spigot. Fill the bag with water, hang it in the sun and voila you have a shower. Sort of.

Women who spend an hour a day putting on their face and shaving can pretend they're European, and guys who hate to shave but feign sensitive skin can let their cave-guy out, grow a beard, a pony-tail, scratch, burp, and generally have a good time. Both sexes can then rag on the other about all of the new body hair and the fact that they're no longer sexually attractive. It'll be fun.

There isn't a whole lot that can be said about hygiene.

If you don't understand it, or you're simply unwilling to practice it, I can't think of anything to say which would light that bulb above your head. If it's important to you now, it will be important to you then.

Survival kit essentials

1. Personal hygiene and grooming items for both sexes
2. Several bars of antibacterial soap
3. Toothpaste (baking soda works well)
4. Toothbrushes (two per person)
5. Finger and toe-nail clippers
6. Wash basin (same as the one for washing dishes)
7. Wash cloths
8. Hand towels
9. Bath towel (optional)

Sanitation

Sanitation and hygiene go hand in glove. They're the same, only different. However, the elimination of dirty bath water isn't the same as the disposal of human waste or garbage. It's not even in the same ball-park.

With the exception of those two weirdo's who live two houses down from you, you probably haven't sat around and pondered the relative merits of human waste elimination since you're civilized and have indoor plumbing and toilets. Push the handle and awaaay it goes. In addition, put the garbage at the edge of the driveway and, when the garbage truck wakes you at 5:00 am, you know your trash is gone.

By this time you're painfully aware there are no garbage trucks and that you no longer have the old ivory throne to sit on. Unfortunately, the waste will keep piling up, and you'll still have to take care of your daily "constitutional."

Now, if you're old enough to remember, you can give a disdainful smirk to all the young whipper-snappers when they ask "what the hell's a chamber pot?" And you can go ahead and tell them that, back in the olden days, a chamber pot was a pot kept near the bed at night in case you had to "go." Back then, people called their bedrooms, bedroom chambers, hence the name chamber pot. (I don't know why it was called a chamber; I'm not *that* old.) Anyway, in the morning someone would (hopefully) empty and clean the pot and get it ready for the next night's use.

Guess what? You're now in the market for a chamber pot. Relax, you don't have to run all over town trying to find a chamber pot. A galvanized bucket will work just fine and it won't stain and absorb odors like a plastic pail will.

I suppose it's perfectly natural for you to ask why you can't just go outside during the middle of the night to "take care of business" instead of using a nasty old bucket. Well, you can. But if it's below zero you might end up with frost-bitten buns, or there might be a raging blizzard in progress, a thunderstorm, swarms of mosquitoes, or a thousand other reasons why you, or your kids, might not want to go outside in the middle of the night. Go buy the bucket. You'll be glad you did. And for those of you who are more delicate, you can purchase a camping toilet that uses chemicals which can be sprinkled on the contents.

For a permanent toilet, there's always that old Halloween favorite, the outhouse. (Don't give'em the opportunity to ask what it is this time, just go ahead and give'em your best exasperated look). Building an outhouse will require some serious work and probably shouldn't be undertaken until the situation becomes reasonably stable. You'll have to dig a pit about six feet deep and, depending if it's a "one-holer," or a "two-holer," from about 4'x4' to 4'x6' . A "one-holer" should be sufficient, though, since I can't imagine why you'd want to perform a dual-dump with someone. You'll need some carpentry skills, nails, hammer, boards, shingles, and a toilet seat, which can be pilfered from any vacant house.

If you come across a bag of lime, sprinkle it on the contents to keep the odors down. If not, use sand. Also, don't forget to provide ventilation of some sort. A PVC plastic pipe extending from about halfway to the bottom of the pit and continuing through the roof with a 90-degree elbow attached will do the trick.

A much easier and more practical survival method of disposing of human waste is the latrine. Just dig a trench around 10' long by a foot or so wide and perhaps 12"-18" deep. The actual size will depend on the number of people who will be enjoying the latrine. Leave the dirt piled up along one edge and, after you make a "direct deposit" or empty the chamber pot into the latrine, cover the waste with dirt. When the latrine is nearly full, dig another one next to it.

If the ground is frozen, you'll have a difficult time getting through the frost, but you can thaw the ground if you have to by building a fire over the area where you want the latrine to be. It might take awhile, but you'll eventually be able to dig deep enough to get the job done. The dirt that you left along the edges will probably freeze, so covering the waste won't be as easy. The upside is that the waste will also be frozen which will eliminate odors until it thaws, and, of course, there won't be a problem with flies in the cold weather. Be sure to locate the latrine a respectable distance from your shelter and in an area that can provide a degree of privacy. You can also rig up a screen of some sort for those who might be a bit sensitive to public displays of defecation. An option to digging a latrine in cold weather when the ground is frozen is to simply go crap in the woods.

Your garbage should be buried or burned daily for the same reasons as you're going to bury your personal waste; insects, odors, and potential diseases.

In addition, if you don't dispose of your garbage effectively, you'll be dealing with animals, both feral and wild, who'll be paying a visit to the area where the garbage was dumped. Burning the garbage is a whole lot easier than burying it, but if you're unable to burn it, by all means, bury it.

If you bury your garbage instead of burning it, be sure you cover it with at least a foot of dirt or the critters will smell it and dig it up. If they do locate your garbage, they'll make a huge mess, and they're likely to come into your campsite, too. You may return from a foray to find they've literally destroyed portions of your campsite. Worse yet is being awakened in the middle of the night by a bear looking into your tent asking where all the food went.

Survival kit essentials

1. Galvanized bucket with bail handle (or porcelain pot) for use as a chamber pot.
2. Toilet paper - (Ratio: 100 rolls per month for females, one roll per month for males)

Childbirth

There's no doubt there will be women who're pregnant in the days BTC. There will also be women who are going to be in labor when it begins, those who will be giving birth within days ATC starts, and some who just found out that they're with child. In addition, there will be others who are pregnant, but aren't aware of it.

If you find yourself in any of these happy situations, your pregnancy and the ensuing birth, or recent birth, of your child will present you with a special and challenging set of circumstances ATC.

Millions of children, maybe billions, have been born down through antiquity without the benefit of professional pediatric care or a hospital environment for delivery. So there's no reason to believe that you and your child can't survive and thrive ATC, as long as you're willing to make some intelligent decisions pertaining to the birth and pre and post natal care.

The thing about babies, as you know, is that when they're ready to see the world, that's it, it's happening. You're going to be a mommy in a short time and there's nothing you can do to stop the event. Furthermore, it won't matter where you are or what's happening around you either.

So if you know you're going to have a baby soon, or if you're planning to have a baby in the near future, start now to prepare for the event out of hospital. Have someone (your husband is a likely candidate) learn how to deliver a baby. It's not all that difficult to do. He just has to stand there looking helpless while you and the baby do all of the work. If he can clear the mouth and clamp the cord, you can do the rest yourself. There are many books on the subject of delivering a baby out of hospital and an equal number of videos showing step by step what to do.

There are also plenty of good books on pediatrics, which you should also read since you're probably going to be your child's pediatrician for an extended period. Overall, a normal birth and a healthy baby won't present any problems whatsoever, and I assure you the fact your baby is born at home or in a tent won't detract one iota from the joys of motherhood.

If you won't be able to breast feed, you'll have to provide a quantity of formula as well as all of the normal baby supplies. Make a list of what you'll need for the baby's first two years and put them in your survival kit.

Okay! Diapers, big problem! You can use the $3,000 you had saved for the down payment on that new car, or you can buy a couple hundred boxes of disposable diapers instead. Then you can figure out where you're going to store them. Here's the solution. Buy several dozen of those nasty old-fashioned cloth diapers in different sizes for less than the price of one box of disposables and still get your new car. Whaddayamean, what're cloth diapers?

Well, Missy, before God invented plastic, babies were diapered using cloth diapers which were washed over and over and over and over and over. That's also where the term wash and wear came from. Cloth diapers are still around, but guys mostly use them these days when they wax their pick-ups.

Seriously, though, cloth diapers are the only thing that makes sense ATC. Buy some disposables for "emergencies" if you wish, but make sure you have several dozen cloth diapers in different sizes to compensate for a growing baby. Don't forget the safety pins and rubber pants either. You'll also need a diaper-pail of some sort to keep the soiled diapers in until you wash them. Here's a note specifically for those moms who have never used a cloth diaper. Your baby can't hang around in a wet one very long without developing a rash and or leaking, so check and change often.

Sex

Every good book these days has sex in it. It's a fun and interesting topic, and everyone wants it. It's also therapeutic, releases endorphins, and eliminates headaches during the act and, believe it or not, sex even has the power to create an instant headache at the mere suggestion of the word. Besides, sex is easy to spell, so I'm going to devote about a half page to the topic of sex, which is about the extent of my knowledge on the subject. You can ask my ex-wives.

Can sex actually create a problem for you ATC? Of course, it can. This is *not* the time for conception, planned or not. And, if I remember correctly, pregnancies are brought about (normally) as a direct result of sex. Therefore, having unprotected sex at this time in your life could result in problems which you won't be prepared to deal with, since you won't have the necessary items and supplies to care for and to feed a newborn baby.

During times of crises, or more specifically power outages, we humans can apparently think of nothing else to do when the lights go out except to have sex. There's always an explosion of births nine months following a major power outage. Should we compare a power outage to a major catastrophe? To the 10th power! The lights are going to be off for a *very long time!* Therefore, it makes sense to provide protection. The type of protection you use is up to you. If you can't do that, you could always find some other form of recreati ... naw ... that ain't gonna happen!

Then there's the subject of teen pregnancies. If you belong to a survival group there will undoubtedly be a number of teens among the members, or at least pre-teens who are the children of adult members. If, for example, you have a teenaged girl who just happens to be the only female teen in the group, and another couple has a teenaged boy, I think it's safe to say they'll end up hanging out.

What occurs next is perfectly natural, of course, but an unnecessary and unwanted teen pregnancy should definitely not be on the agenda. How you prevent that from happening is entirely up to you.

Prescription medications

There isn't a lot that can be said about prescription meds except that if the meds you take are crucial to your health or are keeping you alive, then you need to search for a way to secure a supply that will last you at least ninety days and preferably much longer.

Doctors normally prescribe meds in a quantity that will last for thirty days. If you're in the middle of your prescription just before the catastrophe starts, then you have a fifteen day supply remaining. If the catastrophe started on the 29th day into your supply, then you're effectively out of medications. Talk to your doctor. He may be willing to prescribe a ninety day supply and allow you to continue to pick up your normal thirty day supply each month. That would give you anywhere from 90-120 days worth of meds depending upon the day the catastrophe begins.

You should also ask your doctor what other medications will duplicate or would be capable of replacing the meds you're currently taking. It's just possible that you could locate one of those alternates, or even the original somewhere down the line. There could also be natural remedies for your ailment that could replace some of the meds you currently take. They may not be as effective, but in a pinch, they would definitely be better than nothing.

If the meds you need are pain pills, your doctor might not be able to legally issue you more than a thirty day supply at one time. If that's the case and you're legitimately taking the pills because of pain and not because of a dependency, you can start taking ½ of the pill instead of the entire pill, substituting the other half with an over the counter pain killer such as Tylenol. In a month's time, you'll have gained an extra fifteen days supply of pain pills. This method can work for other types of medications too, but you'd better know what the effect(s) will be if you voluntarily cut the prescribed dosage.

You can attempt to purchase an advanced supply over the Internet, or you can talk to friends or family who may know a doctor who might be sympathetic to your needs.

Since it's going to be critical for you to have a good supply of your prescription medications on hand ATC, you should leave no stone unturned in your efforts to secure an advance supply. Good luck!

Special needs

This subject could be a "sticky wicket," as the English say, because there are undoubtedly those of you who have family members who are handicapped in some way due to heredity, a birth defect, or because of an accident or illness. They could be restricted to a wheel chair, on crutches, blind, or diabetic, the list is endless. In addition, you may be dealing with someone who has a mental condition, or a drug addiction.

The requirements for dealing with the vast array of existing medical and mental conditions, and the methods used to treat them, is beyond the scope of my knowledge. Besides, if I could comment on any of them in an intelligent manner, it wouldn't be feasible to incorporate those comments into this tiny little book. At any rate, most of you who are currently living with someone who's handicapped in some way already know how to do deal with the problem.

But what if someone in your family is seriously injured or hospitalized immediately prior to the inception of the catastrophe? Unfortunately, there's not a lot that you can do if they're not ambulatory. Now I *know* this is going to sound harsh because it is, but you may be forced to make a decision regarding a family member who's hospitalized just BTC begins. If the patient can't be moved, is in critical condition or for any other reason can't be released from the hospital, it may be necessary to leave your loved one behind to save the other members of your family.

That's a decision I hope none of you will ever have to make. I hope I'm never faced with that decision. It would be difficult beyond measure. However, logic would dictate that it wouldn't be prudent to sacrifice your entire family to remain with one member who's in the hospital. Easier said than done, that's for sure.

In addition, someone in your family (maybe you) might be incarcerated and is still in jail when everything begins. That's definitely a problem. Or, perhaps you or a family member was just injured, but is ambulatory, is being treated on an outpatient basis, receiving physical therapy, in rehab, or recently entered counseling. Any of these situations would require changes to your original plan. However, if you planned carefully, the changes, for the most part, shouldn't affect the overall scope of your plan. (Remember, your plan has to be *flexible*.)

Bear in mind the goal of this section is to make you aware of *some* of the things that could affect your plan in the days, or even moments that precede the inception of the catastrophe, and to give you pause to *think* about potential problems you might not otherwise have considered

Burials

Under the best of circumstances, a death in the family is a difficult situation to deal with, and if you're like me, you don't even like to think about it. BTC happened we had funeral homes, family, friends and other support groups to help us get through the difficult and emotional days following the death of a loved one.

Sadly, it's inevitable that someone will be faced with the prospect of burying a family member without the assistance of a funeral home. In the event you're one of those affected by the death of a loved one ATC happens, belonging to a survival group will mean a great deal to you, since you won't have to make all the preparations yourself, and in addition you'll have the emotional support of the group.

However, it's unlikely that anyone (in or out of the survival group) has any expertise or practical experience in the matter of burials, thus some of you will be faced with the prospect of burying your loved one yourself. I don't have first-hand experience in burials either, but the following procedures seem logical to me.

Although it might sound redundant, I believe the first item on the agenda should be to ensure that the person is, in fact, dead. When someone dies, the muscles in the body relax and the eyes are normally open, not closed. The bowels empty, and a pulse is absent. Sometimes it's easy to look at someone and determine that they're dead, and sometimes it's a bit more tricky. It's probably a good idea to record the time, the date, and what you perceived to be the cause of death.

If you're in a warm climate, the body will begin to deteriorate rapidly, which means burial should take place ASAP. You don't want to view your family member in a deteriorated condition. In colder weather, you'll obviously have a bit more time.

Depending upon your location, you might not be able to dig a hole deep enough for burial since the ground may be frozen, too rocky, or simply too difficult to dig in. If you can't dig a grave, you can prepare the body, lay it on the ground, and place a cairn of rocks over it to keep the animals from getting at it. If there're no rocks available, you can cremate the body, but you'll have to have an *extremely hot fire* to accomplish cremation. The only other viable options are to place the body high up in a tree, or to attach weights to it and submerge it in a lake or similar large body of water. If, God forbid, you're in the process of an emergency evacuation, you may have no choice but to leave the body as it is, where it is.

You can make whatever preparations you're comfortable with for burial. Wash and prepare the body if you can, wrap it in a blanket, and have a funeral, saying goodbye in your own way and using words of your own choosing. If you're in a permanent location, you can pick a burial site that you're comfortable with, erect a headstone or monument, and visit the grave whenever you wish. There doesn't seem to be much else you can do.

Seniors

I have a friend in her late 80's who is ill. She wanted to read this particular chapter long before I finished the book. After she read it, she indignantly stated,

"Well, at least you didn't put the chapter on Senior citizens before the chapter on burials," which I know is irrelevant, but I got a kick out of the comment, so I thought I'd pass it along.

I don't know if there are people who actually look forward to old age. I know I don't. Getting old is *not* for wimps. Your mind's generally as sharp as ever, but it's frustrating that your body won't do what your mind's telling it to do. You can't hear worth squat (what?), your eyesight sucks, and your, well . . . I don't want to ruin all the surprises that await you when you gain senior status, so, end of comment.

While aging is inevitable, getting old doesn't automatically mean you've become helpless and incompetent. There certainly are seniors who have difficulty with mobility, eyesight, hearing, and mental faculties, but there are also those who are perpetually young and exhibit few, if any, of the problems associated with aging.

BTC the ability of seniors to live a normal, active, and healthy lifestyle varied dramatically. The ability of those same seniors to function effectively ATC will likely be even more dramatic since the situation will define them as either an asset or an albatross. Now, before anybody gets their panties in a wad over that comment, please understand I'm not calling old people a goofy- looking bird, nor am I intentionally insulting them. I are one, too.

The facts are what they are. Some older people are going to become an extremely heavy burden on whoever's caring for them, and I'm not referring to a physical handicap or a memory loss. Anyone can deal with those conditions. But an irascible, disagreeable, argumentative, complaining, whining, and negative senior, whether it's your mother or your father, could very well create a dangerous situation for you and the rest of your family ATC. If your parent(s) fit that description, you'll soon discover that it'll be necessary to deal with him or her in an entirely different manner than you did BTC. Not out of impatience or disrespect, but out of necessity. If you're reading this and you're one of "those parents," *put a sock in it!*

Conversely, some seniors will be more than capable of carrying their load and probably a significant portion of yours, too. In addition, older people are a virtual gold-mine when it comes to information and experience. You can use that knowledge to help you survive and thrive during the chaos.

Some seniors will know how to can vegetables and fruit, bake bread, make butter, grow a garden, sew, make clothes, raise animals, hunt, fish, and a whole lot more. A vast and critical source of information may be yours for the asking. Do *not* make the mistake of assuming that their knowledge is irrelevant.

If you're a senior(s) and you're living alone, everything in this book applies to you in exactly the same manner as it does to everyone else. Prepare your plan, pack your kit, and prepare to survive. We'll need you around when it's all over.

Infants and toddlers

Caring for an infant ATC won't be a big deal for most of you, but having a toddler with boundless energy and enthusiasm, an innate curiosity about everything, and who's also in the process of discovering his or her independence will probably be the stuff of legends. And somehow, and please don't ask me how, you'll have to incorporate all of the attention that your toddler requires which will allow him or her to grow and prosper, and at the same time fit your new duties into some sort of miracle routine that benefits everyone. Good luck, mom; dad's gonna go catch some fish for supper.

Am I an expert on infants and toddlers? Oh, hell no! But I did raise four of my own, and in doing so I've learned one important thing. I've learned nothing! With the exception that what works for one won't necessarily work for the other. But I can remember living for that afternoon nap, and it was never clear to me who needed the nap more, me or my child. Have things changed since that time? I doubt it. Infants on a schedule are comparatively easy. Feed them, change them, and they go to sleep. Toddlers, on the other hand, are a different story. Watching them sleep, grow, and looking at the wonder in their eyes is priceless, but as anyone who's been there knows, raising a toddler properly isn't for the impatient or the faint of heart.

ATC it's going to be critical for you to channel that energy into some form of constructive outlet. You won't have *Sesame Street* to utilize as a surrogate baby sitter while you do your chores or take a break. So make sure you pack some items that will occupy the toddler for at least a few minutes. It's definitely going to be challenging. It might be a good idea to begin to teach him or her some of the skills that you just learned yourself: gardening, plant identification, fishing, gathering firewood, or anything else that might satisfy the child's thirst for new and satisfying input.

One thing's for certain; there won't be the adaptation problem with the infant or toddler that's going to be present with older children. I would strongly suggest you teach your child, in the form of a game, that there are times when *immediate and silent* obedience is required. IE: obeying hand signals.

Don't forget to pack clothing and shoes for your children that will fit them as they grow, and don't worry if your child is temporarily put-off by the food you're going to be feeding him or her. When they're hungry enough, they'll eat.

Children and teens

Now that you've read my profound thoughts on infants and toddlers, you find yourself looking at the title of Children and teens. I know what you're thinking, too . . . rriiight! This oughta be good. Well, I have one, no, make that two words of advice for you. SELL THEM! Naw, you know I'm only kidding. You should never consider selling your kids. (Unless you can get a *really* good price for 'em!)

Hey, a little change of pace is in order here. I have two questions for you. The first question is, at what age does a toddler become a child? Over two years old, potty trained, in pre-school, or something else? You tell me; I don't know. The second question is; when does a child cease to be a child? At the age of thirteen, sixteen, eighteen, or is it 65? Last week someone told me that I was being childish, and this week that same person told me I was being a baby. So, I'm pretty confused. I thought I was an adult, but last week I was a child, and this week I'm a baby.

Well, the *law* says that anyone under the age of eighteen is a child, which means anyone over the age of eighteen is an adult. I have no problem with that. Never have. Nevertheless, ATC it's going to require a change in thinking as to the time a child becomes an adult. No, I'm not referring to, or advocating any type of sexual activity for anyone under the age of eighteen. I'm alluding to a reasonable expectation of what age we'll be forced to place additional responsibilities upon our children. I think it's safe to say that the sooner they accept the fact that the fabric of their life has changed, the better off the entire family's going to be. This won't be the time to "baby" them. They're going to have to grow up, and grow up fast, regardless of their age.

Younger children are likely to adapt to the new lifestyle more easily, and more quickly than older children. Teens especially are likely to find it tough sledding ATC. No more texting, cell phones, video games, cars, dating, hanging out, school activities, sports, no more anything. Some teens are certain to be mature enough and smart enough to comprehend the problem and are likely to become instant adults. Unfortunately, there'll be those teens who will be belligerent, withdrawn, argumentative, lethargic, and depressed. (Looking at that last sentence, you might be asking yourself, yeah, so what's gonna be different?)

The difference is, if your teen was exhibiting those attitudes BTC, they could probably be chalked up to normal teen growing pains, an overly permissive society, teachers who aren't teachers anymore, schools that are no longer schools, peers that shouldn't be, and parents who don't parent correctly. Whatever the reason, those attitudes need to cease. Now! The whys of your teen's behavior are irrelevant at this time. What is relevant is the fact that your teen will be facing a monumental mental adjustment to his or her life. In fact, your teen may very well feel totally alone with no one to talk to, as well as feeling inept and perhaps even responsible for what happened. In addition, he or she is probably going to be scared to death. This is definitely the time to be your teen's parent.

Anyway, I'm not going to tell you how to raise your children. I do know if you're going to survive, your older children, especially the teens, are going to have to become a fully functional, working member of your family ASAP.

No one should know your children better than you do. Therefore, if they're old enough, it might be a good idea to incorporate them into some of the preparations when you develop your survival plan. Perhaps enlist their aid in researching selected techniques, such as making lye soap, tallow candles or any other survival techniques you'd like to learn more about. If you make them a part of the plan and the learning process, the conversion from life BTC to life ATC won't be nearly as traumatic for them.

Your younger children will have to receive some sort of schooling ATC begins. Someone, probably you, will have to become a teacher. There are many self-schooling books available, or you could simply keep a supply of pencils and paper on hand to teach them the good old three R's. The education of your children is entirely up to you, but I recommend you pack a Bible, a dictionary, a copy of the Constitution of the United States of America, the Bill of Rights, and the Declaration of Independence.

Your entire family should have some form of recreation. Board games, a football, Frisbee, soccer ball, as well as crayons, coloring books, and one or two indestructible toys (if such a thing exists) for the younger kids. In addition, if anyone in the family plays a musical instrument such as a guitar, harmonica etc., those items should also be included. I don't know if kids still play the games we played when I was little; red rover, hide & seek, ring around the rosy, king of the hill and the like, but they were fun back when dinosaurs walked the earth; they'll be fun in the future, too.

CHAPTER 9

NATURES MARKET

MOTHER NATURE CAN PROVIDE EVERYTHING you require to survive and thrive, but you have to know how and where to shop.

Gardening

Planting, maintaining, harvesting and storing the produce from a garden will become the most important aspect of your survival endeavors. Let me put that another way if you don't mind. Growing, harvesting and storing the produce from a garden could be the difference between life and death for you and your family. Therefore, do yourself a favor and don't take this chapter lightly!

It's unlikely you'll encounter major problems securing shelter or locating water, but once the food you've stocked is gone, you'd better be prepared to feed your family from a different source. Remember that the majority of all deaths ATC will be due to starvation.

I have no idea what percentage of the American population has ever planted a fruit or vegetable or has any idea of how to go about it, but I suspect the number is small. After all, why bother messing with a garden when you can visit the supermarket and purchase fruits or vegetables that are imported from a 2nd world country, nearly spoiled, covered in wax, saturated with insecticides, and virtually tasteless? Why would any normal American want to go through the hassle of planting and tending a garden to get fresh, vitamin-packed, insecticide free, and delicious produce that you grew yourself?

"Plant our own garden? That's a great idea Hon, go ahead and start, . . . hey, there's my tackle box!"

Gardening is quite simple. Well, maybe not that simple, but it's not rocket science either. In reality, gardening can be hard work, although it doesn't have to be.

A traditional garden, where all the rows are in single lines, will require a lot of land to qualify as a true survival garden. Traditional gardens are productive, but there's a much easier way of gardening that will produce far more product in less space and require a lot less maintenance than the traditional in-line-row garden. In fact, the method is so effective and so compact, it's almost as though it was developed specifically for our survival needs ATC.

I highly recommend you purchase, or at least read, a book titled *All New Square Foot Gardening*. (Information is located in the appendix). I don't intend to duplicate the information that's contained in this tremendous book, but I'll give you a heads-up on one change that may be necessary. The book will instruct you how to build the framework for your square foot garden using lumber, but you can accomplish the same thing using small logs if there's no lumber available.

Planting a vegetable garden that'll yield enough crops to last from the fall harvest to the following summer simply isn't going to be within the reach of everyone. In addition, if the catastrophe started in mid-summer, planting a garden during the remainder of that year won't be possible except in some areas of the deep South. However, if you're able to plant at the appropriate time in the spring, your summertime diet will receive a major upgrade, and you'll be well on your way to warding off starvation.

Nevertheless, your summertime orgy of fresh veggies isn't going to do you a bit of good during the ensuing winter unless you're able to store some of those crops. Finding a way to store crops for use during the winter is the final key to your successful survival efforts.

There are several ways to store your crops. Dehydration, canning, and root-cellar storage are the most commonly used methods of survival crop preservation.

You can easily accomplish all of them with simple equipment and without the use of electricity.

Almost all fruits and vegetables can be canned, dehydrated, or stored in a root cellar. Root crops are vegetables whose "fruit" grows under the ground, such as potatoes, carrots, turnips, rutabagas etc. and some above ground crops such as squash, pumpkin (pumpkin is a squash), and cabbage can all be stored in a root cellar. Summertime crops such as tomatoes, strawberries, cucumbers, peppers etc. can't be stored in the root cellar. Let's take a brief look at each preservation method.

Canning requires special equipment; a pressure cooker, jars, and lids to name a few. It's possible to can virtually anything, including fish and meat. Canning isn't difficult, and the equipment necessary isn't expensive, but the process won't be within the reach of everyone due to storage and space availability.

If you're comfortable with your choice of a primary survival site and decide to invest in canning equipment, you definitely won't regret the decision. A great book on the subject is *Putting Food By*. (Info in Appendix)

Dehydration is simply the process of removing the majority of moisture from food by drying it. This is accomplished by using the sun and wind to dry out the produce. Different produce (and fish and meat) require different methods of dehydration. Navy beans and peas, for example, placed in single layers on an old window screen, (which you can pilfer from an abandoned house) dry and store exceptionally well.

A small survival dehydrator is available (see appendix) which allows you to dehydrate small quantities of fruits or vegetables by placing the product on trays and hanging the dehydrator from a tree limb or other suitable anchor.

Make certain the produce you're dehydrating is sliced as thin as possible, ensure that air can circulate around the produce, and don't allow the dehydrator, (or the product) to remain in direct sunlight for extended periods. When the produce is dried, simply store it in zip-loc bags or other suitable containers. (We'll cover the smoking and drying of fish and meat in the hunting section of this chapter.)

Corn is another vegetable that's easily dried. Let the corn dry on the stalk well into the fall. When you're ready, pick the corn and shell it, which is farmer speak for removing the kernels from the cob. You'll have to do the shelling by hand, and you'll need either a good sturdy glove or a new thumb when you're finished shelling the corn. (see appendix for corn shelling tools) Dried corn can be ground or pounded into cornmeal and used for cornbread, cornpone, mush, or cereal.

A root cellar is simply a *cool* dark place where the inside temperature remains above freezing. A root cellar doesn't have to be elaborate. If the soil is heavy (not sandy) you can build an effective root cellar by digging into the side of a hill deep enough to allow you to place the produce at the back of the hole. Line the hole with pebbles or small rocks for drainage, and cover the entrance with anything that will provide adequate insulation, such as layers of evergreen boughs. If you have the time and the skill, you can create a much more elaborate root cellar than the *root hole* I just described. Regardless, a root cellar will be mandatory to store your root crops through the winter.

"So, let's see . . . you're saying I need to plant this humongous garden and raise enough crops to feed me, my wife, and 32 kids from September until, what . . . June? That I should have all of this *stuff* so I can dehydrate, can, and store the crop. Is that right?"

Here's the deal. You *do* have to plant a garden. It's going to be tough to survive without one. However, it's probably unrealistic to expect to be able to plant a big enough garden during the first year to provide all the food you'll need. In addition, many of you might not be able to purchase the necessary equipment to plant, harvest, and store the crops that can be grown in a large garden. Fortunately, all is not lost. Your book on square foot gardening will allow you to grow *some* food to help hold you over until the following year. In addition, the survival group you've joined may have an existing co-op garden, root cellar, and all of the tools, canning equipment, and everything else that'll be necessary to grow, harvest, and store the crops.

In the end, you should consider any crops you grow during the first year to be a bonus, even if you can't store them.

As far as gardening tools are concerned you'll need a shovel (which you should have,) and a hoe (no, not that type of . . . nah, can't say it), which can be made from a sharp stick.

If you won't be able to plant a full summer garden, then it makes sense to concentrate on growing items that will last well into the fall and early winter, so concentrate your efforts on those crops that store well. Navy or pinto beans, peas, pumpkin, carrots, potatoes, sweet potatoes, and acorn or butternut squash and cabbage all keep well and would be welcome additions to your winter diet.

A few other gardening techniques you should look into are seed starting, composting (fertilizer), and pest control.

Starting seeds in peat pots in the spring will allow you to get a jump of several weeks on the growing season, since you can plant the pot and plant directly into your garden.

Fertilizer will absolutely increase the yield of your garden. Compost is arguably the best fertilizer in the world and can be created utilizing table scraps and other garbage.

Books on composting are readily available, and I suggest you arm yourself with the basics of composting. The effort will be well worth your time.

The bane of all gardeners is insects and other pests, which include deer, rabbits, etc. Unfortunately, pest control is mandatory. Commercially available Sevin works on about 100 different types of garden insects and is a reasonably effective method of insect control. Natural methods include capturing ladybugs or praying mantis for release in the garden, which is an excellent and natural method of insect control. The problem lies in capturing the ladybugs and the preying mantis in sufficient quantity. Spraying diluted liquid peppermint and sprinkling cinnamon on the plants works better than nothing, but not by much.

You might decide to encourage deer, rabbits, and other garden-marauding animals to visit your garden since their meat will certainly be welcome. Bear in mind, most of those animals will visit during the hours of darkness, which means you'll be standing the night-watch to keep them from ruining your garden, or to harvest them for food.

Alright, seeds! Seeds are *absolutely* the most important aspect of your garden and are one of the most important items you can put in your survival kit.

Almost all of the seeds available today are F-1 hybrid seeds, which means they're one and done. You can't get *viable* seeds for the next growing season from F-1 hybrid plants because the seeds they produce, which are few, are unreliable and, if they do sprout, they won't produce a plant anything like the parent plant. F-1 seeds are effectively sterile.

Heirloom seeds, on the other hand, are seeds that can reproduce themselves exactly. Put another way, heirloom seeds can produce their own seeds and are the ancestors from which all hybrid seeds originated. As a general rule, hybrid seeds are hardier, more disease and insect resistant, and produce bigger crops than heirloom seeds do, but the ability to reproduce themselves has been bred out of them.

To feed the masses, today's farmers use F1 hybrid seeds almost exclusively. Heirloom seeds are not extinct, but genuine heirloom seeds aren't that easy to find either. A supply of heirloom seeds is necessary if you're going to have a reliable source of food ATC. In fact, it's not inconceivable that heirloom seeds will be the gold-standard of the future.

To get the seeds for the next year's planting from heirloom plants simply allow selected plants to "go to seed" rather than harvest their fruits. Harvest the seeds from these plants before the first frost in the fall and store them for use the following spring.

You should consider heirloom seeds to be an absolute necessity for extended long-term survival ATC.

Don't sell F-1 hybrid seeds short, though, since they can still be of value and can provide you with vegetables for at least two years. Here's how. Assume you have two packets of F-1 hybrid cucumber seeds with about twenty seeds per packet. If you planted four hills of cucumbers with three seeds per hill the first year, you'll still have eight seeds left from the first packet and twenty from the second. The next year, since the germination rate of those seeds has undoubtedly dropped by at least 50%, you may have to plant eight to ten seeds per hill to get at least one viable plant. If you opt to use this method, place the un-used seeds in a zip-lock bag and keep them in a cool and dry location. Using F-1 hybrid seeds is a gamble. You're betting the world will be a perfect place again in two short years. If you don't want to take that risk, you should purchase a quantity of heirloom seeds. Heirloom seed sources are located in the appendix.

It's rumored the "Global Elite" are storing heirloom seeds in seed bank vaults near the Arctic Circle. That's what the ad says.

While I can't validate that rumor, I question why the "elite" would construct a vault located near the Arctic Circle. If they're going to store heirloom seeds somewhere, perhaps they should consider putting them in a vault that will allow easy access when they need them. Why the Arctic?

"*Well, since you're one of the sheep, and therefore, a lesser life form, I'll explain it to you. They are in vaults near the Arctic Circle so the temperature can ensure they remain dormant and maintain their potency. In that manner, when we, the all knowing, all-powerful Global Elite, are ready to allow you and your kind to be our subjects, we can control you by using food*".

Oh, excuse *me* your Worship, but aren't you one of the morons screaming about Global Warming? What happens to your precious seeds when the Arctic becomes the new Bahamas? Furthermore, have you ever heard of refrigeration and generators?" Sorry, but the title Global Elite pisses me off.

But, what if it were true. I mean, what if *they* actually were storing seeds somewhere? Would that mean the Global Elitists thought something bad was likely to happen too, and that those seeds would be worth more than gold sometime in the future?

The truth? There *is* a doomsday seed vault near the North Pole. But it was built and paid for by Norway. It's called the Svalbard International Seed Vault. Completed in 2008, it will hold three million seed samples when it's filled. The operation is legitimate and visible to all.

It's definitely not run by the Global Elite. However, it does speak to the doomsday thought process involved in spending millions on building the vault and the millions more that will be necessary to stock and maintain it.

At the end of the day, or in this case, this chapter, I've decided not to incorporate any gardening essentials other than to make a strong recommendation for you to read or purchase the Sq. Ft. Gardening book, and (at least) a supply of hybrid vegetable seeds.

Oh, by the way, what would you like to bet the Federal Government actually does have a huge supply of heirloom seeds stashed away somewhere, and how stupid would it be if they didn't?

Foraging

Times were tough when I was a young boy. Looking back on my childhood, there were far too many days when all I could scrounge up to eat was sugar bread. (Stale bread with butter and sugar on it.) Nevertheless, because I was a kid, I didn't know times were bad, and I'd never even heard the word *diet* before, much less know what it meant. I did know, however, that summertime ushered in a big change in my eating habits due to the proximity of one of our neighbors, Old Mr. Mason. Mr. Mason had a world-class garden and apple orchard. I knew the garden was world-class because he constantly told the neighborhood kids it was. It was like dangling a worm in front of a hungry fish, and summer nights would find my younger brother, two of our cronies, and me foraging in Mr. Masons world-class garden. We'd gorge ourselves on whatever we happened to stumble upon on any particular night, especially the watermelon.

And it was the watermelon that did us in. We didn't know about evidence (trampled vines, etc.), and we didn't know we were foraging; we called it "raiding". The cops informed us that we had been foraging and trespassing. *WHOA*! I couldn't imagine I'd committed a crime as heinous as foraging, so the word got my attention. And even though it didn't roll off the tongue as easily and lacked the macho image of "raiding," it sounded pretty legal. We were thus taken before Lt. O'Brian, whose mere name invoked images of broken and gutted children left rotting in the sun, who proceeded to pull from his belt a *gigantic* three foot long jail cell key. Looking up at that monstrosity, my eyes as big as basketballs, the words foraging, and trespassing began to sound like something out of a nightmare.

Ultimately, with a kick in the butt, and a promise to stay out of Mr. Masons' world-class garden, we were free. We ran home as fast as our little legs could carry us. That humongous key scared the raid right out of us.

Looking back on that event, it was an intelligent and influential way of teaching four young boys a lesson. If that same situation were to happen today, Lt. Obrien would probably be washing dishes somewhere for not contacting my Ma, and Mr. Mason would be penniless, having been sued in Federal Court for a violation of my civil rights for not allowing me to trample and eat his watermelons. As for yours truly, I probably would have gone on to oversee a vast black market crime syndicate that specialized in raided, foraged foods.

In any event, foraging for food in any of your neighbor's survival gardens is a definite no-no, since a load of buckshot would likely replace the three-foot jail cell key and the kick in the butt. Fortunately, there are plenty of other methods of foraging for food that won't get you shot, and the owner, Mother Nature, won't complain to anyone.

Finding wild, edible foods is a whole lot easier than you might think. Natural wild foods are everywhere, and I do mean *everywhere*. The catch is that you have to know what to look for, when to look for them, and how to find them. This is another subject best learned by buying or reading a book, and there are many excellent ones available. A good book on edible wild foods will include pictures and will describe what you can and cannot eat, and why. It'll be an invaluable source of information you'll use repeatedly. (See appendix.)

No matter where you live, there are natural foods available. Just a few are a variety of nuts and berries, apples, peaches, pears, bananas, citrus fruit, strawberries, asparagus, mushrooms, herbs, cactus, maple syrup, and wild plants such as stinging nettle, dandelion, pussy willow, and other "weeds". In addition to foraging for wild foods, you might be close to an abandoned farm that has an apple orchard or even an abandoned home that had a garden with plants still growing in it.

You'll have to do a little research to find out what types of wild and edible plants are native to the area in which you live, but the result will be more than worth the effort.

And while it would be terribly convenient for us to say that the catastrophe will begin in the middle of May when ole Ma Nature is renewing herself, it could just as easily be in the middle of January.

Fishing

So you don't like fish. So what? Fish are like rice; you don't have to like it you just have to eat it, especially since there's a good chance that fish will become one of your main food sources. Fish are everywhere.

They're in freshwater, brackish water, salt water, they're reasonably easy to catch, and they can be caught by a wide variety of methods. Virtually any body of water holds fish. From a two foot wide mountain stream to the mighty Mississippi; from farm ponds to the Great Lakes, and from the brackish backwater sloughs and bayous of the South, to the Gulf of Mexico, and in both the Atlantic and Pacific Oceans, fish are everywhere. However, simply knowing fish are available won't put them on your menu. You need to learn how to catch them first.

Everyone is familiar with sport fishing, which consists of using live or artificial bait and a rod and reel. The most common methods used to catch fish for sport and table fare are: still fishing, with the bait sitting on the bottom or suspended from a cork; by casting a bait toward a point in the water and reeling it back in, or by trolling, which is basically dragging a bait behind a moving boat. You should have a rod and reel of some kind as well as artificial baits, extra line, hooks, sinker, and corks (bobbers) in your survival kit, because it's an effective way to catch fish and, in some areas, it may be the only way you'll be able to catch them.

I don't intend to make this chapter a lesson on how to fish. If you've never been fishing, you definitely need to learn how. Have a friend teach you or attend a fishing seminar where expert fisherman (which is anyone who fishes) will teach you how to enjoy old Isaac Walton's favorite pastime. Actually almost any angler will be more than happy to take you under their wing and teach you how to fish. Just remember to smile and look incredulous when they tell you the story about the big one that got away.

How else can you catch fish other than by the use of a rod and reel or cane pole? Let's take a look.

A casting net is a round net about 8' across with weights along the perimeter and a loop in the center with a rope about 20' long attached to it. The net is thrown so that it lands flat on the water in its full circle form. The weights pull the net down, ensnaring any fish that's unlucky enough to end up beneath it.

The caster then hauls the net in with the rope and, if everything was done correctly, you (the fisherman) have fish for supper or bait to catch a larger fish. This method is most effective if you can see a school of fish prior to throwing the net.

Spear fishing is another method used to take fish and turtles. Spear fishing is especially effective in the springtime when fish move into the shallow water near shore to spawn (lay eggs). A fishing spear consists of 3-4 barbed metal prongs about four inches long and 4"- 6" wide with a metal flange at the other end where a pole is inserted. (A broomstick will work). Insert a screw into the pre-drilled hole on the flange or drive a nail all the way through the broom handle, bending the nail over as it exits the other side. If you fail to bend the nail, it'll work its way out of the broom handle and you'll lose the spearhead.

You can purchase the spearhead and put it in your survival kit, making the handle when the need arises. Fish don't have ears per se, but rather, sense vibrations through a lateral line that runs the length of their bodies. Thus, you'll have to be quiet and walk softly as you approach the water. In addition, your shadow will spook fish that are in shallow water, so make sure the sun isn't at your back.

You may have to stand motionless for some time before you see a fish cruise by, or if the water's muddy, you may only see the wake or even just a shadow. But if your aim is true, you'll have a fish.

Spearing is also used on frozen lakes in the winter, which means you'll have to cut a good sized hole in the ice and wait for a fish to swim by the hole. You won't always see the actual fish, usually just a shadow or a sudden darkening of the water. This method of spearing doesn't work too well south of Tampa Bay.

Ice fishing's a popular sport in some areas of the north and at times can be productive, albeit a bit on the chilly side. Chop a hole in the ice with your axe, which isn't a lot of fun when the ice is 30" thick, drop a baited line into the hole, keep the hole from freezing over, and if you're lucky, you'll catch a fish. (Yes, I know modern ice fishermen use ice-augers, but you only have an axe. It's dull, too. Sharpen it!)

Several productive methods of catching bottom-feeding fish, such as catfish, are jug or setline fishing, and running a trotline. You can make a simple jug line by tying one end of a heavy cord to a milk jug and the other end to a three-way swivel.

Tie another length of cord about four feet long to the bottom eye of the three-way swivel and attach a heavy weight such as a rock or brick to the four foot cord. Now tie a three foot piece of heavy monofilament line to the remaining eye of the swivel, attach a hook, and you have a setline. When placing the setline, bait the hook and lower the weight until it hits bottom, wrap the slack line around the jug, tie it off, and check the line periodically to see if you caught a fish.

Trotlines are another way to catch bottom-feeding fish, but they're a bit more complicated than a jug line. Trotlines aren't difficult to make, but it might be easier to purchase one that's pre-rigged rather than to attempt to make one. A trotline is a long cord or line normally 50'-100' long with 25-50 18" hook-lines spaced 2'- 3' apart that attach to the long line and have hooks at the other end.

You can tie the hook-lines to the long-line, but there are spacer clamps that can be purchased to keep the hook lines from working down the long-line and tangling up. To envision what a trotline looks like, picture a capital letter U. At the top of each U is a jug with a line attached to it (the vertical sides of the U,) that runs down to the bottom of each side of the U, where they each attach to a heavy weight.

The bottom portion of the U (the long hook line) has the hook lines attached and runs from one weight to the other. You'll need a boat, a canoe, or even a heavy plank or a log to paddle out and place the baited trot line. If you're near the mouth of a creek or small river that empties into a larger body of water, you can stretch the trot line across the creek by tying the ends to trees on each side of the bank. Trotlines are a productive method of catching fish, and you don't have to sit and watch them.

If you need to fish deeper water, but can't get to it, you can use a balloon to get your bait a significant distance off shore. If, for example, you're near a river that empties into a lake and the current is reasonably strong, or for ocean fishing when the tide is going out, you can use a balloon as a large bobber. Attach the balloon to your line using a snap clothespin set three to four feet above the baited hook. Throw the entire rig, balloon, weight, and baited hook as far into the current as you can and watch as it floats offshore. This method of fishing is especially good for catching shark.

There are certainly many other ways to catch fish, but the methods that I mentioned will probably be the most practical for the average person ATC. If you're interested in other methods, you can check out the use of seines, gill, trammel, and hoop nets, crab and crawdad traps, dip-nets, and weirs.

A friend of mine, who's a Chippewa Indian, taught me this method of "hand fishing." Stream trout and bass (especially the big ones) are territorial, routinely resting in the same areas; an undercut bank, by a submerged tree, large boulder or similar object. If you can locate a big trout, it's probable that no matter what you dangle in front of him, he'll ignore it. That same big trout, however, will likely be in the same spot every day, moving only to feed at night. Use of this procedure will take a lot of patience, but you can catch him by using it.

If you can get to within three feet or so of the fish, slowly, and quietly approach the bank above the trout and lie down directly above him. With movements so slow as to be almost non-existent, lower your hand and arm into the water as far as you can. Now start working your way S L O W L Y up toward the fish, and under the fish's belly. (If you accidently touch the fish, don't worry, it won't spook him.) Work your hand up toward the head of the fish, and in one quick motion, jam your fingers and hand into the gills and in the same motion, throw the fish onto the bank. I don't know if there's an official name for this particular method but I *can* tell you that, honest-Injun, it works.

Another unorthodox method of catching fish which I'll share with you, and that I discovered purely by accident when I was about eight years old, is to wade in water about three feet deep where you know there are fish. In this particular instance, we're talking about Carp, which were trapped in a backwater of the Mississippi River after a minor flood. Walking slowly along with your hands near the bottom, you can actually touch fish, as long as you do it S L O W L Y and gently. You can perform the same maneuver that I just described with the trout, except the thrust into the gills will come from the top of the fish, as opposed to the under-belly. After you've captured the Carp, and because you *know* it's the greatest game fish of all time, you can put it into the basket attached to your bicycle and pedal furiously to the river to release the "King of all fish" so it can be caught with a rod and reel (by you) on some other day. But in your situation, you might prefer to smoke and eat it instead.

So there a lot of different ways to catch fish and, wait . . . what was that question? What's the easiest fish to catch? That one's easy. Those little three inch bait stealers that you swear at all the time. Use a #14-wire hook and two lb. test leader and you'll catch 100's of them. Fresh or salt water, it won't matter. And just for the record, 100 three inch fish that are cleaned, equals about 100 bites, divided by four people equals 25 bites per person.

If you're hungry, 25 bites per person equals a decent survival meal.

Cleaning the fish after you catch them is everyone's un-favorite thing to do. I'm not going to attempt to tell you how to clean a fish or how to fillet one either, but I will say that a thin, flexible blade fillet knife will make the job easier, and that the fishy taste in fish is usually a direct result of improper care after the fish is caught.

If you don't want your fish to taste like fish smell, make sure you do the following. After you catch the fish, if you're putting it on a stringer or in a bait-well of some sort so you can continue to fish, check the fish often. If the fish dies, remove the gills *immediately*, or at least before they turn pink, since the gills are the first part of the fish to spoil. When you're actually cleaning the fish, try not to rupture any internal organs.

If you caught the fish in muddy water, water that has a lot of tannin in it, or from an area with heavy vegetation, the fish is likely to taste like the environment it lived in. To eliminate the odor and taste, remove the skin. In addition, if the filet has dark lines in it, usually down the middle of the fish, cut them out. You'll enjoy fish that taste like fish and not like fish smell.

If you're a fisherman, you probably have everything you need, or at least you'll know what equipment you need to buy and how to use it. For the novice angler, the choice of equipment is vast. You can use a cane pole or a willow switch to catch fish, but if you decide to use a rod and reel and you're just starting out, you'll have the best luck with a spin-cast rod and reel combo.

Live bait for fish can be just about anything, including pieces of other fish, insects, grubs, worms, night crawlers, minnows (small fish) or guts from birds and animals. You can also use canned kernel corn to catch carp, sucker, and mullet. In the winter, if you're having trouble finding bait, but can locate some goldenrod, check the stalks. If there are bulbs on them, some of them will contain a small grub.

Survival kit essentials

1. 2-pc spin-cast rod and reel with 10-lb monofilament line and one extra spool of line
2. An assortment of hooks and sinkers, including #14 wire hooks and BB split shots
3. An assortment of barrel and three-way swivels
4. A spool of 2-lb or 4-lb test mono for catching bait stealers
5. An assortment of bobbers (corks)
6. An assortment of lead head jigs from 1/32 oz. to 3/8 oz

7. An assortment of plastic jig head tails in white, yellow and purple
8. Spinner bait
9. Spoon bait
10. Crank bait
11. For salt water simply add a stronger rod and reel, heavier line, larger hooks, heavier sinkers, and perhaps a larger artificial bait.

Hunting & trapping

Not bad, Pilgrim! You have a garden planted, you constructed a root cellar, found some nut and fruit trees, you located a pond, and fish are on the menu. Now it's time to add some meat.

You *should* have a .12 Ga. shotgun in your survival kit, since it's your main defensive weapon. It's also an excellent hunting weapon. You can hunt anything from big game like deer and small game such as rabbits and squirrels, and birds ranging from quail to turkey with your trusty .12 Ga. shotgun. It's a highly versatile weapon.

While the .12 Ga. wouldn't be any knowledgeable hunters weapon of choice for big game, it's highly effective on deer-sized animals at ranges out to about fifty yards using a slug, or by using #00 buckshot (which is .30 caliber in size) at closer ranges. However, to hunt different types of birds and small game, you have to use a smaller shot size. The *smaller* the number that's marked on the shot-shell, the *larger* the shot-size, or pellet, will be.

Commonly used shot sizes are BB, which is the exact same thing as the BB your kid shot out the neighbor's window with, #2 shot, #4 shot, #5 shot, #6 shot, #7-1/2 shot, and #8 shot are all common shot-shell sizes. The smaller the shot size, the more pellets there are within the shot-shell, thus there are more #8 pellets in a shot-shell than there are #4 pellets in the same exact shell. Is that confusing?

Let me put it another way. A shotgun shell that has the number four (4) marked on it, will contain larger, but fewer pellets than a shotgun shell with the number eight (8) marked on it. Is that better? When the shotgun is fired, the pellets leaving the barrel are in a dense, almost solid group, but spread, or separate from each other in an ever-expanding cone, or circular pattern. The further the shot moves from the end of the barrel of the gun, the larger the circle becomes.

A shotgun with an improved cylinder (IC) choke and 26" barrel allows the pellets to begin to expand into a larger circle more quickly than a shotgun with a 30" barrel that has a full choke. A full choked shotgun will hold the pellets closer together for a longer distance, thus increasing the distance you're able to hit a target. By contrast, your I/C choked shotgun allows the pellet formation to begin to expand quicker, reducing the effective range, but increasing the probability of putting lead on target at closer ranges.

In other words, the closer the target is to the end of the barrel (muzzle), the more pellets are likely to strike the intended target.

Your I/C choked gun will have an *effective* range of approximately 35 yards on birds and other small game. The larger pellets like #00 buck, BB, and #2 shot will go farther and have the capability to bring down what they hit at a greater distance than smaller pellets due to mass and the effects of gravity on the different size and weight of the individual pellets. I know that information is a bit confusing and probably seems irrelevant, especially if you know nothing about firearms, but it's important that you have a basic understanding of the distances you can expect to hit and kill something with your shotgun and what its limitations are.

As a rule, larger, tougher game such as high-flying geese and ducks are hunted using BB's or #2 shot, while pheasants might be hunted with #4 shot, grouse with #6 or, even #7-1/2 shot, and rabbits and squirrels with #5 or #6 shot. There's no set shot size to use on any particular game. It's left up to the hunter to decide what size shot to use.

Just remember, the larger the shot size, the more pellets there will be heading toward the target, but that those pellets won't have the range or the knockdown (penetration) power of the larger shot with fewer pellets. Think of it in terms of the difference between a punch from an eight year-old child (7-1/2 shot) and that of a 200 lb professional boxer (BB size shot).

A shotgun slug is different from a shot-shell filled with pellets. A .12 Ga. shotgun slug is a solid 1-oz piece of lead and is much like a bullet fired from a rifle. With a shot shell loaded with pellets, you only need to come close, but with a slug, you must hit the target precisely.

If you've added a .22LR to your armory, you have an excellent small game caliber for taking squirrels and any rabbit or bird that might sit still long enough for you to get off an accurate shot. Don't underestimate the effectiveness of the .22LR round.

If you were to hit a deer between the eyes with a .22LR, it might ultimately kill it, but the animal would more than likely be stunned and drop to its knees, or thrash around on the ground for a minute or two. If you're hungry enough, and not squeamish about it, and you can get close enough to the deer, you can shoot it in the eyeball, which should allow the bullet to penetrate the brain, or you can smack it over the head with a log or something. I suppose that sounds harsh, and I might be the recipient of another visit from PETA for writing it, but to echo the most profound of all statements, . . . *whatever*,

"my family's starving and this deer is food."

If you do decide to smack a deer over the head, be mindful of the deer's hooves. They can kick the crap out of you while they're thrashing about. If the deer is a buck, be *extra* careful of the horns. If a buck deer gores you, you could end up dead.

Hunting could easily take up several thousand pages of any number of books, so you might want to devote some study time to the subject of hunting. Before you do, however, you should find out exactly what type of game is available in your primary location and limit your hunting research to those particular animals. If you've never hunted before and you don't know anyone who can teach you, you'll have to learn on the job.

You can't become an expert hunter by reading a book. If you can't take the time to read up on hunting, but can remember and apply these basic principals when hunting, you'll probably do okay.

Animals notice movement immediately, so keep your head and body movements to a minimum and go SLOW. If you think you're going too slow, SLOW DOWN! Be as quiet as you can, and stop, look, and listen often. Be patient. Never hunt with the wind at your back. Animals have a keen sense of smell and will be long gone if they get wind of you. Finally, be aware that animals will be aware of you long before you're aware of them.

Earlier we determined that where you live would be the single biggest factor in your survival. Where you live is also important when it comes to hunting since it will dictate the type of game and the amount of game that's available to you. The western states have many big game animals in the mountains, but probably less small game than the eastern states.

Someone once told me that prairie dog tastes like chicken, and although I can't make an intelligent comment about the taste buds of the shooter/commentator, I'm pretty sure it was beer-induced. Almost all states have an abundance of deer, and in some areas they're approaching pest status. Florida has the mighty gator, which is tasty, and in many of the western states, rattlesnake is easy to come by. Apparently, rattlesnake also tastes like chicken, even to people who are completely sober. Whenever you ask someone what an "exotic food" tastes like, the answer is *never* . . .

"well . . . it sorta tastes like a Big Mac."

The answer is *always* . . . "tastes like chicken!"

Trapping is also a genre unto itself, but the majority of information that you're going to find will pertain to the trapping of fur-bearing animals for their pelts. Methods used to trap or kill animals or man is different from setting a trap to catch a mink or beaver.

Let's take a look at pitfalls.

You've seen pitfalls in the movies. Somebody digs a large hole about 10' deep somewhere on a well traveled trail and covers it with a thin material that matches the trail *perfectly*.

With zero evidence of the 64,357 cubic yards of dirt that was removed, the hero who dug the pit in his spare time with an old spoon, and thus knows exactly where it is, lures one of the dumb-ass bad guys to chase him down the trail.

Because the hero knows *exactly* where the pit is, he rounds the bend, jumps the pit, turns, and watches as the bad guy(s) falls through the membrane, into the pit, and onto the sharpened stakes below. Ouch!

That's pretty much how a pitfall works. The differences are that your pitfall would be on a much smaller scale, and the animal is smarter than the movie bad guy, so you'll probably have to place bait in the center of the membrane to lure the animal onto the trap.

Snares and deadfalls can also be effective traps to kill an animal (or an enemy). You can go online and find detailed diagrams pertaining to the setting of snares and deadfalls.

Removing the guts from an animal after it's been killed (field dressing) is essentially the same for all animals, regardless of their size. Therefore, learning how to field dress one will give you the basic knowledge to be able to field-dress any of them. Skinning an animal isn't difficult, but it does require a sharp knife. Any knife will work, but a special knife with a curved blade, and oddly enough called a skinning knife, works the best. For information on the butchering of animals, and birds check the books in the appendix.

People often complain of the "gamy" taste of wild game and, much like a "fishy tasting fish," a gamy tasting animal is almost always the result of improper field dressing.

During the process of field dressing an animal, it's important to take great care not to puncture the intestines or the bladder. If you do, the contents will contaminate the meat and it will likely have a gamy taste.

After field dressing the animal, the proper care of the carcass is critical. If it's hot out, you should begin to butcher the animal almost immediately. If you let it hang with the hide on in hot weather, it will quickly start to spoil.

If the weather's cold, you can allow the carcass to season for a few days out of the sun by suspending it from a tree limb. To keep wild animals away while the carcass is hanging, make sure it's high enough off the ground.

Two of the preservation methods that you should learn are drying and smoking fish and meat. Different cultures have used these two methods of fish and meat preservation for centuries. They're simple to use and very effective.

Cut the meat or fish into thin strips and hang them by whatever means you can devise to allow the air to dry them. Don't allow the strips to touch anything while they're drying, and be sure to place the strips high enough off the ground to provide protection from wild animals.

Smoking the meat utilizes the same principle as drying except a fire producing more smoke than heat smolders under the drying strips. This procedure allows the air and the smoke to dry and cure the meat. The type of wood used in the smoking of meat is important, since the smoke will impart a flavor. Apple, hickory, mesquite, and cherry are all preferable woods used in the smoking of meats, but won't always be available. When the meat's fully smoked, you'll have jerky.

If you aren't able to purchase all of the books you should or would like to read, or simply don't have the time, you can print the selected website information or visit the library and take notes on those items that are relevant. You can bring library books home and photo-copy the pages you're interested in. Placing all of the printed information and notes in a marked file in your survival kit will give you a handy reference guide when the need to know arises.

Survival kit essentials

You should have at least two good brand name knives since they'll be one of the most useful and important items you'll be putting in your kit. Choose one from makers such as Gerber, Ka-bar, SOG, Cold Steel, Kershaw etc. *Don't cut corners with your knives!*

1. Folding pocket/belt knife with a 3" to 4" blade
2. 6" to 10" blade, fixed blade hunting knife with belt sheath (your main knife)
3. One box (24 rounds minimum) .12 Ga. #5 shot (A compromise) high brass 2-3/4" shotgun shells
4. One bottle gun oil (optional cleaning kit)

The lost arts

Have you ever wondered how American Indians got by so well without the many conveniences we take for granted? They knew how to do things that modern man has never learned. How many people today know how to do *one single thing* that an Indian child knew how to do? Not very many, that's for sure. The simple items that you're placing in your survival kit are probably light years ahead of the meager tools the Indians had to work with, yet they were able to do everything that's been mentioned in this book, and a whole lot that hasn't been.

They could make their own clothing, footwear, design and create their own tools, weapons and utensils, build their own shelters, and provide their own medicines, just to give a few examples. If there's *one skill* you should learn, it's how the Indians did things. In addition to Indian survival skills, you can learn a lot from later generations of Americans, especially the technology used through the latter part of the 19th and the earlier part of the 20th centuries. Check the appendix for books on both of these subjects.

If you start studying how the Indians did things you'll find it to be a fascinating subject, and it's fun to try some of the methods they used. I've tried a lot of them, including making venison jerky, pemmican, and the building of an authentic teepee, but what opened my eyes to how very knowledgeable the Indians were and how incredibly difficult certain aspects of their life must have been was, the moccasins!

I was in my early twenty's when I decided I was going to make an authentic pair of moccasins using the same methods the Indians used way back when. I shot a deer from a distance of about fifteen yards from a tree stand with a long bow and a wooden arrow that I made myself.

I cheated on this part and skinned the deer with a Puma skinning knife, but I removed the hair from the hide by burying it in the ground, broke up the fibers by moving it back and forth over a sharp rock, smoked the hide over a green oak fire, and cut and made a pair of moccasins and lacings. The only modern tools I used were the bow I used to take the deer and the knife I used to skin it with. It would've been a heck of a lot easier to simply buy the moccasins, but it wouldn't have been anywhere near as satisfying as knowing I created those *two left-footed Budweiser moccasins* all by myself. I also learned not to drink "fire-water" when "working" and I gained a new and lasting respect for the American Indian and the skills they used on a daily basis. Or should I say the skills the Indian women used. The men were out fishing or something.

Some of you will be in a position to raise animals for food, so I'll briefly tell you that the easiest animals to raise for food are chickens. They require a minimal amount of care and for the most part they'll feed themselves by scratching around for bugs and such unless it's cold, in which case you'll have to provide them with food and reasonable shelter. You'll also have to protect them from predators such as foxes, martins, and the like, but the eggs alone are worth the effort. If you want chicks, you'll have to provide Ms. Hen with a rooster. When the chicks are old enough, you can butcher and eat any roosters that hatched. By the way, chickens that are allowed to "range" don't taste anything like the chicken you buy at the supermarket. They taste like, well, . . . like chicken.

Rabbits are another animal that can be easily raised for food, and they breed like rabbits.

A goat will provide you with fresh milk and the opportunity to make cheese. You'll also gain a cool family pet.

CHAPTER 10

EMERGENCY RELOCATION

THE LIST OF *ESSENTIAL ITEMS* FOR your survival kit is nearly complete, but having those items scattered around the house won't do any good if you're forced into an emergency evacuation of your primary location. Therefore, it's essential that you keep the *basic survival items* in an easily accessed backpack, or bug-out bag. Many years ago, when I was analyzing and perfecting my own survival plans, I concluded that a packed and readily available bug-out bag was the crucial part of my over-all plan. I could see it, touch it, and if all else failed, I knew that packed bug-out bag was the most dependable option I'd have. That conclusion's still valid today. Go-bag, bug-out bag, ready-bag, it doesn't matter what you call it, that pack is going to be your *best survival option.* Everything you'll ever need to know about Bug-out bags is covered in the *how to* section of the book. For now, though, let's assume you have your bug-out bag(s) packed and ready to go. The questions of *who* or *what* would force you into a relocation phase, and *when* or *why* can't be answered with any degree of certainty at this time, but it seems reasonable to believe that one single event could answer all four of those questions simultaneously. It could be any of the catastrophes listed in the beginning of the book. So we're left with just two questions we can realistically answer. *Where* do you go, and *how* do you get there?

It's a cinch you won't want to wander aimlessly around in the woods looking for a suitable location to pitch a tent. That would be foolhardy as well as dangerous. Therefore it's imperative you know exactly *where* you're going and exactly *how* you're going to get there.

Let's take a look at *where* first, since it's arguably more important than *how.* Knowing exactly where you're going during an emergency evac from your *primary residence* means it will be necessary for you to incorporate an *emergency relocation site* into your overall survival plan. Don't confuse emergency relocation site with a primary residence. They're totally different. If you have to go to your emergency relocation site, it will be *from* your primary residence or safe area, and it'll mean your primary residence is no longer safe or viable.

The search for a suitable emergency relocation site should begin as soon as you know where your primary location or safe area's going to be. The area you choose for an emergency relocation site has to meet the same criteria as your primary location or safe area. It has to be able to provide you with the three *old basics*, and as many of the *new basics* as possible. You'll be carrying your shelter with you in the form of a tarp or a tent, so the emergency site has to be able to provide you with water, the availability of a fuel source, the ability to grow or find food, and it has to be reasonably safe and defensible. Above all, it has to be relatively close to the primary site since the odds are that you'll be walking to it. Close means it shouldn't be more than 25 miles away.

If possible, you should visit the emergency relocation site you've chosen. Paying a personal visit to the site will allow you to locate defensive positions, escape routes, and where to set up your initial campsite. You'll also have the opportunity to scout out the area, check out the flora and fauna, and familiarize yourself with your site selection.

Purchasing a USGC (United States Geological Survey) topographical map of the area will prove invaluable, since it will show every feature of the chosen area, including the location of springs, bodies of water, elevations, abandoned buildings, woods, fields, roads, and in some instances, old logging roads and footpaths.

All of these features and more are displayed on USGC topographical maps, and they're absolutely priceless. They're so accurate you could actually become familiar with the area without a personal visit, although I don't recommend it. Get one that's waterproofed if you can. If not, you can waterproof it yourself. A simple, effective, and enjoyable method of checking out the area you've selected is to take your family on a field trip for a weekend, which will allow you to check out some of your equipment in the process. If the area you've selected is a national or state park, you can visit it on a regular basis and, assuming they allow tent campers, you can spend several weekends fine-tuning your equipment, sharpening your survival skills, and enjoying yourself at the same time.

Once you know *where* you're going, you need to determine *how* you're going to get there. The options, during an emergency relocation, will undoubtedly be limited, but we'll explore those that could be possible.

Will you be able to drive? That question can't be answered right now, but if driving to the site is a possibility, extending the distance of the location out to fifty miles or more might not create an insurmountable problem. Let's assume the location you picked was fifty miles distant and it appeared there was a 75% probability you'd be able to drive to the site. Enter Mr. Murphy and X the unknown factor. Oops, guess you're hoofing it those fifty miles. That's okay. Simply make the journey in stages, even if it takes you a week to get there.

Obviously, you're going to want to get to your emergency site as quickly as possible, preferably in a matter of hours. However, you also need to do it safely. Does that mean you go by horse, by boat, 4-wheeler, snowmobile, vehicle, or private plane? And the answer is, yes. As long as you can do so safely, riding *anything* would beat walking. However, machines make noise, and that noise is going to be more noticeable without the ambient background noises that were always there BTC, but that will now be conspicuously absent.

Those mechanical noises will alert the bad guys that you're in their neighborhood, and they're likely to plan a little surprise party for you. In addition, traveling at night with headlights on would give them a visual to go along with the audio, thus increasing their chances of intercepting you. If you determine it will be safe to drive at night, at least disable your tail and brake lights, take out the interior and exterior bulbs and tape off your headlights, leaving a small rectangular slit in the middle. Then drive slowly and carefully. Keep in mind that nighttime noise travels much farther and can be heard with greater clarity than the same noise created during daylight hours.

Floating to the site in a boat, canoe, or the equivalent, (assuming it's downstream) is actually a good idea. Using a motor to go upstream will definitely tell the scumbags you're on the water and in which direction you're heading. Remember too that sound travels *much farther* and with *much greater clarity* over large bodies of water, such as a lake, than they do on land.

A plane could also work, assuming you could land near, but not too near your actual site. If you flew to within five miles or so of your destination and walked the final distance, you'd probably be okay. Land at, or close to, the actual site and the bad guys will find you.

The bottom line on getting from your primary residence to the emergency relocation site is to do so in the safest manner possible, which is probably going to be on foot.

Walking will allow you to stop, look, and listen. You can skirt those areas that look dangerous and avoid people you see before they see you. In addition, you can stick to whatever cover is available, and if it's raining, you can go as far as you can as fast as you can using the rain as cover, since there won't be too many bad guys out and about until the rain stops.

If you're going to be walking fifty miles or so in the woods, you'll need a decent compass with a declination offset, and you'll have to learn how to use it.

Path finding is an art unto itself, and the best book ever written on the subject, *Be Expert With Map & Compass*, is available almost anywhere, and I highly recommend you purchase it.

Don't start a fire unless there's no alternative, since the light from a night-time fire or the smell of wood smoke created by a daytime fire, are both invitations you won't want to send out.

Remember, if you have to walk *any* distance it's imperative you have good footwear.

Walking *will* get you to your emergency relocation site and while it's true you might arrive exhausted, sore, hungry, wet, cold, and miserable, the point is that you will have survived, and you will have arrived in one piece. And that's the goal!

CHAPTER 11

SURVIVING THE SURVIVORS

WHEN THE INITIAL EFFECTS OF the catastrophe have ended, there will be survivors. However, not everyone who survived the initial catastrophe, whatever it was, will survive the phases that follow. Those survivors who were injured and are unable to receive medical assistance are likely to perish in a relatively short period. A bit further down the time line will be those who contracted a disease and who will die, and those who will starve to death. There will be other survivors who were killed accidentally, and those who were killed intentionally.

It's possible that you'll encounter all of these types of survivors. They'll all pose different threats to you and your family, but as time goes by, their threat will be alleviated through the process of elimination.

The threats created by diseased, dying or starving survivors will occur, not because they're inherently bad people, but because of the condition they're in. In the case of those who are injured, you may want to help them. While there's nothing wrong with that desire, you should be aware that using up your own medical supplies to help a stranger may imperil your own family somewhere down the line. There's probably not going to be much you can do to help survivors who are dying except to make them comfortable and say a few kind words. Be aware however, that friends, and especially family, of an injured or dying survivor may insist that you use whatever medical supplies you have in an effort to heal that person. They may even make that insistence at the point of a gun and even kill you to get your medical supplies.

Diseased or starving survivors are a different matter altogether.

If someone has an obvious disease, there's *no way* you should risk coming in contact with that person and passing the disease on to your family. I would avoid them like the plague. No pun intended. Those survivors who might be starving are also likely to pose a serious and credible threat to you and your family. If they know you have food or even suspect you have food, and you won't give it to them or at least share it with them, they *will* attempt to kill you to get it. Do what you have to do! You planned. They didn't. Too bad!

Ultimately, it seems probable that half of those who survive the initial catastrophe and the ensuing survival phases will be decent, civilized, normal human beings, much like yourself; the "good guys." We could also predict that the other half of the survivors will be those who were unprepared, but were in the right place at the right time, were lucky, or simply took what they wanted in order to survive. It's also likely that half of the "lucky" survivors (25% of all survivors) will be neither consistently good nor habitually bad. They're likely to be easily manipulated and will probably align themselves with whomever they think will provide them with the best opportunity. You can call these survivors whatever you like.

Then there's the remaining 25%, the ones you really need to be concerned with, *the bad guys*! In no particular order, the list would include gangs, drug addicts, crazies, end of the world nuts, those who fancy themselves kings, and anti-social, schizophrenic or homicidal maniacs. Their ranks will likely include prisoners and mental patients who escaped or were released from prisons, jails, and mental institutions. Most, if not all, of these deranged scumbags will have little or no conscience, and you better believe they're *extremely dangerous*. Don't delude yourself into believing or hoping they won't make it through the initial catastrophe. They will!

The majority of the survivors in this category (perhaps as high as 60%-70%) are likely to be mere accomplices to the seriously dangerous ones. Their faux power and the danger they present will come from their collective mentalities. (Yeah, kind of like the Borg.) In other words, they won't be "bad" if they're alone. That doesn't mean they're not dangerous, for they certainly are. They will likely carry out the criminal desires and orders of the leaders.

Without some sort of organization, most of these bad guys won't be around long. They'll be eliminated by the good guys, as well as by other bad guys fighting for "turf."

This brings us to the number of survivors who are genuinely evil and have the intelligence, charisma, and the ruthless personality necessary to control and effectively lead surviving "bad guys." The small handful of surviving sociopaths who might fit that description is probably less than 1/10 of 1%. That percentage, as small as it is, will be more than enough. I'm sure you remember Hitler and Stalin.

As for safe areas across the country, there will be a lot of them, especially in rural or lightly populated areas. It's inconceivable that organized gangs with effective leaders will be in control everywhere.

Be that as it may, the most dangerous time ATC will be during the first few weeks or months. As time goes by, everyone, including the bad guys, will have settled into some sort of routine, and life will begin to take on some sort of order. My advice is to avoid *everyone* during the chaotic period, however long that may last. At some point, you'll be able to recon selected areas, and through observation, locate groups you may want to hook up with.

Eventually, perhaps a year or two later, civilization will re-emerge, and life will begin to take on a semblance of normalcy. Communities will "spring up," trade and barter will begin, and people will once more be able to think in terms of a future.

Monetary System(s)

Will there be legal tender? Yeah, there will be, but it won't be the dollar. It'll be either gold and silver, seeds, or food.

Speaking of gold, I'm sure you've heard the glut of "buy gold now" ads on the radio and TV. I get a kick out of one that states "*and gold has never been worth zero.*" *Reeeally?* Well, neither has a penny or a roll of toilet paper, ever been worth zero. So, I should pay $1400 dollars for an ounce of gold and if I'm lucky, it probably won't ever (maybe) (hopefully) be worth zero?

Is gold really a solid investment for the future? Of course it is. It's never been worth zero. Besides, when a monetary system is re-established, the Vegas odds are that the new monetary standard will be based on gold.

As far as monetary systems are concerned, we'll know the *exact* value of an ounce of gold immediately BTC, but we'll have no idea what that same ounce of gold will be worth immediately ATC. What we will know however is that an ounce of gold won't be worth anything near its value BTC.

Eventually, though, people will acknowledge that gold and old silver coins have a value, and they'll also be aware that a one oz gold coin is worth more than a pre-1964 silver dollar. (Similarly, they're going to realize that a pound of salt is worth more than an ounce of sugar.)

Someone, maybe you, will determine that a one oz gold coin is worth, let's say $100, and that all silver coins are worth 1/10th of their face value set against the one oz. gold coin as the standard. That means a silver dollar would be worth $10, a silver half-dollar would be worth $5, a silver quarter $2.50, a silver dime $1, and a silver war nickel would be worth half a buck. The penny would *finally* be worth zero.

It follows then that the prices "new merchants" charged for items they sell would have to reflect the value of the adopted monetary system.

If you plan to buy gold for use in a post catastrophic world, think about this. In the long term, gold will undoubtedly turn out to be a wise and solid investment, but in the short term, silver coins will be much more practical and easier to use than a gold coin.

"Hey man, how much do you want for that chicken?"

"Half a buck pal."

"Jeez, fifty cents? All I have is this one oz gold coin. Can you make change?"

"Hell no, I can't make change."

"Hey, Jody, I bought us this chicken for supper."

"Whaddicha give for it?"

"Uhhh . . . hey, look, there's my tackle box again. Hey kids, let's go fishin'."

The sad reality is few people will have old silver coins and even fewer will have gold coins. Therefore, even though you may have both and are one of the "Nuevo Riche," the gold coins in particular aren't going to do you a lot of good in your everyday ability to buy or sell, which is where barter and trade come in.

Trade: "I'll trade you three shotgun shells for that snake if it tastes like chicken." Or barter: "I'll give you this carp that tastes like a Big Mac if you'll help me cut a cord of firewood." Alternately, you can mix barter and trade together. "I'll give you this rattlesnake that tastes *exactly* like chicken, plus this almost new chamber pot and a roll of TP for your wife, if you'll help me butcher this big ole turkey."

"That's not a turkey, it's a pigeon, and one roll of TP'd only last my wife a day."

"Really? Ok then, two rolls but, uhh . . . you sure this isn't a turkey?"

Regardless of whether you're trading labor or products, your negotiating skills will ultimately determine if you made a good deal or if the other person got over on you. One thing's for certain; you can only pay $100 for a chicken that's worth fifty cents one time before your wife takes away your shopping privileges.

Here are some inexpensive barter items that people will want and will need, which you can procure for future trade, barter, or sale.

Toilet paper
Iodized salt
Sugar
Bar hand soap
White distilled vinegar
Aspirin
Tylenol
Band-aids
Pepper
Bleach.

You can easily add other items to the list. Simply think about items people will need (or want), but will be unable to find, that will be inexpensive for you to stock.

Pre-1964 silver coins are available from almost any coin dealer as "junk silver coins." You should seriously consider putting some in your survival kit.

CHAPTER 12

NATIONAL NATURAL DISASTERS

SINCE SOME OF THIS INFORMATION was provided in a shortened version in the beginning of the book, I'll try not to duplicate too much of it. For the most part, the information contained in this section has more depth. Where feasible, I've added a survivability rating based upon the probability of the event happening, levels of preparedness, and proximity to ground zero. The ratings are predicated upon the assumption that you and your family are in a life and death survival situation without medical assistance or governmental help of any kind. They're based on a broad range of averages and are a long way from being scientifically accurate. Use them as a guide only.

Any of the disasters listed here could happen. That's not to say any of them will happen. There are a ton of "experts" willing to give endless reasons why a particular disaster will take place, and an equal number who will tell you the disaster in question simply isn't going to happen in our lifetimes.

The fact is, there are few facts pertaining to any of them, particularly of what the results on humanity will be. It's all theory, (an assumption based on limited information or knowledge,) conjecture, (a preposition that's unproven, but appears to be correct and hasn't been disproven), and opinion. (You remember what opinion's are like.)

So while the theories, conjecture, and opinions of bona fide experts with credible credentials are important and should be listened to, the bottom line is, no one knows for certain if any of these disasters are going to happen, when they might happen, and what the results will be if they do happen. Therefore, it's up to you do determine which "expert" you choose to believe. If you lean toward those predicting dire consequences, you could easily spend your life and your last dime worrying about and preparing to survive an event that may never happen. If, on the other hand, you chose to believe those "experts" who tell you not to worry about it, and Yellowstone decides to get nasty, well, the result of that decision is obvious.

One thing's for certain, if a major disaster does occur, it'll be to your benefit to have an understanding of the implications and potential pitfalls that any of them produce.

I'm defining natural national disaster as a disaster that would impact the entire nation in a relatively short time, and I'm utilizing the only information any of us have; the theories, conjecture, and opinions of the "experts."

Infectious Diseases

From a survival standpoint, infectious disease has the potential to become a huge problem in your survival life. While the exotic diseases, such as Ebola, garner the majority of the headlines, the odds of contracting Ebola are remote. Conversely, the odds of encountering more common diseases and sicknesses such as pneumonia are well above the norm, and the odds of dying from one of them is correspondingly high.

The diseases we're concerned with are caused by either a virus or a bacteria, and without going into the differences between the two, the important thing to remember is this. *Doctors sometimes have trouble determining whether an illness is due to a virus or bacteria without ordering tests.* The rule of thumb is: Antibiotics *don't* kill viruses. They're used to treat bacterial infections. Colds, flu, most coughs (including bronchitis,) and sore throats (except those resulting from strep) are caused by a virus and *can't* be treated with antibiotics. These are (some) of the infectious diseases that are legitimate cause for concern following a national disaster.

Cryptosporidium (Crypto)

Crypto is a gastrointestinal disease whose primary symptom is diarrhea. In most healthy people a crypto infection produces a bout of watery diarrhea, and the infection usually goes away within a week or two. If you have a compromised immune system, a crypto infection can become life-threatening. In addition, the danger from dehydration is real. You can help prevent crypto infections with good hygiene habits and by avoiding drinking water that hasn't been boiled, filtered, or treated. The main cause of crypto infection is from drinking *bad water*. If you treat your drinking water properly, you should have little or no problems with Crypto.

Survival rating for Crypto

Probability of contracting	High
Danger if prepared	Low
Danger if unprepared	High
Survivability	Good to excellent, depending upon health

Pneumonia

Pneumonia is an inflammation of the lungs, usually caused by infection. Bacteria, viruses, fungi, or parasites can all cause pneumonia. Pneumonia is of particular concern if you're older than 68 or have a chronic illness or an impaired immune system. Pneumonia can also occur in young, healthy people. The seriousness of Pneumonia can range from mild to life-threatening and is often a complication of another condition, such as the flu.

Pneumonia is a definite concern in a survival situation, and the best approach for you to take will be to attempt to prevent infection. Antibiotics will treat most bacterial strains of Pneumonia, so it's important to make an effort to secure some sort of antibiotic for your survival kit. Since prevention is key, it's important to make an effort to keep your immune system in good shape.

Survival rating for Pneumonia

Probability of contracting	Moderate
Danger for healthy person untreated	Moderate-high
Danger for unhealthy person untreated	High
Danger if treated	Moderate
Survivability	Poor to good, depending upon health

Colds and seasonal flu

Everyone's familiar with colds and flu.

The common cold is a viral infection of the upper respiratory tract; your nose and throat. A cold's usually harmless, although it may not feel that way. Because of the 200+ viruses that can cause the common cold, the symptoms tend to vary greatly.

Adults are likely to catch a cold two to four times a year, and children, especially preschoolers, may have a common cold as many as six to ten times a year. Most people recover from the common cold in about a week.

The seasonal flu is also a viral infection, but it attacks the respiratory system, including the nose, throat, bronchial tubes, and lungs. People who're generally healthy and catch the flu are likely to feel sick for a few days, but probably won't develop complications or need professional medical care. If you have a weakened immune system or a chronic illness, the flu can be fatal.

And therein lies the problem. Regardless of your current health, but especially if you have health issues, you'd be wise to give both the common cold and the seasonal flu a bit more respect during a survival situation. I'm not going to give a survival rating for a cold or the flu.

Hepatitis A-B-C-E

Hepatitis is an infection caused by a virus that directly attacks the liver. Chronic cases of viral hepatitis can lead to life-threatening liver cirrhosis, liver failure, and liver cancer.

Unless you already have hepatitis B, you don't have to be concerned with hepatitis D.

Both hepatitis B and C are spread through contaminated blood and needles. In addition, hepatitis B can be spread through sexual contact. Hepatitis A is spread through contaminated food and water, and through feces, and hepatitis E is spread through contaminated water.

Your main concerns should be with hepatitis A and E since water is a source for both viruses, and to a lesser extent you could be at risk for hepatitis B, if for example you treated a wound or injury of someone you didn't know who was infected with the disease.

In a disaster situation, you shouldn't be overly concerned with hepatitis as long as you treat your water properly, be careful of the food you eat (especially if it's given to you by someone you don't know), and if you're treating a wound, take the precaution of wearing latex gloves

Hepatitis *cannot* be passed on by hugging, sneezing, coughing, sharing food, water, cutlery or by casual contact.

The signs and symptoms of hepatitis include:

A short mild flu-like illness
Nausea, vomiting and diarrhea
Loss of appetite
Weight loss
Jaundice (yellow skin and whites of the eyes, darker urine, and pale feces)
Itchy skin
Abdominal pain

Survival rating for hepatitis

Probability of contracting	Moderate
Danger if contracted	Short term, medium/Long term, high
Survivability	Short term, high/ long term, low

Strep Throat

Strep throat is a bacterial infection that can make your throat feel raw. The bacteria is found in an infected person's saliva. The bacteria becomes air-borne when the infected person talks, coughs, or sneezes. Treatment for strep throat requires an antibiotic. Most sore throats are caused by viruses and usually go away on their own. Only a small portion of sore throats are the result of strep.

It's important to identify strep throat for a number of reasons. If untreated, strep throat can sometimes cause complications such as kidney inflammation and rheumatic fever. Rheumatic fever can lead to painful and inflamed joins, a rash, and even damage to heart valves.

Strep throat is most common between the ages of five and fifteen, but it affects people of all ages.

It's possible to have many of the signs and symptoms of strep throat, but not have strep throat. The cause of the signs and symptoms could be a virus, tonsillitis, or other illnesses. A doctor will generally test specifically for strep throat to determine if the illness is indeed strep throat. It's also possible to have the bacteria that can cause strep in your throat without having a sore throat. Some people are carriers of strep, which means they can pass the bacteria on to others, but the bacteria do not make them sick.

You might have strep throat if any of the following are present.

A sore throat without cold symptoms such as a runny nose.
A sore throat accompanied by tender, swollen lymph glands.
A sore throat that lasts longer than 48 hours.
A fever higher than 101F in older children, or any fever lasting longer than 48 hours.
A rash.
Problems breathing or difficulty swallowing anything, including saliva.
A cola-colored urine more than a week after a strep infection may indicate kidney inflammation.
A fever or pain or swelling in the joints, shortness of breath or a rash after a strep infection, even as long as three weeks can indicate rheumatic fever.

As you can see, strep throat can be a serious problem during a survival situation, especially since you can't see a doctor. Limiting contact with other people will minimize the possibility of contracting the bacteria, and making sure you have surgical masks available in case someone is coughing or sneezing will also help minimize the possibility of contracting strep throat

Survival rating for strep throat

Possibility of contracting	Moderate
Danger if contracted	Moderate to high
Survivability with no treatment	Fair
Survivability with treatment	Good

Meningitis

Meningitis, sometimes referred to as spinal meningitis, is an inflammation of the covering of the brain and spinal cord. It can be caused by viruses, parasites, fungi, and bacteria. Viral meningitis is the most common and is the least serious, while bacterial meningitis is the most common form of serious infection with a potential for serious, long-term complications. Meningitis is an uncommon disease, but requires urgent treatment with antibiotics to prevent permanent damage or death.

Fortunately, none of the bacteria that cause meningitis are as contagious as the common cold or the flu, and they're not spread by casual contact or by breathing the air. The germs live naturally in our noses and throats, but they don't live long outside the body. They're spread when people exchange saliva (kissing, sharing drinking containers, utensils etc.) The germ doesn't cause meningitis in most people. Instead, most people become carriers of the germ for days, weeks, or even months. Bacterial meningitis rarely overcomes the body's immune system to cause meningitis or other serious illnesses.

Meningitis shouldn't be a concern during a survival situation as long as you follow these simple procedures when interacting with other survivors.

Don't share *food, drinks, utensils, toothbrushes, cigarettes,* etc. In addition, you should avoid, or at least limit, kissing someone who's not in your immediate group and whom you don't know well.

It's easy to mistake the early signs and symptoms of meningitis for the flu.

The symptoms are:

A high fever
Severe headache
Vomiting or nausea with headache
Confusion or difficulty concentrating or an inability to maintain eye contact
Seizures
Sleepiness or difficulty waking up
Stiff neck
Lack of interest in drinking and eating
Skin rash
Leg pain
Ice cold hands and feet
Abnormally pale skin tone

Newborns and infants may exhibit the following signs:

Constant crying
Excessive sleepiness or irritability
Poor feeding
A bulge in the soft spot on top of the head
Stiffness in the body and neck

Survival rating for Meningitis

Probability of contracting	Low
Danger if treated	Low to moderate
Danger if untreated	High
Survivability if untreated	Low

Typhoid

Typhoid fever is rare in the United States and is caused by a bacteria. I'm listing it here because it's spread through contaminated food and water, and because a re-appearance of the disease can't be ruled out as a potential threat. In addition to food and water, Typhoid can also be spread through close contact with someone who's infected.

Signs and symptoms usually include:

High fever
Headache
Abdominal pain
Either constipation or diarrhea
When treated with antibiotics, most people feel better within a few days, although a small percentage may die of complications.

Survival rating for Typhoid Fever

Probability of contracting	Low
Recovery if treated	Excellent
Recovery if untreated	Fair to good

West Nile virus

West Nile Virus is transmitted by mosquitoes and has been found in all 48 contiguous states. Exposure to mosquitoes where West Nile Virus exists increases your risk of getting the disease, which means, of course, your chances of contracting West Nile Virus during a national disaster will be dramatically increased.

Prevention is again the keyword. Head-nets, insect repellent, and proper clothing will reduce the risk of contracting West Nile Virus.

There's no specific treatment available for this disease. Mild infections go away on their own. Severe cases of encephalitis are treated with supportive care in a hospital, which involves helping the body fight the illness on its own. Hospital treatment includes IV's, ventilators, and prevention of secondary infections. Most infected people have no signs or symptoms.

About 20% develop a mild infection which includes:

Skin rash
Headache
Fever
Diarrhea
Nausea
Vomiting
Backache
Muscle aches
Loss of appetite
Swollen lymph glands

Less than 1% of infected people exhibit the following symptoms:

High fever
Severe headache
Stiff neck
Disorientation or confusion
Stupor or coma
Tremors or muscle jerking
Signs and symptoms similar to Parkinson's Disease
Lack of coordination
Convulsions
Pain
Partial paralysis or sudden weakness

Survival rating for West Nile Virus

Probability of contracting	Moderate
Treatment	None available
Survivability	Fair to good

Rocky Mountain Spotted Fever

Rocky Mountain Spotted Fever, herein after referred to as RMSF, is a potentially serious bacterial infection transmitted to humans by tick bites. The illness occurs when an infected tick attaches to your skin and feeds on your blood. The infection then has the potential to spread to your bloodstream and to other areas of your body.

RMSF doesn't spread directly from person to person. If treated promptly, a case of RMSF is usually fairly mild. In a small number of people, the disease can be serious, or even fatal, especially in older adults. RMSF progresses rapidly, and although many people experience symptoms within the first week after being bitten, the illness could incubate for up to fourteen days after the tick bite.

You should consider RMSF to be life-threatening. In a survival situation where professional medical assistance isn't available, contracting RMSF could prove fatal.

As always, prevention is the best cure. If possible, avoid areas where ticks are prevalent, especially in the woods in the spring of the year. Wear a protective hat and keep your clothing tight around the waist and ankles. The use of insect repellent and head-nets will also prove beneficial.

In most cases of RMSF, a red blotchy rash develops on the wrists and ankles, spreading to the palms of the hands and soles of the feet. This usually occurs between days three and five of infection. The rash often spreads up the arms and legs to the torso. A few people who are infected don't ever develop a rash. If your skin's darkly pigmented, a rash might not be readily apparent. However, the absence of a rash doesn't indicate a milder form of the illness and may make the condition more difficult to diagnose.

Initial signs and symptoms of RMSF often are nonspecific and can mimic those of other illnesses.

Those symptoms can include:

High fever of 102F or greater
Chills
Severe headache
Sensitivity to light
Nausea and vomiting
Abdominal pain
Loss of appetite
Fatigue
Later on the following symptoms can develop:
Red spotted or blotchy rash on the wrists or ankles
Widespread aches and pains
Diarrhea
Restlessness
Delirium

Survival rating for Rocky Mountain Spotted Fever

Probability of contracting	Moderate to high (depending on location)
Survivability if treated	Very good
Survivability if untreated	Fair

Lyme Disease

Lyme Disease is a tick-borne illness that causes signs and symptoms ranging from rash, fever, chills, and body aches to joint swelling, weakness, and temporary paralysis. Lyme Disease is caused by a bacteria. Deer ticks, which feed on the blood of animals and humans, can harbor this disease and spread it when feeding.

You're more likely to get Lyme Disease if you live or spend time in grassy or heavily wooded areas where ticks carrying the disease breed, which means, of course, that in a survival situation a lot of you may be living (temporarily) in tents in the woods. Therefore, it's important to take extra precautions in those areas where Lyme Disease is prevalent. If treated with the appropriate antibiotics in the early stages of the disease, you'll most likely recover completely. However, some people have recurring or lingering symptoms long after the infection has cleared.

The signs and symptoms of Lyme Disease vary widely because Lyme Disease can affect various parts of the body. Not everyone with the disease will have all of the signs and symptoms.

In general, Lyme Disease can cause:

RASH - A small red bump may appear within a few days to a month, often at the site of the tick bite, often in your groin, belt area or behind your knee. It may be warm to the touch and mildly tender. Over the next few days, the redness expands forming a rash that may be as small as your fingertip or as large as twelve inches across. It often resembles a bull's-eye, with a red ring surrounding a clear area and a red center. The rash is one of the hallmarks of Lyme Disease, affecting 70-80 percent of infected people. If you're allergic to tick saliva, redness may develop at the site of a tick bite. The redness usually fades within a week. This is not the same as the bulls-eye rash described above.

FLU-LIKE SYMPTOMS - A fever, chills, fatigue, body aches, and a headache may accompany the rash.

MIGRATORY JOINT PAIN – If the infection isn't treated, you may develop bouts of severe join pain and swelling several weeks to months after you're infected. Your knees are especially likely to be affected, but the pain can shift from one joint to another.

NEUROLOGICAL PROBLEMS – In some cases, inflammation of the membrane surrounding your brain (meningitis), temporary paralysis of one side of your face (Bells Palsy), numbness or weakness in your limbs, and impaired muscle movement may occur weeks, months, or even years after an untreated infection. Memory loss, difficulty concentrating, and changes in mood or sleep habits can also be symptoms of late-stage Lyme Disease.

Less common signs and symptoms can include heart problems, such as an irregular heartbeat, several weeks after infection, but this rarely lasts more than a few days or weeks. Eye inflammation, hepatitis, and severe fatigue are possible as well.

Lyme Disease can obviously cause some real problems. If you're surviving in tick country and it's tick season, especially in the spring, you can minimize your exposure by making sure your pant-legs fit snugly around your ankles (you can tie them with cord or fishing line), keep your shirt tucked inside your *belted* pants, wear a hat, use insect repellent, and check yourself every day to make sure a tick hasn't imbedded itself into your skin. If you discover a tick has attached itself to you, *don't* pull it off. Doing so will break the tick in two, leaving the head imbedded in your skin, which may cause infection. Put a match or something hot to the tick and it'll back out on its own. Immediately cleanse the area of the bite and check it daily.

Survival rating for Lyme Disease

Probability of contracting	Moderate to high
Survivability if treated	Good to very good
Survivability if untreated	Poor to fair

Hantavirus

Hantavirus pulmonary syndrome is an infectious disease characterized by flu-like symptoms that progress rapidly to potentially life-threatening problems.

Deer mice excrete the virus in their urine, saliva, and droppings. A person may be exposed to hantavirus by breathing contaminated dust after disturbing or cleaning rodent droppings, or by living or working in rodent-infested settings.

Treatment options for Hantavirus are limited. The virus progresses through two distinct stages with the first signs and symptoms appearing between one and five weeks after exposure.

Because you may be living in areas where deer mice are prevalent, the potential for exposure to Hantavirus will be increased. Prevention as always, is the best cure. The best and perhaps *only* realistic measure you can take to prevent exposure to Hantavirus is to be aware of heavy rodent droppings in any buildings you decide to stay in. *Don't disturb the droppings.* If you see heavy rodent droppings, it would be a good idea to seek shelter elsewhere or find an area within the building free from droppings.

Signs and symptoms of early stage Hantavirus include:

Fatigue
Fever
Chills
Muscle aches (especially large muscle groups such as the thighs and back)
Bubbling or rattling sounds in your lungs
Abnormally fast breathing
Abnormally fast heartbeat
Headache
Dizziness
Nausea
Vomiting
Diarrhea
Abdominal pain

Cardiopulmonary stage signs and symptoms include:

A cough that produces secretions
Shortness of breath
Respiratory failure (shock)
Build-up of fluid in the lungs (Pulmonary Edema)
Acute respiratory distress
Multi-organ failure
Low blood pressure

Survival rating for Hantavirus

Probability of contracting	Moderate
Danger if exposed	High
Survivability	Low

Rabies

Rabies is a deadly virus spread to people through the saliva of infected animals. It's usually transmitted through a bite.

Animals most likely to transmit rabies in the United States include bats, coyotes, foxes, raccoons, and skunks, although any animal, including cattle, horses, rodents, and cats can transmit the rabies virus. Humans can also be infected and pass on the disease through their saliva.

Once a person begins showing signs and symptoms of rabies, the disease is *almost always fatal!*

Animals infected with rabies may become aggressive, combative, and highly sensitive to touch. They also can become vicious. This is called the "furious" form of rabies, but there's also the "dumb" form. In the dumb form, the animal is likely to be lethargic, weak in one or more limbs, and unable to raise its head or make sounds because the throat and neck muscles are paralyzed. Most human victims, and apparently animals as well, suffer excruciating pain on swallowing liquids. Though they may suffer from thirst, both animal and human rabies victims can be terrified by the sight of water, hence rabies is sometimes called Hydrophobia.

The incubation period for rabies can range from ten days to an astonishing one year or more, but the average incubation period is thirty to fifty days. The length of the incubation period apparently depends on both the location of the wound (the farther from the brain, the longer the incubation period), and the dose of virus received.

No matter where the wound is located, the first and most valuable preventive measure is thorough cleaning of the wound with soap and water.

Bats that fly into a room (or a tent) while people are asleep can bite you without waking you up. If you awake to find a bat in your room or tent, assume you've been bitten. Also, if you find a bat near a person who can't report a bite, such as a baby, small child, or disabled adult, assume that person has been bitten.

Rabies victims won't show any signs or symptoms until the disease is in the later stages, often just before death.

Rabies signs and symptoms may include:

Fever
Headache
Agitation
Anxiety and confusion
Difficulty swallowing
Excessive salivation
A fear of water
Hallucinations
Insomnia
Partial paralysis

During a survival event, the potential for an encounter with a rabid animal is definitely higher than normal. Prevention of rabies is the *only* cure! If you encounter a wild animal that exhibits abnormal behavior, such as showing no fear of humans, is acting erratic, or appears to be abnormally aggressive or lethargic, *stay away from it!* The same advice applies to domestic animals, especially dogs that may have gone feral.

Survival rating for rabies

Probability of contracting	Moderate to high
Survivability	Zero

Pandemics

A pandemic is defined as an epidemic of infectious disease that's spreading through populations across a large region; for instance, a continent or worldwide. A flu pandemic doesn't include the seasonal flu. A pandemic can start when three conditions have been met; the emergence of a disease that's new to the population, the agent is infectious and causes serious illness, and the agent spreads easily and sustainably among humans.

There've been several major pandemics in recorded history. They include diseases such as *typhoid fever*, *bubonic plague*, *smallpox*, *cholera*, *measles*, *tuberculosis*, and of course *flu*.

There are currently two active pandemics. *Aids*, and the *Swine Flu*.

Aids is easily controlled by the practice of safe sex and by avoiding the blood from an infected person. If you're not part of the high-risk group and you practice safe sex, the likelihood of contracting aids is remote.

The H1N1 virus, or Swine Flu doesn't appear to be an especially virulent form of the flu, but is now found worldwide and has been declared a pandemic. Common sense precautions and a vaccine are available to combat the swine flu.

There's concern among health officials of a future pandemic involving Viral Hemorrhagic Fevers, such as Lassa Fever, Rift Valley Fever, Marburg Virus, Ebola, and Bolivian Hemorrhagic Fever, since all are highly contagious and deadly diseases. Fortunately, all of these diseases are currently limited in their ability to spread efficiently enough to cause a pandemic since their transmission requires close contact with the infected person and the person only has a short time before death. Genetic mutations could occur, which could elevate the potential of these diseases to cause widespread harm.

There's also concern that antibiotic-resistant "super-bugs" could contribute to the re-emergence of diseases that are currently well controlled. Some of the diseases which are cause for concern are tuberculosis and plague. Other diseases which have the realistic potential to become a pandemic and to wreak havoc on the human population include: SARS (Severe Acute Respiratory Syndrome) which is a new and highly contagious form of atypical pneumonia, and the H5N1 AVIAN Flu, or "Bird Flu." It would be beneficial to keep a close eye on these two diseases as they probably have the most realistic potential to cause a new and deadly pandemic.

With the relentless advance of man into regions of the Earth that are relatively free from the effects of civilization, specifically areas in Africa and in South America, the possibility of the emergence of a heretofore unknown virus or bacteria will remain a realistic and potential threat to humans.

During a survival event, a pandemic could become a serious threat. While we can't project what a pandemic during a survival event might entail, we can use common sense to help prevent exposure. Since interaction between humans will be curtailed by default, the odds of a pandemic affecting you personally are probably less than BTC.

Survival rating for pandemic

Probability of contracting	Low to moderate
Survivability	Unknown

Sunspots and solar flares

Unfortunately, sunspots and solar flares happen regularly and they wreak havoc with the earth. What are they exactly?

A sunspot is a storm on the surface of the sun that's cooler than the surrounding material. The cooler temperature results in increased magnetic activity that allows charged particles to escape from the Sun's atmosphere. These particles are called a solar wind. Sunspots normally occur in seasons of eleven year cycles. The new cycle, which was supposed to begin in 2009 hasn't happened yet.

The primary effect of sunspots on the Earth is on the upper part of the atmosphere (Ionosphere). The particles in the solar wind can interact with storms in the Ionosphere and create problems with communications systems such as background static in data transmitted from satellites and destruction of GPS data. In extreme circumstances, high levels of solar wind can bring about a solar storm where large quantities of charged material is sent into the earth's atmosphere. Although this material isn't physically dangerous, it does cause the Ionosphere to swell in response to extra heating. The swelling can promote the decay of satellites in the Earth's lower orbit.

Overall, then, sunspots aren't all that dangerous or destructive. Solar flares, on the other hand, are a different story. The biggest sunspots generally create the most intense solar flares.

A solar flare is defined as a sudden, rapid, and intense variation in brightness. The amount of magnetic energy released from a solar flare is the equivalent of millions of 100 megaton hydrogen bombs exploding at the same time. As the magnetic energy is being released, particles, including electrons, protons, and heavy nuclei, are heated and accelerated in the solar atmosphere. This energy is ten million times greater than the energy released from a volcanic eruption, but is also less than one-tenth of the total energy emitted by the Sun every second.

What effect does all of this extra solar energy have on the Earth? The precise effects are hard to determine. In the short term, the aftermath usually involves disruption of all forms of electronic communications with a severe threat to all space satellites and telecommunications.

The long-term effects aren't easy to categorize either, but they probably include highly disturbed weather patterns with a greatly increased risk of earthquakes and volcanic eruptions in vulnerable locations.

There's some evidence to support the theory that solar flares can have intense medical and emotional consequences on human beings.

On a larger scale, research shows that solar activity has the potential to trigger general social unrest including wars, riots, revolutions, and a deteriorating state of international harmony.

So, could a solar flare actually destroy life on Earth? The potentially troubling answer is, yes. Although the sun is remarkably stable, it does go through phases of increased activity. It's believed (theory) that a lethal solar flare explosion could conceivably erupt at any moment. The fact we haven't seen one for many thousands of years means nothing. An extreme flare-up could happen before this sentence is finished.

From a survival perspective, a solar flare is no different than any of the other natural events that *could* happen. There's nothing we can do to prevent it from happening. Is it going to happen? No one knows for certain.

Survival information for sunspots and solar flares

Probability of an occurrence	Possible at any time
Survivability of ensuing problems	Good (prepared)
Survivability of ensuing problems	Poor to good (un-prepared)

Meteorite, Asteroid, Comet impact

A "rock" in space is called a *meteoroid.* When the rock enters the Earth's atmosphere and is heated up, it becomes a *meteor*. If the meteor hits the ground, it's known as a *meteorite.*

An *asteroid* is a tiny, rocky planet that orbits the sun. Most asteroids are located in space between the orbits of Mars and Jupiter. This is known as the Asteroid Belt.

A *comet* is simply an asteroid with an electrical tail caused by a sufficiently elliptical orbit.

A large number of asteroids enter the Earth's atmosphere every day. Most are small, just a few milligrams each. Only the largest ones ever reach the surface to become meteorites. The largest meteorite ever found weighs 60 tons. By comparison, the largest know asteroid is called Ceres and is 933 kilometers across, which is similar in size to Pluto's moon, Charon. There are hundreds of thousands of asteroids in sizes ranging from ten kilometers across, and possibly millions that are one kilometer and smaller.

Meteor Crater near Winslow, AZ was formed about 50,000 years ago by an iron meteorite about 30-50 meters in diameter. The crater is 1200 meters in diameter and 200 meters deep. There are about 120 meteorite impact craters identified on Earth.

A more recent impact occurred in 1908 in Western Siberia in Russia. Known as *Tunguska*, the meteor was about sixty meters in diameter and probably consisted of many loosely bound pieces. The meteor exploded before hitting the ground, so there's no crater. Nevertheless, all the trees were flattened in an area eighty kilometers across, and the sound of the explosion was heard halfway around the world in London.

The effects of meteorites and asteroids impacting the Earth can range from almost un-noticeable to extinction events.

Should you prepare to survive a meteorite or asteroid impact? That's one of the 64,000 dollar questions. The odds of being hit by a small to moderate size asteroid are surprisingly high. Getting nailed by one of the big boys, while possible, isn't all that probable; at least not in our lifetimes.

Here are some simple examples of meteorite sizes and the equivalent yield of the impact in megatons with frequency and projected consequences.

78 meter meteorite	10 to 100 megatons.	Similar to Meteor Crater. (Every 1000 years.)
160 meter meteorite	100 to 1000 megatons.	Would destroy an area the size of Tokyo. (Every 5000 years.)
700 meter meteorite	10,000 to 100,000 megatons.	Would destroy an area the size of Virginia (Every 63,000 years.)

Asteroids impacting the earth would have the following projected consequences:

A small asteroid of *1000 yards in diameter* would severely impact the strike area to a distance of up to 300 km. For the most part, the damage would be local or regional in nature.

An asteroid of *three miles in diameter* would have far greater consequences with an immediate impact out to 5000 km. While not a total extinction event, an asteroid impact of this size would be difficult to survive by those outside the impacted area who were unprepared to survive.

A *six mile diameter* asteroid would impact with the force of 100 million megatons of TNT. The effects of an asteroid of this size impacting the Earth would be felt globally in a matter of hours, and would create global mass extinctions. Since human beings aren't dinosaurs, the human race would probably survive in some form, but at a tremendous cost. Only a small percentage of the words total population would likely survive.

Is it possible to survive such a devastating event. Yes, it's possible. But you'd have to be in the right place at the right time, have the proper survival supplies and a lot of luck.

No survival ratings are given.

Super volcano

Three of the known seven (7) super volcanoes are located in the United States. Yellowstone caldera, which is the best known and is also the most likely to erupt, is in Wyoming. Long Valley Super Volcano in California and the Valles Caldera Super Volcano in New Mexico are the others. The worlds other super volcanoes are Lake Toba in Indonesia, Taupo Super Volcano in New Zealand, Aira Caldera Super Volcano in Japan, and the Siberian Tarps Super Volcano in Russia. The Siberian Tarps Super Volcano is by far the largest of the super volcanoes and is often referred to as Yellowstone's "big sister."

According to the "experts," the eruption of a super volcano will happen sooner or later, and will chill the planet and threaten human civilization. The bad news is, there's not a thing we can do about it.

A super volcano eruption would dwarf the eruption of Mount St. Helens. The eruption would be about 100 times larger and would likely devastate an area the size of the United States with pronounced deterioration of the global climate for years following the eruption. It would likely result in the devastation of world agriculture and severe disruption of the food supply, which would result in world-wide mass starvation.

Some computer models predict the earth would be plunged into perpetual winter, causing plant and animal species to disappear forever.

So, a super volcano eruption is apparently inevitable. The question then becomes, when will the eruption occur? And the answer is, no one knows. It could happen tomorrow or it could be 100,000 years from now. Either way, there's nothing to be done about it.

Let's assume it happens in two or three years. Is it survivable? Well, yes, and no. It all depends on which volcano erupts and where you are in relation to the volcano. The latitude you live in, the quantity of supplies you have, and the type of shelter you're going to attempt to survive in will all play a part in your final outcome. If Toba erupts, the initial impact on the United States won't be as bad as it would if Yellowstone were to erupt. If you live in Minnesota, the impact from a Yellowstone eruption will probably be felt more acutely than if you lived in Key West. Of course, if Yellowstone does erupt and you live in Wyoming, you're probably toast. Be that as it may, if you have an underground shelter with several years worth of supplies (i.e., food) you might end up a survivor. If you live in a normal American home and you have a case of beans on hand, you'll probably end up going the way of those good folk in Wyoming. Maybe not as quickly, but I wouldn't be making any long-range plans.

So like it or not, surviving a super volcano eruption for the average person isn't probable.

Survival rating for a super volcano eruption

Probability of an eruption in our lifetime.	Fifty-fifty
Survival chances if prepared	Poor
Survival chances if unprepared	Almost zero

Pole shift

In scientific jargon, a pole shift occurs when the Earth rotates on its axis 180 degrees. In simplistic terms, a pole shift means the North Pole becomes the South Pole and vice versa.

There are simply too many "experts" with an opinion to list. However, two of the more notable are Nostradamus and the Mayans, both of whom predict a pole shift on 12-21-12 due to astrological alignments. In between we find a plethora of "experts" who have a theory on when, why, and how a pole shift will occur and what the consequences will be.

There's just one thing they all agree on. *The results will be astonishingly devastating*.

If a pole shift occurs, do you really give a damn what caused it? I don't. I'm concerned with the effects and the steps I could take to survive it. But therein lies the problem. The movie *2012* shows the consequences of Hollywood's version of a pole shift. If you do a bit of research, you'll find so many different theories pertaining to the actual consequences, you'll likely throw your hands up in disgust and walk away from your computer.

Here are the real facts. *No one knows for sure what the consequences will be*! Common sense, however, tells us the consequences aren't going to be pretty.

What *is* the worst case scenario? Let's come up with our own. The worst case scenario is the total destruction of the human race. If that's the case, and you subscribe to that "theory," then there's no sense in making any type of preparation to survive it. You have a couple of years to live. Have fun! How about a scenario where there are 1000 humans left alive when the dust settles? Do you want to be one of those 1000 survivors who will endure untold hardships on a daily basis? Even if belonging to that exclusive little club will require an incredible amount of good luck?

How about 95% of the human race perishes? You're one of, what, 400,000 or so (I don't know how many people were born in China yesterday, so it's kinda hard to pin it down) survivors living underground in a frigid and desolate Miami or a balmy and subtropical Minneapolis. Take your pick. Come up with your own end result. Your guess will be as good as any of the "experts."

The point is, do you want to attempt to survive a pole shift, and, if you do, what preparations can you make to have a realistic shot at surviving. If the other experts are right, there's really nothing you can do.

But look at it this way. If you spend a reasonable amount of money preparing to survive a pole shift and it doesn't happen, you'll have everything you need to survive the myriad other disasters that could befall us. And if a pole shift does happen, you'll either survive or you won't.

Hydrates

Methane hydrates are a solidified form of natural gas trapped in ice and buried in the ocean floor and under the Arctic permafrost.

It's estimated there are more methane hydrates available than the combined totals of all natural gas, coal, and oil deposits in the world.

With the world's relentless demand for energy and, given the fact that sooner or later, oil will cease to be a viable option, man is looking at methods to harvest the Methane gas from the depths.

Normally, the pressure of hundreds of meters of water keeps the frozen methane stable, but heat flowing from oil drilling and from pipelines has the ability to slowly destabilize the methane, with potentially disastrous results. Melting Methane Hydrates could trigger massive underwater landslides as it decomposes. In fact, scientists are reasonably certain that 8,000 years ago, decomposing hydrates helped generate a gigantic landslide under the North Sea.

The resulting tsunami scoured the Norwegian fjords and scattered seafloor sediment across Holland and Scotland. Then, too, there's always the realistic possibility of an underwater slide causing enormous environmental damage from oil spills that couldn't be easily stopped. As a matter of fact, the Deep Sea Horizon rig that blew up in the Gulf of Mexico just recently was caused by an explosion of Methane Hydrates.

Another danger from the frozen hydrates is the fact that methane is a potent greenhouse gas. Some geologists have suggested that methane could accelerate global warming if the rising ocean temperatures eventually released the methane gas in large enough amounts. Rapid, methane-driven global warming has occurred before in Earth's history, causing mass extinctions both 55 million and 600 million years ago.

And last, but not least, is the "bug burp" theory. The world ends due to a huge release of Methane Gas into the atmosphere (a big burp) where it's ignited by a bolt of lightning and explodes with more force than the combined nuclear arsenals of the entire world.

So, lots of theories, few real facts. Should we be concerned? Can it happen? There's no guarantee either way. We simply don't know.

From a survival perspective it wouldn't make a lot of sense to worry about methane hydrates. There're definitely other events that have a much more realistic chance of causing you to implement your survival plan.

No survival rating for Methane Hydrates.

Gamma Ray Burst

Gamma Ray Burst, or GRB, are the result of an exploding star and are the most powerful explosions in the Universe. Most of the energy is released as gamma rays in short bursts lasting from micro-seconds to as much as 100 seconds, hence the name Gamma Ray Burst. The GRB's are released in a focused beam much like the light from a laser and are sometimes referred to as death rays. Since the GRB's that have been observed happened million of years ago to stars millions of light years away and, since the chances of a focused GRB from one of those explosions hitting the Earth is almost non-existent, there's little to be concerned about.

If, however, a star within our own Milky Way Galaxy were to explode, and it was close enough, within about 6,000 light years, and the focused beam of Gamma Rays were to hit the Earth, it *could* trigger mass extinction.

The absorption of the radiation from the GRB's in the upper atmosphere would cause the nitrogen to generate nitric oxide that would act as a catalyst to destroy the ozone layer. With even one half of the ozone layer destroyed, the direct UV irradiation from the burst combined with additional solar UV radiation passing through the diminished ozone layer would have significant impact on the food chain thereby triggering the mass extinction by starvation.

NASA scientists are positive this type of mass extinction occurred on Earth hundreds of millions of years ago. Their models show that a GRB originating within approximately 6,000 light years and lasting for just ten seconds can cause years of devastating ozone damage.

The most extreme theory is that a huge GRB hitting the Earth from within our own Galaxy would instantly kill everything on Earth, but we wouldn't know anything about it since it would be over before we knew it began.

What are the chances of a GRB hitting the Earth in our lifetime? What are the chances of winning the lottery or getting hit by lightning? It could happen, it is possible, but like every other extinction event we're looking at, no one really knows.

Is it possible to survive a GRB? Sure. But as is the case in any of the other extreme natural disasters, it would require a lot of luck, being in the right place at the right time, and having the necessary supplies to be able to survive until things returned to normal, which would probably take centuries. In addition, it would probably be necessary to reside underground during that time period. For the average person, the probability of surviving a GRB is pretty much nil.

No survival information for this event seems necessary.

Peak Oil

Peak oil is defined as the point in time when the *maximum* rate of global petroleum extraction is reached after which the rate of production enters terminal decline. In English, Peak Oil means there's not enough oil left in the world to supply the demand so the total amount of oil available starts to go down.

Peak Oil will allegedly be reached around 2020 and begin to decline. Pessimistic predictions of future oil production operate on the theory that either the peak has already occurred, oil production is on the cusp of the peak, or that it will occur shortly. A global depression is predicted, perhaps even initiating a chain reaction of a decline in industrial civilization, potentially leading to large population declines within a short period.

Personally, I have a difficult time accepting the concept of Peak Oil by 2020 unless those making that prediction can state with a degree of certainty they know where every oil field on earth is and how many total barrels of oil is available. Well, they don't. That's why oil companies explore for oil. So I think it's all a crock of crap. But in case I'm wrong, and I have been twice in my life, (I divorced them both) here's what we might have to look forward to shortly after Peak Oil is reached.

Gas rationing and long waits at the pump.
Gas prices that are off the charts
Rationing of electrical power
More expensive products and food
Riots, curfews, increased crime, decreased food production, hunger and starvation, war (over oil)

Survival rating for Peak Oil

Probability	50-50
Danger if it occurs	Ultimately very high
Survivability if prepared	Good
Survivability if unprepared	Poor to fair

Global Warming

(AKA the theory of Gore)

Is Global Warming actually happening? Well . . . maybe it is, maybe it isn't. Is it caused by man? Hmm . . . maybe, maybe not. Is it a natural cycle of the Earth? Ah . . . yeah, I think so, I mean ... maybe, but then again, maybe not.

Regardless, here's the information on those events Global Warming could ultimately be responsible for.

Ice Age

Whenever I hear the term Ice Age I invariably picture Woolly Mammoths, Saber Toothed tigers, and hot cave girls running around in Leopard skins. You probably do, too. But a new ice age, in addition to not having elephants, tigers, and cave-girls (oh my), probably wouldn't be anything like the last ice age. At least not while anyone reading this book is around.

Strange as it may sound, an ice age is the one disaster that could easily take place in the near future. In fact it may already be underway.

The normal state of the Earth's climate has always been an Ice Age. We're currently living in an interglacial, a brief (by geological standards) period between long ice ages. Interglacial periods last for about 10,000 years, followed by a period of 100,000 years of ice age. Guess how long it's been since the last ice age ended? Yep. 10,000 years.

During the current interglacial period, there was a mini ice age which started in the 14th century. In Northern Europe the mini ice age started with the Great Famine of 1315. Crops failed due to cold temperatures and incessant rain. Desperate and starving, *parents ate their children* and *people dug up corpses for food.* In jails, inmates instantly set upon new prisoners and ate them alive. The Great Famine was followed by the Black Death, the greatest disaster ever to affect the human race. Fully one third of the human race died; terror and anarchy prevailed. (The current world population is roughly seven billion. If a third of the people on the planet perished today, we'd have more than twice as many bodies than there were people on Earth during the period of the Black Death.) By the mid 17th century, glaciers in the Swiss Alps advanced, wiping out farms and entire villages. In England, the River Thames froze during the winter, and in 1780, New York harbor froze.

The fact is the oscillation between ice ages and interglacial periods has been the *dominant* feature of Earth's climate for the last one million years.

Our climate is controlled by the Sun, not by man. Every other factor, compared to the Sun, is trivial. The coldest part of the Little Ice Age, during the 17th century, was marked by the nearly complete absence of sunspots. August of 2008 was the first month since 1913 that no sunspots were observed. The Sun is quiet again. Is the Ice Age coming?

Is a mini ice age or a full blown ice age possible? Unfortunately, yes. To both. Will it happen in our lifetime? Unknown. Should you prepare to survive an ice age? That's up to you, but since you're preparing to survive a national and world-wide depression with the ensuing consequences, you're already ahead of the game if a mini ice age occurs. Is an ice age survivable? Of course it is. Would a good time be had by all? Definitely not.

Gulfstream Shutdown

A lot of people are worried about the Gulfstream shutting down. While it is possible, there's no credible scientific evidence to support that statement. Zero. Nada. Nyet.

In fact, there's a great deal of uncertainty as to what the effects of a diminished Gulfstream flow would entail. Some models show that Europe would be cooler. Others show it would be warmer. At any rate, a slowdown of the Gulfstream will apparently occur over a period of several decades to a few hundred years, if it occurs at all.

From a survival viewpoint, it appears a shutdown of the Gulfstream isn't going to happen.

Glacier/Polar ice melt and sea level rise

Are the polar caps really in danger of melting and causing the oceans to rise?

To begin with, the Earth's main ice-covered landmass is *Antarctica*, at the South Pole with about *ninety percent of the World's ice and seventy percent of its fresh water*. Antarctica is covered with ice an average of 2,133 meters (7,000 feet) thick. If all of the Antarctic ice melted, sea levels around the world would rise by about 200 feet. But the average temperature in Antarctica is -37 degrees Fahrenheit, so the Antarctic ice is in no danger of melting. In fact, in most parts of the continent, it never gets above freezing.

At the other end of the world, the North Pole, the ice isn't nearly as thick as it is at the South Pole. In addition, the ice at the North Pole floats on the Arctic Ocean. If the Arctic ice melted, sea levels wouldn't be affected since the ice is already in the water.

There's a significant amount of ice covering Greenland, which would add another twenty feet to the oceans if it all melted.

However, there may be a less dramatic reason than ice melt for the recent increase in ocean levels; warmer water temperatures. Water is most dense at four degrees Celsius (39.2 degrees F). Above and below that temperature, the density of water decreases. (The same weight of water occupies a bigger space.) That means as the overall temperature of the water increases, it naturally expands, making the oceans rise.

Do rising sea levels present an immediate threat to your survival? Hardly. Long-term, if you live on the coast and the oceans rise, you'll be forced to move. If the oceans do rise, even a few feet, there will be insane competition for living space due to the millions of displaced people. That migration inland could definitely have an adverse affect on humanity. Picture the population of your town doubling in a few years while the jobs and available housing remain relatively static.

Plant and animal extinctions

Dramatic climate change would have an effect on 25 of the 34 globally outstanding biodiversity hotspots. (Areas containing a large number of species unique to those regions, yet facing enormous threats.) These hotspots, according to scientists, are refugee camps for many of the planet's most unique plant and animal species. If those areas are no longer habitable due to global warming, then the last sanctuaries many of these species have left will be destroyed. These biodiversity hotspots make up about one percent of the Earth's surface, but contain 44 percent of all terrestrial vertebrate species and 35 percent of the world's plant species. Some of these areas include the tropical Andes, the Cape Floriatic region of South Africa, Southwest Australia, and the Atlantic forests of Brazil, Paraguay, and Argentina. These areas are particularly vulnerable because the species in these regions have restricted immigration options due to geographical limitations

Some species of animals, birds in particular, would be able to adapt to temperature and climate change more easily than would the majority of mammals, reptiles, and amphibians. Some species of animals that live in cooler climates would be forced to seek out higher altitudes to survive. On the other side of the coin, plant, and animal extinctions would probably be more dramatic if the world were to enter a sustained cooling period, or another ice age.

Either way, plants and animals have gone through many extinction phases during the course of life on Earth. It's safe to say that if we do lose species, eventually Mother Nature will introduce others to take their place.

Will plant and animal extinctions have a dramatic impact on your survival? Perhaps. But not initially. And not for some time.

(For information on a *Mega Tsunami*, see the section on Tsunami in Chapter 14.)

CHAPTER 13

National Man-made Disasters

Terrorism

IF YOU WOULD HAVE TOLD someone on September 10, 2001 that terrorists would fly planes into the World Trade Center the next morning, they would have looked at you like you were nuts. Ten years later, the concept of terrorists killing themselves to kill us is a readily accepted thought process, even though that thought process doesn't compute to the Western mind.

Those involved in hunting down terrorists on a daily basis understand too well that Muslim terrorists will never stop trying to kill us. The general public has pretty much shoved that thought to the back of their minds, and Congress is too busy covering their own asses and kissing others to give our guys the tools necessary to effectively deal with these killers.

Until now, Muslim terrorists have gone for the "big one." That may change soon. It's inconceivable they're all morons, and sooner or later they'll figure out the methods they're using *is not* the way to spread terror or to bring our country to its knees. I won't tell you the way they could do it just in case they haven't figured it out yet. No sense giving them a blueprint. They don't understand the way we think any more than we can comprehend their twisted thought processes.

At this time, as long as you don't live in New York or DC, and don't spend a lot of time in the air, the odds of being involved in a terrorist attack are small.

Nuclear terrorism

A terrorist attack involving a nuclear weapon would have catastrophic consequences indeed. The question is, do they have access to a nuclear weapon, or will they have that access in the near future?

We'd be foolish to assume they don't, or won't. Nor should we assume they don't have the ability to transport a nuclear weapon into the United States and to arm and detonate that weapon.

This may shock you, but there are over *200 documented cases* of persons attempting to purchase special nuclear bomb making materials or tactical nuclear weapons on the black market.

That's *documented cases* mind you! In addition there are *over 100 suitcase nuclear weapons* missing from the Soviet nuclear inventory. That's right, over 100, which could be 101 or 10,000, it doesn't matter. It only takes one!

Alexander Lebed, the former head of Soviet National Security, has testified before Congress. He stated that the missing devices measure approximately 24" x 16" x 8" and can be set off by one person in less than thirty minutes, producing a one kiloton yield. Such an explosion in New York Harbor would produce a wave of fifteen to twenty feet that would destroy New York City. Other sources have confirmed that the number of suitcase nuclear weapons missing from the Soviet inventory is correct.

Detecting such a small device would be extremely difficult. Without going into the scientific description of gamma rays and spontaneous fission that produces detectable neutrons, suffice it to say that the radiological signature of a "suitcase nuke" could easily be shielded by a few inches of lead or tungsten. In addition, four or five inches of steel would effectively reduce the radiations to background. The device could be shielded and placed inside the hollowed out engine of an automobile being imported into the United States.

It's absolutely impossible to search every ship, every container, every piece of air cargo, every car, every piece of luggage, every cruise ship, fishing boat, private yacht, and every person that comes into the USA on a daily basis. The nuke could also be brought across the border at any of the crossings since only a few of them are equipped with dosimeters. Plus, if the device is properly shielded, the instruments would be worthless anyway. Additionally, the ease of crossing the border from Mexico is well documented. In fact, getting across the Mexican border into the USA is much easier than we've been led to believe.

The bottom line on getting a suitcase nuke into the country? Not much of a problem.

In addition to the threat of a thermonuclear explosion, there are three additional nuclear concerns.

1. A terrorist act at a nuclear facility, fuel enrichment or fabrication plant, or a university reactor. (See Nuclear Plant Accident in this section for more detailed information.)
2. The explosion of a "dirty bomb" in a public place such as a major city, amusement park (can you say Disney?), a sports stadium, or an airport.
3. Release of a radioactive aerosol or other airborne radioactive material into the air intake of a major building or the release of a radioactive material into the water supply of a major city.

While the effects of any of those three concerns would be disastrous and would undoubtedly kill several thousand people, the end results pale in comparison to the effects of a thermonuclear explosion in a major U.S. city.

What would the government's response be to a nuclear terrorist attack? Without doubt there would be martial law in the impacted area, perhaps nationally, and checkpoints and curfews would be established. Those controls would remain in effect for at least a week, and possibly a lot longer. (See martial law, curfews and riots in this section.)

Survival rating for nuclear terrorist attack

Probability	Good
Survivability @ ground zero	Almost none
Survivability	Odds increase as the distance from ground zero increases
Danger from fallout	Extremely high if downwind
Danger from aftermath	Moderate
Impact on the nation	Extreme

Biological terrorist attack

As opposed to general terrorism, biological terrorism is a giant step up the terrorism ladder of destruction. While the "targets" are likely to be the same, the methods of delivery will be quite different. For a biological terrorist attack to be successful, the entire cell will require a lot more intelligence, considerably more expertise, and a much larger network than a "normal" terrorist cell has at its disposal.

There are a number of possibilities for weaponized forms of biological agents. They include anthrax, Ebola, Marburg virus, plague, cholera, Typhus, Rocky Mountain Spotted Fever, Tularemia, Yellow Fever, Smallpox, and several lesser known but equally contagious and deadly diseases.

It's safe to assume our government, the old Soviet Union, China, and a handful of western nations have some, if not all of these diseases in weaponized form. Why? Because we do. What difference does it make? We aren't going to use them, we just have them.

What biological agents, if any, do the Muslim terrorists have access to or have stockpiled? If they don't have them, can they get them? If so, can they weaponize the agent, or can they hire someone to do it for them? Can they build an effective containment vessel, and can that container be delivered undetected into the target area? Last, are they capable of releasing that agent?

That's a lot of questions, and I don't want to guess at the answers. It seems logical, though, if they do have one, and if it is weaponized, there's still the difficult problem of getting it into the country, delivering it to the target area, and detonating it with a dispersal system that will kill the most people. Not impossible, but certainly not as easy as getting a nuclear device on target.

The logical answer, from the terrorists' perspective at least, would be to procure the weapon from a disgruntled scientist or employee with access to that type of device, although that's an almost impossible scenario since the security surrounding biological agents is unbelievable. (And rightly so.) So in the end, a high-tech biological attack doesn't seem to be a plausible terrorist attack scenario. A low tech biological attack, however, is definitely possible.

The release, however small, of a biological agent in a major American city would wreak havoc by causing panic, shutting down schools, commerce, transportation, and almost everything else we use, perhaps for as long as a week or more. That alone would be devastating.

Survival rating for biological terrorist attack

Probability	Small to moderate
Danger if exposed	High
Survivability if exposed	Poor to fair (depending on the agent etc.)
National impact	Impossible to calculate

Domestic terrorism

The majority of American citizens have as much difficulty understanding how someone who was born and raised in this country could become a terrorist as they do understanding how a Muslim terrorist thinks. Neither one computes. Although a domestic terrorist who might be of Arabic origin, is a Muslim, and was recruited by the Muslim terrorists to further their agenda has to be considered dangerous, the fact is that most of those type terrorists aren't likely to shed their Western ideals and attain the same degree of commitment the radical Muslim terrorist portrays.

This type of terrorist's main value to the Muslim terrorist organization(s) lies in their freedom of movement, their ability to blend in, and their knowledge of all things American. These people are usually young, Arab-American, male, and are impressionable and/or idealistic. Regardless of what you hear or read, people who fit that type of profile are kept tabs on by the FBI. We also have "snitches" who relay information to the FBI regarding potential terrorists and terrorist activity at mosques, etc. I have absolutely no problem with that, and you probably don't either. The real danger from these type(s) of terrorists is the possibility they may act on their own by striking a blow against the infidel, in the name of Allah, the 10,000 virgins, or whatever.

A more insidious, and much more dangerous type of domestic terrorist is the Timothy McVeigh type. You remember McVeigh, an Army veteran who, in 1995, blew up the Alfred P. Murrah building in OKC because of a gripe against a tyrannical Federal Government.

This type of terrorist doesn't include the occasional nut-job who goes on a shooting rampage. Those are crimes, not acts of terrorism. Yet, it's almost a certainty there are a lot more Timothy McVeigh-type terrorists actively thinking or planning some sort of violent response against government, minority groups, schools, or even individuals.

The list is virtually endless. This type of terrorist is arguably more dangerous than a Muslim terrorist who was born and raised in the USA, since the target of their grudge could be anything. Here's the real problem with a domestic terrorist. Not one of them considers themselves to be a terrorist, and they don't think killing innocent people is an act of terrorism. They tend to think of themselves as patriots. And they're not all weird either. Most appear perfectly normal. On the plus side, it's pretty difficult to plan and carry out a terrorist attack without some authority learning about it beforehand, unless the individual(s) involved were totally self-contained and capable of keeping their mouths shut, which isn't likely since they tend to brag to their girlfriends, wives, etc. about their potential patriotic exploits.

If that makes you feel more secure, it shouldn't. It's not within the power of the combined local, state, and federal agencies to identify, catalog, monitor, and apprehend every head case who pops up on the radar, much less those who don't.

Should you worry about domestic terrorism? No. But you should be aware of their existence. The odds of you being involved in an attack by a domestic terrorist are small.

Nuclear plant accident

Although an accident at a nuclear power plant is a local or regional disaster, I'm including it under man-made disasters.

There are many different nuclear facilities in the United States which include processing plants of various types and disposal sites for low-level nuclear waste in three states, whose location is classified. There's also the fact that nuclear waste products from all nuclear reactors are transported (usually by truck) throughout the United States. In addition, there's the high level waste disposal site at Yucca Mountain in Nevada (temporarily on hold) and approximately 32 test reactors at various locations which include a number of universities. (Yeah, you read that right; nuclear reactors at universities!)

As of 2008 there were 66 nuclear power plants in the United States with a total of 104 nuclear reactors in 31 different states. The majority are east of the Mississippi River, and the preponderance of those are clustered in the northeast. (The area, coincidentally, with the highest population density in the country.) The list of nuclear reactors is in a constant state of flux as some are in the process of being decommissioned while others have new reactors under construction.

The point of this information is that even though you may feel safe from the effects of a potential accident at a nuclear power plant, the routes of disposal trucks, university test locations (which aren't really secret, but aren't advertised in the local college rag either,) and the location of processing plants and disposal sites could easily impact you and your family if there was an accident or a terrorist attack at any of them. In fact a terrorist attack at one of these facilities is a major concern of the DOE. (Department of Energy.)

So even though you may not live in the vicinity of a nuclear power plant, you shouldn't feel as though you're off the hook. One has only to check Chernobyl to see what the effect of an accident at a nuclear power plant could entail. The Chernobyl accident released 400 times more fallout than the Hiroshima bomb, with "nuclear rain" falling as far away as Ireland. It caused the resettlement of 336,000 people (from a sparsely populated area.) As of 2005 WHO has attributed 56 direct deaths to the accident and has estimated there may be an additional 4,000 cancer deaths among the approximately 600,000 most highly exposed people.

Certain areas of Chernobyl are still off limits today. A similar accident at a nuclear plant near a big population center could have catastrophic fatalities.

Survival information for nuclear plant accident

Possibility	Low
Successful terrorist attack	Low
Natural disaster	Low to moderate
Survivability	Unable to calculate

Stress, ASR, PTSD

This particular section could have been placed under any of the disaster categories. However, I decided to place it under man-made disaster because man is most likely to cause the disaster we're planning to survive. It only seemed fair.

The depression and stress referred to isn't the anxiety you feel when you find out your mother-in-law isn't coming for that two week visit after all, but is, in fact, moving in with you. This is a different type of stress entirely and is one which you shouldn't take lightly.

Without getting clinical, we're talking about the following conditions.

Depression

While everyone experiences the symptoms of depression a bit differently, the symptoms are generally considered to be sadness, a loss of interest in things you once enjoyed, feelings of guilt or worthlessness, restlessness, and trouble concentrating or making decisions. Physical symptoms can include fatigue, lack of energy, and changes in weight or sleep patterns. In addition, those suffering from depression may have vague aches and pains, show irritability, anxiety, and have thoughts of death or suicide.

Acute Stress Reaction (ASR)

The symptoms from ASR typically include an initial state of "daze" with some constriction of the field of consciousness and narrowing of attention, inability to comprehend stimuli, and disorientation. This state may be quickly followed by either further withdrawal from the surrounding situation (to the extent of a dissociative stupor) or by agitation and over-reactivity, anxiety, impaired judgment, confusion, detachment, and depression.

The symptoms usually appear within minutes of the impact of a stressful event, and may disappear within days, but often dissipate within hours. In addition, partial or complete amnesia pertaining to the episode may be present.

Post Traumatic Stress Disorder (PTSD)

PTSD is a severe anxiety disorder that can develop after exposure to any event which results in psychological trauma. The event may involve the threat of death to you or to someone else. PTSD is also referred to as "shell shock" or "battle fatigue." Related symptoms include slowing of reaction time, slowness of thought, difficulty prioritizing tasks, difficulty initiating routine tasks, preoccupation with minor issues and familiar tasks, indecision and lack of concentration, loss of initiative, and exhaustion.

In addition, those suffering from PTSD can experience an extreme feeling of losing control, confusion, a mistrust of others, disruptive behavior, thoughts of suicide, loss of adaptability, anxiety, a heightened sense of threat, depression, and irritability. Physical symptoms may also be present and, among others, can include headaches, back pains, shaking and tremors, sweating, nausea and vomiting, abdominal distress, urinary incontinence, heart palpitations, hyperventilation, dizziness, and insomnia.

Battle-hardened soldiers are susceptible to PTSD and in a disastrous survival situation where you may have lost everything you had, your way of life, witnessed someone you know or love killed, were nearly killed yourself etc. It's almost certain that most people who have been sheltered from this type of trauma will suffer some of these conditions to one degree or another. If you experience any form of stress after a disastrous event, the critical decisions you'll be required to make to ensure your family's safety will be severely hampered or non-existent.

The period immediately following a major disaster is critical in more ways than one. A bout of ASR and PTSD has the potential to become a bigger threat to your survival than the event itself.

War

Conventional, chemical, biological, and nuclear war involving the United States and another country, while not impossible, is difficult to imagine. The only realistic scenario would involve a nuclear war with Mother Russia, which would almost certainly be caused by an accident of some sort, since I'm sure they're painfully aware that a pre-emptive nuclear strike on the United States would be cause for the destruction of their entire society, and probably of the world, too. It just wouldn't make any logical sense. But then what does make logical sense these days? At any rate, I wouldn't stay up nights worrying about this type of war.

There are, however, two types of warfare that are cause for concern and may be happening even as we speak.

Psychological Warfare

This is a VERY interesting topic.

The official definition from the U.S. Department of Defense defines psychological warfare (PSYWAR) as: *The planned use of propaganda and other psychological actions having the primary purpose of influencing the opinions, emotions, attitudes, and behavior of hostile foreign groups in such a way as to support the achievement of national objectives.*

The Encarta definition is:

1. WARFARE BY PROPAGANDA: Tactics that use propaganda to try to demoralize an enemy in war, usually including the civilian population.

2. NON-MILITARY PSYCHOLOGICAL UNDERMINING: The use of psychological tactics to disconcert and disadvantage an opponent in an everyday or a business context, e.g. by causing the opponent to feel fear or anxiety.

Do we have justifiable cause for concern that an enemy from outside the United States may attack us using psychological warfare tactics? No, we don't, but just for the heck of it, let's change a few of the words in the definition and see what happens.

DOD DEFINITION OF PSYWAR: *The* planned *use of propaganda and other psychological actions having the primary purpose of influencing the opinions, emotions, attitudes, and behavior of a segment of the population in such a way as to support the achievement of a political agenda.* (Oh, oh, we might be under attack from the left. But let's check out the revised Encarta definition again before we go bonkers.)

ENCARTA DEFINITION OF PSYWAR: Non military psychological undermining*: the use of psychological tactics to disconcert and disadvantage a citizenry in an everyday context, e.g. by causing the citizen to feel fear or anxiety.*

Ops, we may be under attack by both the left and the right!

Cyber Warfare

Cyber warfare is an increasing problem in the United States and throughout the world.

Cyber attacks that can take down, even temporarily, any part of our infrastructure (especially the power grid) could make our lives miserable as well as dangerous. In addition, a well orchestrated cyber attack could wreak havoc with the financial system (not that it would require much to accomplish that) and could infect and disable critical business computer systems as well as disruption of the Internet.

A cyber attack could also be mounted against personal computers causing untold damage. If the attack was sophisticated enough to get into the military and law enforcement computers, the potential damage could be catastrophic.

It's a certainty cyber attacks occur regularly. It's also a certainty the government and the military are on top of it. While the danger of such an attack is real, there isn't anything we can do to prevent it except to hope our guys are smarter than their guys.

Socialism

It appears the average person isn't overly concerned with the possibility of the USA becoming a socialist state, possibly because, although the word is bandied about incessantly, the actual definition of socialism hasn't been adequately explained to the American populace.

SOCIALISM IS DEFINED AS: Any theory or system of social organizations in which the means of producing and distributing goods is owned collectively or by a centralized government that often plans and controls the economy. Or, the stage in Marxist-Leninist theory between capitalism and communism, in which collective ownership of the economy under the dictatorship of the proletariat (the poorest class of working people) has not yet been successfully achieved.

To more fully understand socialism, its stated goals, and the dangers it represents to a free society, you should be aware of the two distinct, yet separate methods of achieving those goals. *Democratic Socialism* and *Social Democracy* are both political movements propagating the ideals of socialism within the framework of a parliamentary democracy through *trade unions*, *labor* and *political parties*.

Democratic Socialism is more left-wing and supports a fully socialist system, seeking to establish the socialist system by *gradually reforming capitalism from within.*

Social Democracy, on the other hand, is a form of *Democratic Socialism* that's more centrist and supports a broadly capitalist system with just a few socialist elements thrown in to make it more equitable and humane.

Both forms of socialism typically advocate at least a *WELFARE STATE!*

If you're poor, uneducated, ignorant, or just plain lazy, *socialism* probably sounds like a good idea. And for you, it probably is. Those who are educated, creative, intelligent, hardworking, and who earn the money they make won't find socialism at all attractive, since they'll be supporting those people in the first category. If you're one of the people who believe success requires hard work, socialism should scare the hell out of you.

At any rate, the definition of socialism certainly sounds like the intent of the Obama Administration and the left wing Congress doesn't it? You'll have to make up your own mind on that. The fact is, a move toward socialism has been underway long before President Obama came onto the scene and has the potential to endanger your way of life, as well as your physical well being. It's not a reach to believe the next step in the process would be to some form of Marxist-Leninist Communism.

Marxist, Leninist Communism

Communism is a political way of thinking and an idea of how society should work and be organized. Communism is a kind of socialism that says there shouldn't be social classes or states. Communism says that the people of any and every place should all own the tools, factories, and farms that are used to produce goods and food. This social process is known as common ownership. In a communist society, there's no private property.

That's an outdated definition. There aren't too many factories or farms left in the USA, while tools undoubtedly refer to farming equipment and factory machines.

How about this? Communism is a political thought process that organizes the working class of people into "worker bees" with common sharing of all goods, services, and food while providing a select few with unlimited power and wealth.

This social process is known as common ownership and strips the worker of an identity and a future, but provides them with the basics of life. There's no private property in a communist system.

Sounds more modern and accurate to me. The dangers of communism needn't be explained further.

Riots

There are riots, and then there are riots! We aren't talking about the occasional riot involving a couple of hundred disgruntled or misguided demonstrators disrupting a meeting or breaking a few windows. We're referring to major rioting on a regional and perhaps national level.

Could that type of rioting take place in the United States? Sure it could. For those of you who think that's a lot of malarkey, you might be in for a rude awakening in the not too distant future.

It would be nice to think the current situation in the country is a short-term anomaly, that when President Obama is out of office things will return to normal. But what if they don't? What if it's too late? Put another way, what if unemployment, foreclosures, the economy, and the lives of the average American citizen continue to deteriorate with no end in sight?

How long will it be before there's a situation, or an event, that sparks local rioting on a grand scale? Will that local riot take on national overtones? What happens when Hyper-Inflation hits us like a ton of bricks? Will people tolerate and endure paying $12 bucks for a gallon of gas, especially on a reduced income, or worse yet, with no income at all?

Will that happen? Hope not. But the odds are 50-50 it will, and if it does, riots such as the country has never seen are likely to take place.

The danger from the rioters will be real. Curfews and marital law could be imposed on a significant portion of the country, creating additional hardships for the average citizen. Since there are no facts pertaining to this type of event, the best advice I could give you is to stay as far away from the scene of a riot as you can get.

Curfews and Martial Law

A curfew could be imposed locally, regionally, or nationally at any time, for any number of reasons. The curfew could be in effect during the hours of darkness (likely) or during certain hours or even days of the week.

Although a curfew wouldn't be the end of the world, it would definitely disrupt your life and would certainly be a pain in the butt. Curfews could also be used in conjunction with martial law (the military is in charge and is the law of the land during the imposition of martial law. The only rights you have are those the military allows you to have.) Martial law is a serious event. It means something calamitous has occurred. Martial law could also entail the use of checkpoints, special identification, or travel papers.

Curfews could be in place for a few days to indefinitely, and martial law, once imposed could last for a very long time.

Keep your fingers crossed.

Survivability for rioting, curfews and martial law

Current national probability	low
Potential in the future	Low
Current local probability	Low to fair
Danger if implemented	Low to moderate
Disruption of life	Medium to high

CHAPTER 14

LOCAL AND REGIONAL NATURAL DISASTERS

I'LL BET YOU THOUGHT YOU could cruise through this section without paying much attention to it. No chance! While the odds of a natural disaster, such as a super volcano eruption is small, the odds of a local or regional disaster is high. Additionally, nothing will impact your overall survival chances more than local, everyday weather. The good old summertime thunderstorm can pose significant problems for you during a survival event, as well as present imminent danger.

Living in a house during a thunderstorm, hail-storm, tornado, flood, heat wave, cold snap, blizzard, etc. is one thing. Enduring a severe thunderstorm in, let's say, a tent, while simultaneously trying to survive, is a different breed of cat altogether. The normal, everyday "weather" that was nothing more than a temporary pain (or even enjoyable) BTC now becomes a potential killer.

Remember, you're not going to have a weather forecast available.

Let's start with that summer thunderstorm you used to enjoy so much since they impact the majority of the country on a regular basis.

Thunderstorms

Thunderstorms affect relatively small areas when compared with hurricanes and winter storms. The *typical* thunderstorm is fifteen (15) miles in diameter and lasts an average of thirty minutes. Despite their small size, all thunderstorms are dangerous. Of the estimated 100,000 thunderstorms that occur each year in the United States, about ten percent are classified as *severe*. In addition to heavy rain, thunderstorms can and often do produce tornados, lightning, damaging hail, high winds, and flash flooding.

Straight-line winds

Winds in a thunderstorm can exceed 100 mph and are responsible for most thunderstorm wind damage. One type of straight-line wind, the downburst, is a small area of rapidly descending air beneath a thunderstorm. A downburst can cause damage equivalent to a strong tornado and can be extremely dangerous to aviation. A dry "micro-burst" is a downburst that occurs with little or no rain. These destructive winds are most common in the western United States. The State of Florida has more thunderstorms each year than any other state.

Lightning

Every year lightning causes an average of about sixty fatalities and 300 injuries. Lightning occurs in all thunderstorms. There are about 25 million lightning strikes each year around the world. (Florida has the dubious honor of receiving more lightning strikes per year than any other place on Earth.) The energy from one lightning flash could light a 100 watt bulb for more than three months. Most lightning fatalities and injuries occur when people are caught outdoors in the summer months during the afternoon and evening. Especially around the 14th hole.

Lightning can occur from cloud-to-cloud, within a cloud, cloud-to-ground, or cloud-to-air. Lightning is also responsible for many of the fires that happen annually in the western United States and Alaska. The air near a lightning strike is heated to 50,000 degrees F, hotter than the surface of the sun. The rapid heating and cooling of the air near the lighting channel causes a shock wave that results in thunder.

Flash flooding

Flash flooding is the number one cause of death associated with thunderstorms with more than 140 fatalities per year. Most flash floods occur at night, and most victims are people who become trapped in automobiles. Six inches of fast-moving water can knock a person off their feet. Two feet of fast moving water will cause most vehicles to float.

Hail

Strong rising currents of air within a storm, called updrafts, carry water droplets to a height where freezing occurs. Ice particles grow in size, becoming too heavy to be supported by the updraft, and fall to the ground as hail. Hail causes more than one billion dollars in damages to property and crops every year. Large hail-stones fall at speeds that exceed 100 mph.

The average hailstone is approximately .75 inches in diameter, or about the size of a golf-ball. Hail-stones can reach sizes of 14 inches in diameter or more. Yikes!

Tornados

Although tornados occur in many parts of the world, they're found most frequently in the United States. A tornado is a violently rotating column of air extending from a thunderstorm cloud to the ground. Tornadoes cause an average of seventy fatalities, 1500 injuries, and billions of dollars in damages each year. The strongest tornadoes have rotating winds of more than 250 mph and can be up to one mile wide and stay on the ground for over fifty miles. Tornados may appear nearly transparent until dust and debris are picked up or a cloud forms within the funnel. The average tornado moves from the southwest to the northeast, but tornados have been known to move in any direction. The average forward speed is 30 mph but may vary from nearly stationary to 70 mph. Waterspouts are tornadoes which form over warm water. Waterspouts can move onshore and cause damage to coastal areas.

If you're living in the woods in a tent, suffice it to say the "average thunderstorm" is no longer average. Be sure you don't pitch your tent under the tallest tree or in an area that may be susceptible to flash flooding, and be aware and alert. (And hope the hail doesn't shred your tent.) Stay dry!

Blizzards

Remember that big snow storm back in '83? The one that dumped 30+ inches of snow on your garden in April and kept you snowbound for three days? That wasn't a blizzard. It was just a big snow storm. A blizzard is a violent winter storm with winds in excess of 35 mph and visibility of less than one-quarter mile for three hours or more. Blizzards are almost always accompanied by very low temperatures.

Another form of blizzard is a ground blizzard which is characterized by no falling snow, but with extremely high winds that blow the snow that's on the ground. Regardless of the form the blizzard takes, they can bring whiteout conditions, restricting visibility to near zero.

Blizzard conditions (and heavy snowfall too) during a survival situation can bring dangerous conditions to an already serious situation. (If you're in a tent in the winter, you're not having fun).

Ice storms

Have you ever had to live through a severe ice storm? One that coated everything with a couple of inches of ice? Have you sat in your home with no power, in the dark, and listened to the tree limbs cracking like gunshots as they fall to the ground from the weight of the ice? Were you unable to open your car door, knowing, if you did, it'd be impossible to go anywhere anyway? Not a good time, to say the least.

In the north, east and mountainous west, expect the majority of ice storms to occur from about November thru March with late spring being the most common time for an ice storm to occur. Ice storms can happen as far south as the Florida panhandle.

The good news? You won't have to worry about scraping ice off the windshield of your car.

Extreme Cold

A cold wave is defined as a rapid fall in temperatures within a 24 hour period requiring substantially increased protection to agriculture, commerce, and social activities. The precise criteria for a cold wave is determined by the rate at which the temperature falls and the minimum to which it falls.

The minimum temperature is dependent on the geographical region and time of year. Now in English; when it gets a *lot* colder than is normal for where you live, that's a cold wave.

When the temperature drops to freezing, or just a bit below in southern Florida, it's considered a cold wave. In the middle of winter, in Minnesota, those temperatures would indicate spring was just around the corner. So cold is a matter of perspective and location. However, 32 degrees is still 32 degrees whether it occurs in south Florida or in Minnesota.

The United States has experienced many severe cold outbreaks over the last 100+ years. The winter of 2008-2009 saw a host of record low temperatures and, if the start of the winter of 2009- 2010 is any indication, 2010 will see more record lows across the nation.

Severe cold causes a lot of damage psychologically and physically. It kills livestock and animals as well as unprepared humans. Extremely cold temperatures cause metal to shrink, things to break, and trees to fall. In addition, it causes water pipes, both residential and commercial, to break. I'm not sure if the exact financial toll from a severe cold snap has ever been calculated, but I'm sure the total would open some eyes.

Extremely cold weather can cause hypothermia in a short time, and will freeze exposed flesh in a matter of minutes. Most people don't look too good with frost bitten fingers and toes, especially if they require amputation.

There are a lot of precautions that can be taken to ward off the effects of severe cold. A few I know about from personal experience is *don't* take a deep breath of extremely cold air. Breath through your gloved hand, a muffler, or face mask. *Don't* grab anything metal with your bare hand, and *don't* put your tongue on the handle of the pump.

The actual coldest air temperature ever recorded in the United States is -80F in Prospect Creek Camp, AK on 1-23-71. The coldest ever recorded in North America was -81F at Snag in the Yukon Territory, Canada, on 2-3-47.

In the lower 48 it was -69F at Roger's Pass in Montana on 1-20-54, and east of the Mississippi River, it was -60F in Tower, MN on 2-2-96.

Incidentally, the coldest temperature ever recorded in the northern hemisphere was -90F in, you guessed it, Siberia.

For the record, the coldest official temperature ever recorded on Earth was on 7-21-83 in the Antarctic at Russian Vostok Station. An incredible -128.6F, and in the winter of 1997 (July) that same station recorded an unofficial temperature of -132F.

Wind and the resulting wind-chill causes the actual temperature to feel much colder and has a cooling effect on exposed flesh. For example, an air temperature of thirty (30) degrees F with a wind of just ten (10) mph will have the same effect on exposed flesh as an air temperature of 21F. The higher the wind, the more profound the effect. To illustrate this point, an air temperature of zero degrees F with a wind of 30 mph will have the same effect on exposed flesh as an air temperature of -26F.

How does this information relate to a survival situation? You won't know when a cold snap is going to be paying you a visit until after the fact. Cold can kill you quickly. Take the appropriate precautions. And stay warm!

Extreme heat

Heat waves are much like cold waves in so far as they're subjective. What constitutes a heat wave in one location is just another day in paradise in another. Nevertheless, the term heat wave is reserved for periods of abnormally high temperatures in areas that don't normally experience them at the time they occur. Heat waves aren't normally contributors to a disaster but a prolonged or especially vicious heat wave could have severe consequences to your health during a survival event. Avoid abnormal exertion during periods of extreme heat, avoid dehydration, and attempt to do your survival chores early in the morning or after sundown. You should also avoid exposure to the rays of the sun if possible.

Severe drought

Droughts are usually connected to water shortages, but the effects of a severe drought aren't limited to water shortages. Droughts cause vegetation, particularly in western states, to become exceedingly dry, increasing the likelihood of fires. Forest fires are an annual event in the west, causing billions of dollars in damages and forcing the evacuation of thousands of people. Seasonal or drought-induced dry spells are also responsible for thousands of small brush or roadside fires in the rest of the country.

Severe droughts are caused by weather patterns, usually a high pressure gradient that refuses to move, which forces summer storms to move around the system instead of moving across the area that the high encompasses.

It's all tied into weather patterns, and there's nothing that can be done to change the pattern of the weather.

During drought conditions, you should be alert for fires caused by lighting or other survivors who may have been less cautious with their fires than you. You may also be forced to move locations to secure water.

Water shortages

Potential long-term water shortages in parts of the USA is a genuine problem. It's happening now, particularly in California and other areas of the West. It's been estimated that Lake Mead, which supplies most of the water to southern California, the Las Vegas area, and parts of Arizona, will be dry in six to twelve years. While that may or may not be true, it's a sad fact those areas are experiencing seasonal and severe water shortages, even though a portion of that shortage is caused by the "greenies" efforts to save a two inch fish from extinction.

There are several reasons for water shortages. One is drought. Extended periods when there's no rain obviously contributes to the problem. Seasonal run-off from mountain snowpack melt is one of the biggest contributors to the water problem in the West. El Nino, sun spots (or lack thereof) and other naturally occurring events also contribute to drought.

Regardless of the reason, at some point in time, man will have to start regarding water as something other than water.

Water shortages occur in other parts of the country too, not just in the West. Aquifers in some areas are low, and seasonal restrictions on water usage is commonplace, particularly in the summer months. A national water crisis of unprecedented proportions may be just around the corner. It shouldn't come as a shock to anyone if, in the not too distant future, the cost of water is on a par with the cost of gas.

Desalination plants work, but we don't build them. Well, Tampa, FL built one. And it can produce up to 35 million gallons of pristine water per day. But no one else that I'm aware of is seriously considering desalination. I seem to recall a high school science class that taught us that every drop of water that ever existed still exists. Is that true? Alright then, someone has more than their share. Where is it? Oh, yeah, I forgot. It's in the oceans. What were we talking about? Desalination?

How do you protect yourself from future severe water shortages? That's a tough one indeed. Perhaps it won't come to that. Maybe the powers that be will show us some water intelligence and foresight by fixing the problem before it becomes critical. Who wants to pay $3 for a gallon of water? Wait a minute. Who owns the rivers, lakes, and salt water coastline out to 200 miles? Oh yeah. The Federal Government.

Floods

Floods occur regularly in the United States and range from major flooding, such as the great Mississippi River flood of 1993, to flash-floods that take place frequently in normally dry areas of the West. In between are a wide variety of floods that occur due to extended periods of heavy rainfall or seasonal snow melt. You should definitely consider flooding to be a concern during a survival situation.

Most people who live in flood prone areas are aware of the dangers, yet many of those same people appear surprised when a flood happens to them. Flooding can happen in any area and to nearly everyone for a wide variety of reasons, and at any time. Some of the causes include seasonal ice melt, severe thunderstorms, prolonged periods of heavy rain, hurricanes, and tsunami.

If you're surviving in a tent, near a river, and it starts to rise (due to whatever)—move the tent!

Earthquakes

Say the word *earthquake* and you immediately think of California or the Pacific northwest. However, the West Coast doesn't have a monopoly on this devastating event.

Earthquakes can occur over the majority of the USA including the Midwest and eastern seaboard states. Earthquakes, as anyone who's experienced one knows, can represent a major local disaster.

It would be redundant to attempt to explain everything there is to know about earthquakes, their causes and effects. Unless you've been Rip Van Winkle-ing it, you should at least have some idea of the damages an earthquake can cause.

For the best information available anywhere on earthquakes, visit the USGS National Earthquake Information Center (NEIC).

Volcanic eruptions

Volcanic eruptions are the most powerful natural event on our planet. There are approximately 1500 volcanoes that have been active during the last 10,000 years and perhaps an *even larger number* of underwater volcanoes. Presently, there are about 600 volcanoes that have had known eruptions during recorded history and approximately sixty that erupt each year. At any given time there is an average of twenty volcanoes that are erupting.

Volcanic eruptions are generally a local or regional event, but they do have the potential to create national and even world-wide problems by blocking sunlight and creating an event like that caused by the massive eruption of Mt. Tambora in April of 1815. Mt. Tambora is a volcano on an Indonesian island that exploded on that date, blowing off 4000 feet of the volcano.

Of the 12,000 inhabitants of the island, only 26 survived. The ensuing eruption ejected an estimated 28 cubic miles of debris into the stratosphere that took months to settle back to the ground. The event Mt. Tambora caused is referred to as: 1816, the year without summer. It caused near famine conditions in parts of Europe and severely curtailed crop growth and production in the United States.

There are approximately sixty (60) known volcanoes in the lower 48 United States, with an additional 55 in Alaska, and about 21 in Canada. Mexico has around 44, Central America about eighty, and the West Indies 17. That's a lot of volcanoes whose eruption(s) would pose immediate danger to those living within a hundred miles of the volcano. Most aren't active, but then it only takes one.

Hurricanes

Hurricanes are justly infamous for the amount of damage they cause and in the huge toll in misery they extract from the populations of affected areas.

A hurricane dwarfs every other storm, with sustained winds approaching 200 mph and storm surges exceeding 25 feet. A Category 5 hurricane is an unbelievably powerful force.

The United States has had three Category 5 hurricanes make landfall since 1900. The Florida Keys Hurricane of 1935, Hurricane Camille, and Hurricane Andrew.

The most deadly hurricane to hit the United States was the Galveston Hurricane of 1900. It killed an estimated 8,000 to 12,000 people.

The most costly hurricane prior to Katrina was Hurricane Andrew. Andrew caused 28.5 billion in damages. Katrina caused an astounding 75 billion in damages and killed 1200 people. Katrina also set the dubious record for the highest storm surge at Pass Christian, MS of 27.8 feet and set the high water mark of 34.1 feet at Biloxi, MS.

Since 1900 the USA has experienced approximately 35 landfalls from hurricanes and/or intense tropical storms; approximated because some of those hurricanes made landfall more than once. Using that figure, and that data, we could state that the United States is hit by a hurricane once every three years. But we all know that's not a reliable figure due to weather cycles, El Nino, and other influencing factors.

Of those approximate 35 hurricanes to make landfall in the USA, 17 of them made landfall in Florida, six in Texas, six in North Carolina, and surprisingly enough, four on Long Island, NY. Louisiana also has seen four direct hits. Those figures are somewhat misleading, however, since a lot of the landfalls impacted adjacent states as badly, if not worse, than the state in which the hurricane made landfall.

The advent of technology precludes being taken by surprise by a hurricane. We currently have plenty of warning. During a survival situation there won't be any technology available to you, so it's back to the drawing board.

If you're on the coast and the winds pick up dramatically, get inland, fast. Remember, although hurricane force winds are extremely dangerous, nine out of every ten deaths in a hurricane are caused by the storm surge.

Tsunami

Tsunami is a set of ocean waves caused by any large, abrupt disturbance of the sea surface. If the disturbance is close to the coastline, local tsunamis can demolish coastal communities within minutes. A large disturbance can cause devastation and export tsunami destruction thousands of miles away. Tsunamis rank high on the scale of natural disasters. Since 1850 alone, tsunamis have been responsible for the loss of over 420,000 lives and billions of dollars in damages to coastal structures and habitats.

Most of these casualties were caused by local tsunamis that occur about once a year somewhere in the world.

For example, the December 26, 2004, tsunami killed about 130,000 people close to the earthquake that caused it, and about 58,000 people on distant shores. This particular earthquake measured 9.3 on the Richter scale and produced a tsunami in excess of thirty meters (100 feet) along the adjacent coastline. Traveling at speeds up to 500 km an hour (the speed of a commercial jet-liner) the tsunami struck Thailand, Sri Lanka, and India within two hours.

Tsunamis can be generated by underwater landslides, volcanic eruptions, earthquakes, and asteroid impacts.

The eruption of Krakatoa in the East Indies in 1883 produced a thirty meter tsunami that killed over 36,000 people.

In 1997, scientists discovered evidence of a four km diameter asteroid that landed offshore of Chile approximately two million years ago that produced a Mega tsunami that swept over large portions of South America and Antarctica.

Tsunamis are most prevalent in the Pacific, but they can occur in the Atlantic as well.

Anyone living on or near the coastline of the United States should be aware of the danger that a tsunami presents.

Mega Tsunami

Mega Tsunami could have been placed in the national natural disaster section just as easily as this one, since a Mega Tsunami would, indeed, have national consequences.

The difference between a *mega tsunami* and a normal tsunami is the size of the tsunami (length) and the height of the wave. A mega tsunami would likely generate a wave of about 100 meters or 300 feet and could ultimately be a thousand miles long.

To date, we've never experienced a mega tsunami. A lot of experts predict the fractured seaward slope of the active volcano Cumbre Vieja in Lapalma, the Canary Islands in the Atlantic, or Kilauea, in Hawaii, in the Pacific, will slide into the sea during an eruption, generating a mega tsunami. The prediction is that the eruption and ensuing slide of the volcanic slope into the ocean could happen at any time. However, there are other experts who tell us there will be no mega tsunami because greater source dimensions and longer wave periods are required to generate a tsunami wave that can have significant impact on distant shores.

For the record, the prediction of damages from a mega tsunami caused by Cumbre Vieja would spare no coastline in the North Atlantic. Britain, France, Spain, Portugal, and North Africa would all be hit by 100 meter waves. In hours, the wave would hit the Caribbean and Brazil. The east coast of the United States would be hit by a wave that was *only* fifty meters (150 feet) high, but many kilometers long, allowing it to sweep up to twenty miles inland, destroying everything in its path. Virtually every coastal city from Boston and New York and south to Miami would be wiped off the map and nearly every person in those cities would be killed.

The consequences of such a disaster are incalculable. That's one prediction. The other is: "Not gonna happen."

CHAPTER 15

HOW TO

A WELL THOUGHT OUT BUG-OUT BAG (backpack) and a survival knife are both critical survival items. Secondary choices, such as a survival tent and an adequate medical kit, are almost as important.

The following sections will provide you with information to select, pack, and use all of them.

All about bug-out bags

Since a packed bug-out bag is your survival Ace-In-The-Hole, it makes sense to select a good one and to learn to pack and use it effectively. A bug-out bag should be packed and ready to go even if your plan is to *survive in place.*

Let's take a moment and define exactly what a bug-out bag is and examine its survival function.

A bug-out bag is a back-pack loaded with the *basic* items necessary to survive for an indefinite period of time on your own and without assistance from any facet of society. The amount of time you can survive with the items in a bug-out bag will be determined by what you put in it, the severity and type of event that caused you to grab the bag and "bug-out," the amount of survival skill you possess, your location, and many other X factors. A bug-out bag doesn't provide any survival guarantees it merely gives you the opportunity to survive.

The following information will explain how to select, pack, and use a bug-out bag effectively. The list of essential survival gear *is not* a list of recommended survival items for a primary residence or safe area (even though you'll use all of them); rather it's a list of *basic survival items* that should be placed in the bug-out bag(s).

The best bug-out bag is a backpack with an internal or external frame. That sounds relatively simple, and on the surface, it is. In reality, choosing the right size and style of bug-out bag is a matter of critical importance.

Consider. With the exception of food and water, *everything* you need to survive for X amount of time, except for those items you can put in your pockets and carry in your hands, HAS TO FIT IN THE BACKPACK. This is where it gets complicated.

The items you're going to need are largely dependent upon the area of the country where you live and the size of your family.

People living in warmer climates will have an easier time making gear selections than their northern neighbors, since (extra) cold weather clothing is going to take up a significant amount of space. As we progress through this section, remember one size, one type, and one list won't meet everyone's requirements. The contents of your bug-out bag must be tailored to fit your individual needs.

The most popular type of backpack today is one which has the frame inside the bag. In other words, the frame and bag are an integral unit. *Internal frame backpacks* come in a wide variety of styles, sizes and colors.

The other type of backpack has the frame and bag as separate (stand-alone) units. The bag is attached to the frame with a series of heavy duty pins. *External frame backpacks* also come in a wide variety of styles, sizes, and colors.

Both types of backpacks have pros and cons. While *internal frame backpacks* are sleek and don't snag up on branches as easily as an *external frame backpack*, the frame itself takes up a lot of room within the bag.

Although most good *internal frame backpacks* provide lashing points which allow bulky gear to be "strapped" to the bag, you can lash a ridiculous amount of large, bulky, or long items, including saws, axes, fishing poles etc. to an *external frame backpack*. External frame backpacks also allow a tent and/or a sleeping bag to be carried on the top of the bag or below the bag on the bottom of the frame. In addition, the shelf (the bottom portion of an external frame that the loaded bag rests on) is handy for carrying heavy loads, like wood, elk quarters, etc. by using the frame without the bag attached.

Either type backpack works and works well. The choice is a matter of personal preference. Personally, I prefer the external frame pack for the versatility it provides.

The most important thing to remember when choosing a backpack is to make certain the frame fits your torso. Most good backpacks have *adjustable frames*. If the backpack you're purchasing doesn't have an *adjustable frame*, made certain it fits your torso.

Measure your torso from the waist to the "big bone" at the base of your neck. That's your backpack torso length.

When it comes to weight, common sense should tell you that a man who's 6'6" and in shape can carry more weight than a female who's a petite 5'2" and weights 100 lbs.

A man who's in reasonably good shape should be able to handle weights up to fifty lbs without too much trouble. If you're a 5'2" petite female mom, the bag you'll be carrying will be smaller, because the frame and bag will also be smaller, and because (thankfully) you're not loaded with testosterone.

Unfortunately, most people, regardless of their size, aren't capable of carrying a backpack for any length of time loaded to a weight of much more than fifty lbs. The weight you'll be able to carry in a good backpack will be determined by the type of terrain you'll be traversing, the shape you're in, and other less significant factors.

Make an effort to envision the items you'll be carrying in your pockets, on your belt, and those items you'll have in your hands, such as a firearm. A fifty pound pack with the additional weight of clothing etc. can quickly reach 75 pounds or more. In addition, you may be walking through deep snow, wearing snowshoes, or walking in sand. In case you've never experienced it, waking in snow or sand carrying anything more than a beer is tiring all by itself, let alone carrying an additional 75 pounds (or more) of gear. Is it difficult? Absolutely! Impossible? No! With the right equipment, a lot of practice, and a sincere effort to get in shape, it can be done.

When selecting a backpack for use as a bug-out bag, purchase the biggest and best one you can afford that will fit your frame. There's no shortage of quality, big-name backpacks available, and any of the name brands will do the job since they all (for the most part) use exactly the same materials. Construction is also almost identical. The only meaningful difference is price. The higher end expedition backpacks that are used on Everest and K2 expeditions aren't necessary, while the low-end (can you say cheap) backpacks simply aren't going to provide you with the comfort, load carrying capacity, quality, and durability you're going to require. Everyone in the family who can carry a bug-out bag should have one. They don't all have to be the same size, or even the same quality. The main backpack (the largest one, which will carry the heaviest gear) is available from a wide variety of sources in the $150 to $200 MSRP price range. Other good, but smaller bags can be purchased for $100 to $150 MSRP. If you can't afford that type of bag, you can still find a decent bag (without some of the extra features) in the neighborhood of $100 MSRP. It's not realistic to expect to find a good backpack that can be manufactured and sold for much less than $75 MSRP, even if it's made in China. You certainly don't want the bag to rip, spilling the contents along the way.

Forget about packs with hydration bladders. They're great for regular backpacking, but you need the space they take up. Besides, that's why God invented canteens and water bottles.

Any reasonably good knapsack or day-pack will work well for children who're capable of carrying lightweight items, even if it's only their own clothing. Make certain the pack fits snugly and comfortably. Under no circumstances should you overload a child's pack.

Color is irrelevant, although personally I prefer a pack that doesn't scream "TARGET!"

Backpack bags are all made from tough water-repellent nylon, the keyword being *repellent*. A waterproof poly-coated backpack cover that covers the entire pack and provides waterproofing for the entire bag is a worthy accessory. Additionally, a waterproof cover in camo or green eliminates the color issue as well.

Experience in packing and unpacking my bug-out bag has taught me the best way to go about it. I've had one packed for years. It sits patiently in my bedroom closet ready to go. If the situation warranted, I can pick up my bug-out bag, the gear I intend to carry, and the clothes I'll be wearing, and be out the door in a matter of minutes with everything I need to survive on my back.

You can achieve the same thing. It won't come easily, of course, and it's not exactly cheap, but it's certainly attainable. Experimentation is the key. Once you've selected your bug-out bag and determined what survival items you're going to need, and after you've made those purchases, lay everything out on the floor in separate "category piles" for each backpack in your inventory. Select the clothing everyone will be wearing (which will vary depending on the season and your location) and the gear you intend to carry, such as firearms, ammo, belt knives, canteens, binoculars etc. Include *every* item no matter how small it is.

Now stand back and take a look. . . . *Whoa!* I had the same reaction the first time I did it, too. Don't be dismayed. Attempt to pack all the items. The chances are almost 100% the gear you've laid out won't fit in the backpack(s). Or even a dozen backpacks. So it's reality time and back to the drawing board.

Start eliminating. Begin by removing the least important items first. Do you really need that extra chamois shirt and second set of long-johns? Clothing will take up most of the room so begin there. Eliminate as much as you can and repack. Still too much gear? Probably.

It's likely you'll have to repeat this process several times before you get everything of importance into the bag(s).

Packing the bug-out bag is a much simpler process than trying to decide what to put in it. If the bug-out bag is loaded correctly, not only will it be more comfortable and allow you to carry heavier loads, but it will be much better balanced. A backpack that's loaded incorrectly will not only cause you pain, it'll present balance problems when climbing or traversing uneven terrain, wading creeks etc.

If your pack has an internal frame, start by packing your sleeping bag at the bottom of the bag. If your pack has an external frame, the sleeping bag will go on the shelf below the bag. For an internal frame pack, place the tent floor saver, (if you're packing one) or the tarp, over the top of the sleeping bag. If the pack has an external frame, the tent will go on the very top of the bag. For either type of pack, the heaviest items should come next. They should be placed as close to the back of the bag as possible, and no higher than your shoulders. Above the heavy items, and toward the front of the bag (away from your back,) place lighter items such as clothing.

Use the side pockets (you can get a "ton" of gear in most of them) for those items you think you'll use on a regular basis. Compass, lighter, matches, flashlight etc. Once the bag is loaded, tighten the compression straps to stabilize the load and to keep it from shifting. Pull it as close to the back as you can (toward the frame.) If you're using an external frame pack, lash your tent and floor saver on top of the bag. Now lash any items such as saws, axes, fishing poles, etc. to the frame. Follow the instructions that came with the bag pertaining to waist-belt and shoulder-strap adjustments.

When the bag(s) are packed, it's time to weight them.

Weigh yourself (naked), then dress in full survival mode with the clothing knives, guns, ammo, and everything else you plan to carry. Put on the pack and weigh yourself again. Okay chubby, time to go for a walk. See if you can make it to the front door.

The fact is, it's likely you'll be returning to the drawing board and/or visiting the gym, maybe both. But you do have options. You can re-think the entire package in an effort to lighten the load and reduce the bulk. Try not to eliminate the basic survivals items, and remember, this isn't a weekend hiking trip. You're probably going to have to make several attempts at packing the bag, but if you stay with it, eventually you'll get it just right. When you finalize the load, put *everything* that could be damaged by water into heavy duty freezer bags and repack the bag.

Place the bag in a secure, handy location, and update the contents as necessary.

A word of caution is in order. Don't make the same mistake I made when I was learning how to use a bug-out bag. I refused to think I couldn't handle a pack that exceeded a hundred pounds. And since I was full of testosterone induced foolishness, I proceeded to load my pack to around 150 lbs and set off on what I intended to be a five mile hike. In less than ten minutes I was a soggy mass of estrogen, whining like a puppy. It took months of conditioning and weight reduction before I could comfortably carry the current load for a couple of hours at a crack.

The point is, don't let your mentality overrule your physical capabilities.

Essential gear list

The following list consists of items everyone will require. The list doesn't include *food, clothing, footwear, personal medications, toiletries, personal papers, or necessary personal items such as eyeglasses, contact lenses, hearing aids etc.*

Important papers, including all licenses, birth, death, and marriage certificates, inoculation records, passports, deeds, pertinent medical records, and other important papers should be photocopied and placed in a 100% waterproof pouch, along with a few selected pictures. The pouch should either be put into the bug-out bag or placed in an area that would allow quick and easy insertion into the bug-out bag.

I know I've mentioned it before, but there are simply too many variables to attempt to incorporate food, clothing, footwear, toiletries, fire-arms, ammo etc. into the list. There are two areas of note; toiletries and ammo. To begin with, you won't be as squeaky clean then as you are now, nor do you need to be. Eliminate colognes, perfumes, make-up etc. (oh, alright, one little packet! No more!) You don't need them. In fact, they could end up causing your death. (Cologne and perfume can be smelled from long distances in an environment devoid of those types of odors.) Ammo is heavy. Take what you deem practical, but in the event you have to eliminate extra weight, start with *some* of the ammo.

Here's the list. There are items on the list you don't absolutely have to have, but there are also items, such as a tent, that aren't on the list. You'll have to mix and match. Experiment to find what you can and can't get into the bag and adjust accordingly. If you can fit in a good lightweight tent instead of a tarp, the additional weight of the tent will be worthwhile.

By the way, it's not necessary to pack the *exact* item, just get close.

Backpack (one per person). Consider a waterproof cover as an option
Poncho (one per person). Rain jacket as an option
Lightweight mummy sleeping bag (one per person)
Sleeping bag pad (short, closed cell foam or self inflating)
10'x12' HD reinforced nylon tarp with grommets
5'x8' HD nylon tarp with grommets (ground cloth)
50 feet 3/16" diameter nylon rope for tarp/tent centerline
two packs nylon parachute cord (or equivalent) for tent stakes and clothesline
12 metal tent stakes
10" mill file w/handle
Knife sharpener
5" to 7" blade, fixed blade survival knife w/sheath (main knife)
3" to 4" blade folding (pocket) or belt knife (one per person)
Binoculars
Compass
Entrenching tool (folding shovel)
Folding camping saw
Camp axe (3/4 sized)
.12 Ga. pump action shotgun
1 box (24 rounds) .12 Ga. #00 buckshot
Small bottle of gun oil/cleaning rag
LED flashlight (AA batteries) (one per person)
Extra AA batteries (two per light)
Two 2" pillar candles
One box large stick matches in double-bagged zip lock freezer bags
Two disposable lighters
Tinder (newspaper strips) in gallon sized freezer bag
No-see-um head net (one per person)
Small AM/FM radio with AA batteries
Extra AA batteries for radio
Notes, or photocopied pages (How to)
One canteen or water bottle per person
Packable rod and reel with line
Extra spool of line for reel
Small fishing tackle assortment (sinkers, hooks, swivels, corks, jigs, jig-tails)
Pint of unscented chlorine bleach
Pack of cheesecloth

Eyedropper or one-half teaspoon measuring spoon (for water treatment)
Collapsible water container
Collapsible bucket (optional)(for hygiene & dishes)
HD steel cooking grate
50′ roll HD aluminum foil
HD bowl, cup, plate (one per person)
HD cutlery (spoon and fork or spork) (one per person)
2 dish cloths
1 face-cloth/1 hand towel per person
Large metal or plastic spoon
Can opener (small)
Nesting cook set
Waterproof medical kit: band-aids, band-aid sutures, band-aid pads, Kling bandages, sterile pads, roll medical tape, ace bandage, small scissors, Neosporin, aspirin, Tylenol, antibiotics (other as you determine)
Mosquito repellent with maximum DEET
one bar of anti-bacterial soap per person
Small bottle of liquid detergent (dish washing)
Toilet paper (you determine the amount)
Seeds (various kinds; F1 Hybrid seeds are okay for this bare-bones list)
Two watches that are not battery operated
A perpetual calendar
Copies of: The Constitution of the United States, Declaration of Independence, Bill of Rights
Copy of all Amendments to the Constitution of the United States
Holy Bible
Deck of playing cards or similar game (pastime)
Notebook and several pencils and one or two pens
Relevant map(s)
Old silver coins
Gold coins

Optional gear list

Depending upon the size of your bag(s), you may be able to substitute or add items from the following list(s). Don't forget those items that aren't on the list such as clothes, food etc still have to be packed before you start adding additional items.

Solar AA battery charger and matching solar panel
Ni-cad rechargeable AA batteries (replaces any alkaline cells you have)
A packet of sourdough starter (fresh sourdough bread forever)
50′ length of 5/8 nylon climbing rope (for hoisting etc.)
Upgrade the medical kit
Add extra fishing equipment
Add extra ammo
Backpacking tent (see the section on choosing a survival tent)

Katadyn micro-filter—The Katadyn Pocket micro-filter is the best of the best. Not cheap, but the best never is. You won't regret purchasing one. (Filters approximately 13,000 gallons of water.)

Add items from the safe area list and/or increase quantities of selected items from the *essentials* list.

Safe area list.

The list of items that would be useful in a primary or safe area is endless. I won't be listing items you undoubtedly have, such as hammers, gardening tools, perhaps chainsaws, and other household tools and equipment since they'll automatically become part of your overall survival kit.

If you attempted to purchase every item on this list, let me warn you, it would cost a bundle! If you can afford to spend that kind of money, and you have the area to store these items in, you certainly won't regret it if a catastrophe happens.

The following items are *suggestions only*. They will definitely increase the chances of your survival.

.22LR pistol and ammo	9mm Auto and ammo	.308Win scoped rifle/ammo
Extra .12 Ga. shot-shells	Trip wire, extra rope	Ammo belts, pouches
Gun cleaning supplies	Night vision device (NVD)	Binoculars
Extra knives	Extra flashlights	Machete
Rechargeable batteries	Extra Ni-cad batteries	Full size axe
Aladdin lamp & accessories	Solar storage battery	Solar panel(s)
Kerosene for Aladdin	Multi tool	Short-wave radio
2-way radios	Sewing kit and awl	Ice pick
20 gal. water barrels	Water barrel siphon pump	Cast iron cookware
Natural dehydrator	Felling Wedges	Bucksaw and extra Blade
Extra shovel	Duct tape	Large nails or spikes
Compass	Kinetic watch	Slingshot and accessories
Stick matches	Blankets/bedding	Gore-Tex rain gear
MREs	Honey	Cleaning supplies
Heirloom seeds	F-1 hybrid seeds	Salt
Parachute cord	Sevin bug powder	Archery equipment
How to books	Text-school books	Pens and paper
Children's books	Dictionary	Games, balls, etc.
Toiletries	Medications	Cooking and dining items
Wheat grinder	Rolls n rolls of TP	

You should also consider:

Roll Visqueen (clear drop-cloth, for making windows etc.)
Enhanced fishing gear (seine, trot lines, ice fishing gear etc.)
Inflatable boat
Appropriate clothing and footwear
Enhanced medical, dental, surgical kit
1 year supply of survival food for the entire family

As you can see, the possibilities are literally *endless.* Adding even a few of the items mentioned above will increase the chances of your survival and make your survival "life" more bearable.

All about survival knives

A survival knife is arguably the single most important piece of survival gear you can own. If you have a good survival knife you can build a shelter, craft weapons, clean fish and game, gather firewood, and hundreds of other survival necessities in order to stay alive.

When it comes to the selection of that all-important knife, the average person is clueless as to what constitutes a good one . What do all those terms mean? Is AUS8 steel better than 440 stainless steel, and if so why? Does it really matter? If a knife cuts, isn't that enough?

"Wow, this cool looking knife from All Points Survival uses BSL black coated 767 stainless steel with an HRC of 40. The blade's 9-1/8" long and the knife only weighs 1.5 oz too. Not only that but the handle's made from genuine Mandarin CH45 space age plastic and it has a genuine Musaka inlay. Don't know what all that means, but I like the way it looks, and best of all it's only $14.95."

Translation? A cheap Saturday Night Special with inferior steel that won't retain an edge and couldn't cut hot butter. In addition, the tip will break the first time you attempt to pry something with it. Definitely *not* a knife you want in your survival kit. And by the way, that little "survival fishing kit" in the hollowed out handle means the handle is just as weak as the blade. (The fishing kit sucks, too!)

But perhaps a worse description is where the knife's being touted as superior, but makes no mention of the type of steel, HRC, coating, handle material etc. A picture of a knife is *not* worth a thousand words. *Never* buy a knife based on looks alone

To make an intelligent decision about an item as critical as a survival knife, it's imperative you arm yourself with the knowledge that will allow you to make an intelligent decision.

To keep things simple, I'm only listing the most commonly used terminology, as well as the most common and useful types of steel, finishes, blade types etc. that're used in the manufacture of today's knives.

Terminology

OVERALL LENGTH: Refers to the length of the entire knife from the tip of the blade to the end of the handle.

BLADE LENGTH: Refers to the length of the blade from the tip of the blade to the beginning of the handle.

BLADE THICKNESS: This term isn't always used but when it is, it refers to the thickest part of the blade, usually the "top" or "backside" of the blade. Obviously a thicker blade won't break as easily as a thinner blade of equal quality.

EDGE OR EDGE TYPE: Refers to the type of edge on the cutting portion of the blade.

GRIND: This term isn't always used, but when it is, it's referring to the "shape" of the cutting edge of the blade.

EDGE ANGLE: This term is also not used extensively. It references the bevel used when the blade was sharpened at the factory. It's also the recommended angle for re-sharpening.

WEIGHT: The actual weight of the knife without a sheath.

HANDLE: The type of material used in the construction of the knife handle.

FINISH: Normally refers to the finish of the blade, but sometimes refers to the overall knife. A coating is an application put on the finish.

LOCKING MECHANISM or LOCK: References the type of locking mechanism used to open/close a folding knife and to "lock" the blade in the "open position."

RCH or RC: The number assigned a knife blade referencing the hardness of the steel. A number below 56 means the blade won't hold an edge very well, while a number over 60 means the steel is becoming (or is) brittle.

SHEATH: Refers to the type of sheath (carry method, if any) supplied with the knife.

All of these terms are important when choosing a survival knife. However, some are more important than others. If the knife was manufactured by a *reputable* knife maker, it'll have the proper RC and will do what it was designed to do. Aesthetics aside, (which are meaningless when choosing a survival knife) you should determine what function(s) you expect the knife to perform. If you intend to fillet fish with an expensive fixed blade survival knife you can do that. But that big survival knife won't do the job well because it wasn't designed to fillet fish. A much better choice would be an inexpensive fillet knife. The topic of how to choose the right survival knife will be covered in more detail later on.

Blade steel

Knowing what type of "chores" you're going to use your knife for, and the environment you'll be using it in, is the first step in determining what type of steel the blade should have. One type of knife blade won't excel at every conceivable chore. That's not to say the steel in a blade designed for use in a salt-water environment, for example, won't work anywhere else. It will. Simply put, different types of steel are better suited for different types of chores. Manufacturers select the type of steel for a blade based on the following steel characteristics:

Hardness (the ease in which the steel can be hardened)
Strength
Ductility (flex)
Toughness
Initial sharpness
Edge retention
Corrosion resistance
Wear resistance

and last, but by no means least, *manufacturability* (the ease in which the steel can be made into a knife and the price range the knife will be marketed in.)

Once a steel is selected, alloys are added to the steel to achieve the proper characteristics.

Commonly used non-stainless steels

10 SERIES STEEL: 10 series steel is any steel that begins with 10. The most popular 10 series steel is 1055 carbon steel. It's a simple steel but performs well. 10 series steel goes in order from 1095 to 1050 (from the most wear resistant to the least, and from tough to toughest.) In other words, 1050 steel wears better and is tougher than 1095 steel.

1095 HIGH CARBON TOOL STEEL: This 10 series steel (not the same as 1095 steel) hones to an incredible edge and retains that edge much better than other 10 series steels. It's also easier to sharpen than most stainless steels. The big drawback to 1095 High Carbon Steel is that it'll discolor over time, and it's susceptible to rust. Oiling the blade will help keep the rust and discoloration to a minimum. It's worth noting, however, that neither the discoloration, nor a bit of rust will affect the performance of the blade.

A2 STEEL: A2 steel is tough and abrasion resistant. It also holds an edge well.

D2 STEEL: D2 steel is sometimes referred to as semi-stainless. It's more stain and rust resistant than A2 or 10 series steel and has excellent wear resistance. D2 is also much tougher than premium stainless steel, but not as tough as many of the other non-stainless steels. D2 steel offers a combination of excellent wear resistance, almost stainlessness, and good toughness.

5160 STEEL: This steel is used in bigger blades requiring more toughness. It has good wear resistance, is especially tough, and performs well over a wide range of hardness's.

Commonly used STAINLESS steel

420 STAINLESS: A knife blade made from 420 stainless steel is a poor choice for a survival knife. 420 stainless is soft and doesn't hold an edge well. However, it's extremely stain resistant and thus is often used

for diving knives. It's also (normally) the steel used in those spectacular $14.95 survival knives.

420HS STAINLESS: Not to be confused with 420 stainless! 420HS stainless is an excellent knife blade steel. It displays excellent rust resistant characteristics, is easy to re-sharpen, and has good edge retention. It's roughly comparable to 440 stainless steel.

440A-440B-440C STAINLESS: The 440 series of stainless steel is probably the most popular blade steel in use today. 440C is an excellent *high end* stainless steel and is usually hardened to 56-58RC. 440C is also tough and has good edge holding characteristics. 440A stainless is the cheapest of the 440 series and, while all three 440 stainless steels resist rust, 440A is the most rust resistant, while the more expensive 440C is the least rust resistant. Generally speaking, 440A is good enough for everyday use, 440B is a solid all around performer, and 440C should be considered an excellent high end choice.

AUS-6, AUS-8, AUS-10 STAINLESS: Also known as 6A, 8A and 10A, these Japanese steels are roughly comparable to the 440 series of stainless steel. The difference is the addition of vanadium to the AUS stainless. Vanadium improves wear resistance, increases toughness, and enhances the ability of the blade to retain a keen edge. AUS-6 is the lower end steel, AUS-8 is in the middle tier, and AUS-10 is a high end stainless steel and competes with ATS-34 and 154-CM.

ATS-34 & 154-CM STAINLESS: These are both high-end stainless steels and are normally hardened to RC60. Both steels hold their edge well and also display good toughness even at that level of hardness. Both are rust resistant, but neither is as rust resistant as the 400 series of stainless steels.

VG-10 STAINLESS: This high end stainless steel contains Vanadium. Due to the Vanadium content, VG-10 stainless steel takes and holds a killer edge. It's also tougher and more rust resistant than ATS-34.

BG-42 STAINLESS: This stainless steel is similar to ATS-34 except BG-42 holds a significantly better edge and has more toughness.

S30V STAINLESS: This is an excellent all around stainless steel with outstanding edge retention properties.

There are other knife blade steels in use, but these are the most popular. As you can see, there's a lot more to a knife blade than meets the eye. While your choice of blade steel is important, you should be aware a knife blade made from one of the high end steels is going to cost more (maybe a lot more) than a blade made from a lesser steel.

Blade and point types

Knife blades and point types are designed for a specific purpose. An example would be a skinning knife. A skinning knife has a blade shaped to facilitate the removal of skin from an animal. Because the knife has the title of skinning knife doesn't mean it can't be used for anything else. It simply means the primary function of a skinning knife is to allow the user to skin animals easier than by using a knife designed for stabbing.

The marketing techniques used to sell a knife are no different than those used to sell anything else. The success of a product usually depends on how effective it was marketed. There are a lot of knives being advertised (marketed) using the word *tactical.* While there certainly are knives specifically designed as tactical knives, the majority of knives marketed as tactical knives are simply general purpose knives dressed in black. Which is okay I suppose. I mean, after all, who wants a hunting knife with a satin finish when, for a few bucks more, you can have the exact same knife with a sinister black coating on the blade and the catchy title of tactical. Actually the black coated blade on a tactical knife does have a function beyond looks. More on that later.

Blade shapes

DROP POINT: This is one of the most popular and versatile blade shapes in use today. A drop point blade has a strong tip and allows for good control when using the knife. It's good for all kinds of cutting activities and is especially useful for slicing.

CLIP POINT: A clip point blade is the most commonly used blade shape. Picture the tip of a spear. Now picture a "bite," or "clip," cut out of the top part of the spear point. Or picture the point on a traditional Bowie Knife. A clip point blade isn't as useful as a drop point blade for a survival knife since you can't abuse the tip. There are clip point blades that have a shorter and straighter clip which creates a cross, or hybrid, between a clip point and a drop point.

SPEAR POINT: The name spear point is self explanatory. The point, or tip, of the blade, has the same shape on the bottom as it does on the top. The spear point is designed for general cutting. While not as useful as a drop point, the spear point is arguably more useful than a clip point blade since the tip is stronger.

TANTO POINT: The Tanto style blade is inspired by traditional Japanese blade designs. Tanto blades have a strong point, making them extremely useful for heavy duty stabbing, for piercing hard materials, and for prying. There are several variations to the Tanto blade. Some are clipped or semi-clipped, while others are semi-dropped. The Tanto style blade is an excellent choice for a survival knife blade.

There are other blade styles such as *Skinner*, *Trailing Point*, *Straight Point*, *Spey*, *Hawkbill*, *Coping*, *Wharncliff*, *Dagger*, *Scimitar*, *Sheepsfoot*, and *Ulu*, but none are equal or superior to the Tanto or drop point blade for a survival knife.

Blade types

Blade types are different than blade styles. A blade type is the cutting edge style of the blade. Generally speaking, there are four different types of edges commonly used on today's knives.

SINGLE EDGE: Most knives sold today are single edge blades. A single edge blade means the bottom of the knife blade is sharpened, while the top portion of the blade is thicker and is not sharpened. When you picture a knife blade, you're undoubtedly thinking about a single edge blade.

DOUBLE EDGE: Refers to a knife blade that's equally sharp on the bottom as well as on the top. The double edge blade is normally used on daggers etc. Using a double edge knife as your only survival knife isn't a good idea.

PLAIN or STRAIGHT EDGE: Normally refers to a single edge knife blade without serrations or "teeth" on the cutting edge of the blade.

SERRATED or PARTIALLY SERRATED EDGE: Refers to the cutting edge of a knife blade that has serrations or "teeth" cut into the blade. The serrations can be a small section toward the back of the blade, or in some instances can encompass half of the blade. Serrated blades come in handy for sawing through tough material, but they don't cut thin material well at all. The blade serrations tend to snag on materials like paper, fishing line, etc. and they have a tendency to tear or rip instead of cutting them. Be that as it may, a serrated blade can be very useful on a large survival knife. Just remember not to use the serrations for cutting paper, fishing line, or other thin material.

Serrations on a small knife blade, in my opinion, are virtually worthless since the serrations take up too much of an already short blade thus limiting your ability to use the entire length of the blade for the chores you normally associate with a short blade knife.

Typical knife blade grinds

A knife blade grind is the type of edge on the blade of the knife, axe, machete, etc.

HOLLOW GROUND: This is the most common grind used on mass produced, factory knives.

The chances are good your knife blade is hollow ground. The hollow grind produces a sharp edge, but because it's so thin, the edge is more prone to rolling or damage than other grinds. It's not suited for heavy chopping or cutting hard materials, and because of the concavity of the blade, it can be difficult to maintain the bevel when sharpening.

FLAT GROUND: Flat ground blades taper all the way from the bottom edge of the blade to the top (spine) on both sides. Because a lot of material is removed in the process, the blade sacrifices edge durability for one of sharpness. This grind is the easiest to sharpen.

SABRE GROUND: Similar to the flat grind except the bevel starts at about the middle of the blade, not the top. The saber grind produces a more lasting edge at the expense of some cutting ability.

CHISEL GROUND: The chisel grind, or single bevel, is generally found on Japanese culinary knives and can be ground for left or right-handed use

DOUBLE BEVEL: Also referred to as a *compound bevel*, it's similar to a saber or flat grind, but the bevel is put on the blade *behind* the edge bevel or cutting surface. This back bevel keeps the section of blade behind the edge thinner, which improves cutting ability. Because it has a less acute angle than a single bevel, sharpness is sacrificed for resilience. This type of grind is much less prone to chipping or rolling than a single bevel blade. Double bevels are common in a wide variety of edge angles as well as back bevel angles.

CONVEX GROUND: The taper of the convex ground blade is curved, but in the opposite direction of a hollow grind. This type of grind keeps a lot of metal on the blade making for a strong edge while still allowing a good degree of sharpness. This grind is often used on axes, and, in fact, is sometimes referred to as an axe grind. Convex ground blades usually require thicker stock than other blades using other grinds. In addition, this grind requires a fair amount of skill to reproduce the edge when sharpening with a flat sharpening stone.

It's possible to combine varieties of grinds. Some blades, for example, might be flat ground for part of the blade but convex ground towards the edge. If you want to maintain the edge your knife came with, it's helpful to know what type of grind the blade was manufactured with. And by the way, there are few factory knives that are actually sharp out of the box. Your mass-produced knife will almost certainly have to be sharpened. If you don't know the grind, you can't know the angle, and if you don't sharpen your new knife at the correct angle, you'll not only end up changing the angle, you'll end up changing the grind, thereby changing what the knife can or cannot do effectively.

Blade finishes

A finish isn't the same as a coating. A blade finish is the final polish of the blade and is accomplished by repeated sanding with ever finer grit sandpaper to produce the desired finish. Finishes are usually high gloss (which isn't the recommended finish for a survival knife) or satin, which produces a subdued gloss. Another finish which has recently gained popularity is the bead blast finish. Bead blasting consists of small glass beads sprayed onto the steel under high pressure to produce a matte finish to reduce glare.

Blade coatings

There are four coatings which are consistently used on knife blades. Although a coating can be produced in any color, the vast majority of knife blade color coatings are black. A black coating on the blade eliminates glare and coincides with the public's love affair with all things tactical. A black knife just looks, well, . . . bad.

POWDER COAT: Powder coating has been around for a long time. It offers corrosion protection. looks nice, and reduces glare. Powder coating is probably the least effective method of coating a knife blade.

ZINC OXIDE COATING: This type of coating provides good corrosion and weathering protection, and also provides increased protection against salt water and solvents.

TEFLON COATING: A popular and effective coating for knife blades. Teflon offers good protection against corrosion, looks great, reduces glare, and makes cleaning the blade a snap.

TINI COATING: Titanium nitrate is an *extremely hard ceramic* material and actually improves the blade's surface properties. It's alleged the coating can actually help hold a knife's edge. Whether that's true or not, TINI is definitely an exceptional coating for a knife blade, particularly for tactical, military or survival knives.

Knife handle materials

Is the material used in the construction of the knife handle really important? Absolutely.

Knife handles have been made using just about every type of material imaginable. A good modern knife is handle-specific (requiring a specific shape and type of handle material) to perform efficiently. The modern knife handle should be tough, won't rot, check, or crack. In addition, it should be virtually indestructible, comfortable, non-slip (even when wet or bloody,) and shouldn't get too hot nor too cold when gripped with the naked hand. The handle should also "give" just a fraction when gripped, and it should be ergonomically adaptable to fit a wide variety of hand sizes. That's a pretty tall order, wouldn't you say? Believe it or not, there are materials used in the construction of knife handles that meet all, or at least most, of those criteria.

While some people will prefer knife handles made from black or white mother of pearl, stag, bone, wood, ivory, or old woodpecker bills, the majority of us will want our survival knife handle to be made from one of the following materials.

KRATON: Kraton is made by Kraton Polymers and is a synthetic rubber which offers many of the properties of natural rubber, such as flexibility, high traction, and sealing abilities, but with increased resistance to heat, weathering, and chemicals. Kraton is an *excellent* material for a survival knife handle.

CARBON FIBER: Carbon fiber knife handles are composed of thin strands of carbon fiber woven tightly together in a weave pattern and set in resin. Carbon fiber is probably the strongest material currently used in knife handle construction. It's an excellent knife handle material, but it's labor intensive, which increases the cost of the knife dramatically.

G-10: G-10 is a fiberglass based laminate. Layers of fiberglass cloth are soaked in resin, compressed and then baked. The result is a hard, lightweight and strong knife handle. Surface checkering, or texture, is then added. G-10 is an ideal material for a fixed blade or tactical folder because it's durable and lightweight.

MICARTA: Micarta is similar in construction to G-10 except the material is usually linen instead of fiberglass. Micarta handles have no surface texture and are extremely smooth. Micarta handles also require a lot of manual labor to produce which translates into a higher priced knife. Nevertheless, Micarta is a popular knife handle material. In addition to being tough and stable, Micarta is impervious to water, can be gripped when wet, and is an excellent insulator.

TITANIUM: Titanium is harder but lighter than steel and provides the knife handle with the toughness and durability of a metal handle without as much weight. Titanium also offers the most corrosion resistance of any metal. It has a good feel and is an excellent knife handle material.

STAINLESS STEEL: Stainless steel offers the same durability and corrosion resistance as a stainless knife blade. The biggest drawback is the increased weight of the knife. Stainless steel knife handles usually have another material such as Kraton, rubber, etc. as an insert in the handle to facilitate the grip and to reduce weight.

ALUMINUM: The aluminum used in a knife handle is actually durable and provides a solid feel without the extra weight. In addition, aluminum can be formed into shapes which allow a comfortable grip. Most aluminum handled knives are anodized to add color and protection.

ZYTEL: Zytel is a thermoplastic nylon material developed by DuPont. Zytel is an excellent material for everyday knife handles since it's virtually unbreakable and is abrasion-resistant. To improve grip, the handle is usually given some sort of surface texture. Zytel is also one of the least expensive of the synthetic handle materials to produce, which means the cost of the knife could be less.

ABS PLASTIC: This material is usually reserved for cheaper, everyday knives. It's a decent handle material since it's extremely tough.

Other materials such as leather are nice to look at, but leather-handled knives should be epoxy coated since leather isn't nearly as durable as the other handle materials available.

Locking mechanisms

Locking mechanisms apply to folding knives. There are four basic types of folding lock mechanisms, and although different companies refer to their locking mechanisms by different names, they're all a form of one of the following.

SLIP JOINT: The slip joint is used almost exclusively for traditional pocket knives. The opened blade doesn't actually "lock" open, but is held in place by a spring device which allows the blade to fold if a certain amount of pressure is applied.

LOCKBACK: A lock-back is a type of folding knife where the blade "locks" in the open position. When opened, a locking folder provides much of the confidence derived from using a fixed blade knife, yet enables the operator to fold the blade for safety and carrying convenience. Opening the blade causes a rocking lock plate, visible on the back of the handle, to lock against the blade as the blade is locked into the open position. Pushing down on the rocker at the back of the handle releases it and enables the blade to be closed. Lock-backs require two-handed closing, although there are a few that can be closed using one hand.

LINER LOCK: The liner lock is one of the most common locking mechanisms used on today's folding knives, especially tactical folders. The main advantage of a liner lock is that it allows the lock to be disengaged with one hand. It consists of a liner that's bent so that when the blade opens, the bent liner presses against the rear of the tang (that portion of the blade that connects to the handle), preventing it from swinging back. To disengage the lock, the liner is pressed to the side of the knife and the blade can then be folded back into the handle. The liner lock is the easiest of the locking mechanisms to use and can be opened quickly and with a minimum of movement.

FRAME LOCK: A frame lock operates like a liner lock, only the lock's a tensioned part of the handle frame with an open channel. When the blade opens, the frame lock moves into the handle opening and locks against the frame. Pushing the lock to the left releases it from the locked position so the blade can be closed.

Carry methods

There're many different ways to carry a knife. A pocket knife, of course, can be carried in your pocket. Some folding knives can also be carried in a pocket, although most are carried in a belt holster. If the knife has a lanyard hole in the handle, a lanyard (cord) can then be attached to the knife, and it can be carried around the neck, or anywhere else you choose to attach it. A sheath will allow the knife to be carried almost anywhere, including the inside of a boot (boot knives). A fixed blade knife is almost always carried in a sheath, which protects the blade, allows for easy access, and helps secure the knife against loss. Sheaths will allow you to carry the knife tip up, tip down, sideways etc.

How you decide to carry your knife is an important consideration. Since your survival knife is (again) arguably the most important of all your survival tools, you'll want to protect it and ensure it against loss. Therefore, the type of sheath you use is almost as important as the knife itself. A cheap sheath with a snap that breaks, causing you to lose your most important survival tool, would create a huge hardship for you.

The bottom line? If you didn't scrimp on a knife, don't start now by using a cheap sheath. Most good knives come with an equally good sheath, but not all. Here's the lowdown on the different types of sheaths as well as their pros and cons.

NYLON SHEATHS: Nylon sheaths, whether made from *Cordura* or *Ballistic* nylon, are excellent and inexpensive methods of carrying a knife. Nylon sheaths are tough, strong, rot and mildew resistant, and aren't affected by water. They're also scuff and tear resistant, and they're relatively quiet. Nylon sheaths will stretch a bit over time, which means, sometime in the future, your knife may not fit as snuggly as it did when the sheath was new.

LEATHER SHEATHS: Leather sheaths are tough and strong. They aren't impervious to water, although they can be treated to be water repellent to a degree. Like nylon, a leather sheath will stretch a bit over time. Additionally, leather will scuff, cut, and stain, and the stitches can tear out, which won't affect the function of the sheath at all since it can be re-sewn and the stains etc are irrelevant. The nicest thing about a leather sheath is, they're silent, and although irrelevant, they take on character over the years.

PLASTIC SHEATHS: Unless the knife in question is a fillet knife, forgetaboutit!

KYDEX SHEATHS: Kydex is a high performance thermoplastic that's unaffected by water, blood, and most chemicals, including skin acids. Kydex holds its shape and will not stretch or shrink under normal conditions. It's hard, with a Rockwall hardness rating of 90. Even though a Kydex sheath is all the rage right now, they're not perfect. A good one, and I want to emphasize the word *good*, can be superb under certain conditions.

But don't let the marketing blitz fool you. A mediocre Kydex sheath can be nearly worthless. The cons to any Kydex sheath are: they're noisy. Simply withdrawing the knife from the sheath makes noise. Banging the sheath into a tree etc. makes even more noise. They're also not easy or comfortable to carry. If the sheath isn't of the highest quality, the knife usually fits too tight, or too loose in the sheath, both of which are a pain. In addition, Kydex will usually dull the edge of the knife every time you put the blade into or take it out of the sheath, since the sheath is much harder than the knife blade.

So taken as a whole, you might think a Kydex sheath is worthless, but providing the Kydex sheath you're going to use is of the highest quality, you'd be wrong. If it's of lesser quality, then you'd be right.

Regardless of what type sheath you ultimately select, remember that the sheath is only as good as the method used to secure the knife in the sheath. A sheath with a single snap over the butt of the knife isn't the best method available. This type of fastener can be unsnapped by a branch or brush and you can unknowingly lose the knife. Velcro is a much better method of securing the knife in the sheath, and a lanyard (loop) over the butt of the knife used in conjunction with Velcro is even better.

Ultimately, the choice of a survival knife comes down to a compromise. I've yet to find a knife that meets every criteria I'd prefer. Finding one that meets most of them isn't all that difficult to do. But since you should have more than one survival knife you can end up with two or three knives that will meet your requirements.

Remember, the survival knife will be your most important survival tool. Make that selection wisely, even if a good one (or two or three) will cost you more money than you imagined. Having the right survival knife in your possession will give you a *survival tool* that could definitely save your life.

Knife sharpening

Congratulations. You now have the *perfect* survival knife. If it's going to do you any good, it has to stay sharp all the time! If you don't know how to sharpen a knife, then you have to learn how. If not, you might as well lash that knife to a tree branch and use it as a spear. If it's dull and you can't sharpen it, it definitely won't work as a survival knife.

Sharpening a knife on a whetstone is kind of an art form. I can't tell you how many blades and arrowheads I destroyed when I was young learning how to sharpen them. In those days Al Gore had yet to invent the Internet, no one had ever heard of a diamond whetstone, and barbers stropped their straight razors on a leather strop. What did we use? Good old oil whetstones, which is what I still prefer today, probably because it's what I'm used to. Anyway, I suppose I looked pretty weird walking around with patches of hair missing here and there from the back of my hands and my forearms from constantly checking the sharpness of the blade. I eventually used the hair on my legs when the arm hair was gone, but that wasn't a big deal since no guy in his right mind would even think about wearing a pair of shorts back then.

Today, you can buy a sharpening system that takes all of the guesswork, mystique, and romance out of knife sharpening. A sharpening system will allow you to use the correct angle to sharpen any type of grind on almost any knife imaginable.

It would still be a good idea to learn how to sharpen a knife (or axe, or machete) the old fashioned way using a whetstone, or even a sharpening steel. But regardless of how you choose to do it, "just getter done, "as the man says.

Degrees of sharpness

Any of your knives can be sharpened to any of the following levels.

CHOPPING: For heavy duty tools like axes or perhaps machetes.

SLICING: A knife that will be used for slicing should be sharp enough to cut paper and for general usage.

SHAVING SHARP: A knife that's shaving sharp will shave most of the hair off your arm (or leg) in one stroke. Or it's sharp enough that you can (sort of) shave with it.

RAZOR SHARP: A blade that's razor sharp will shave all the hair off your arm in one stroke. You can definitely shave with a knife that's razor sharp.

Remember this. You can't fell a tree with a razor, nor shave with an axe. Both blades require different degrees of sharpness since they're expected to perform different functions. If you have more than one survival knife, (and you should have) you can delegate different chores to different knives and sharpen them accordingly.

Based on the type of usage, here are the recommended sharpening angles that correspond to the aforementioned degrees of sharpness.

30 DEGREES: A 30 degree sharpening angle will provide you with an adequate and durable edge. A blade sharpened at this angle is a good rule of thumb for all blades that will be used for general cutting. In addition, it's the preferred sharpening angle for axes.

24 DEGREES: This sharpening angle is for heavy duty chopping chores and for machetes.

22 DEGREES: Use this angle for pocket knives and small folding knives. If you want the knife to be sharper, use a 20 degree angle.

18 DEGREES: An 18 degree sharpening angle will produce an edge that's razor sharp. Definitely use this angle for fillet knives.

All about survival tents

Let's start with a definition of the word survival. According to the dictionary I use, survival is defined as: "the act of living or continuing longer than another person or thing" or "the continuation of life or existence." Since a tent is actually a shelter, a *survival tent* then translates into "*A shelter that will allow you to continue life or existance,*" or "*that will allow you to live longer than another person.*"

About fifteen years ago, I spent over a year camping throughout the United States and I pitched a tent in every environment and in every weather condition imaginable, from high elevation, primitive areas, to severe cold weather camping in the upper Midwest, to family style campgrounds and beach camping in Florida, and everything else in between. I camped in snowstorms, monsoon rains, desert heat, severe thunderstorms, high winds, you name it, I camped in it. (Okay, no hurricanes or tornadoes.) Don't ask me *why* I did it; I'm not sure myself. It doesn't matter. What does matter is the amount of information I gained about tents and tent camping via hands on use and experience. And boy did I learn a lot! I also went through several inferior tents before I found out what *actually* worked, and what was marketing BS.

Survival tent designs

There're a lot of tent types on the market today, but generally speaking there are only three tent designs, the A-frame, the dome, and the cabin. For the most part, every tent's a variation of those three designs.

All three tent designs are made in sizes ranging from single person tents, through large 8+ person tents. Additionally, most of the three tent designs can be purchased in either three or four season configurations.

A-FRAME TENTS: The A-frame tent design has been around a long time, and with good reason. They're effective, easy to pitch, and for the most part are inexpensive. The one drawback to an A-frame tent is the steeply angled sidewalls preclude using the entire space within the tent efficiently. Providing the tent is taunt, an A-frame will shed snow and they're reasonably stable in high winds.

CABIN TENTS: When you think of a large family tent, you're probably picturing a cabin tent. They're available in many configurations, and the good ones do what they're supposed to do. That is, they provide an enjoyable time for a family at the old campground. However, as a survival tent, most of the family style cabin tents on the market won't work very well, if at all. There are exceptions. Heavy canvas "outfitter" cabin tents are *exceptional* survival tents. The problem is they weigh more than my mother in law. A good one is also expensive. Setting up a cabin tent takes a lot more time than the other designs, and cabin tents require a significant amount of staking to maintain tautness and stability in high winds.

Most family cabin tents *don't* provide a full cover fly, which is a prerequisite for an effective survival tent. Depending upon where you live and the weather conditions you're likely to encounter, a three season cabin style tent can make an okay survival tent. Due to the high side walls, cabin style tents allow you to utilize the entire floor space of the tent. In addition, the big ones usually have a center height of six feet or more, allowing an adult to stand up-right.

DOME TENTS:

Dome tents come in many configurations, which include geodesic, and are the best tent design for a survival tent. They're also available as large family tents. The good ones allow you to use the entire interior of the tent, and readily shed rain and snow. The smaller dome tents are available with full-cover flies, offer vestibules for storing additional gear, for keeping wet or muddy clothing and footwear, and allow you to cook in inclement weather. They're easy to pitch, are stable (depending on the pole configuration used,) and even the larger ones are relatively light.

Survival tent sizes

Tent manufacturers are either small people or they've never slept or camped in a tent, especially one of their own. If a tent is designated a four person tent I assure you, you won't be comfortable sharing that tent with your wife, and Uncle Buck and his girlfriend, unless you *really* like each other a lot.

Why do tent manufacturers over-rate the number of people their tents can sleep? It's called marketing. Ideally, your survival tent will not only (comfortably) sleep the required number of people (horizontally,) it should allow you to keep your gear in it as well. You're also going to be using your tent during the daytime for various survival chores, for cooking and eating, and you'll likely be spending extra time in it during periods of extended inclement weather. If you have four people, and we'll simply say four adults, you won't be happy with a four person tent. It's just too small. Go at least one size bigger. Two sizes if you can carry the extra weight. A four person tent for two adults and two small children will work okay.

When deciding how big your survival tent should be, take into consideration not only how many people will be using the tent, but also how big those people are.

If you intend to use the tent as a temporary shelter to get from point A to point B, or for a short time period, then "cramming" might not be a factor. If you're with a group that has a big base-camp tent for daytime activities and you're only using your tent to sleep in and to store your personal gear, then a smaller survival tent *might* be okay for four adults, depending on their size.

In short, before you can decide what size tent to buy, you have to attempt to define how you plan to use it, how many people will be using it, how big those people are, and perhaps where you'll be using it.

To decide what size tent to buy, try this. Let's say you need a tent that'll shelter two adults and two children, and you intend to use the tent for the duration of the survival event, or until you can secure a suitable permanent shelter. You're considering a quality four person dome tent with a floor size of 6' x 8'.

Using masking tape or something similar, mark off a spot on your carpet measuring 5'-6" x 7'-6" to represent the floor of the tent.

The 6" differential is compensation for a tent that doesn't have vertical sidewalls, and/or to allow a buffer zone to keep gear, including sleeping bags, from touching the interior walls of the tent. (More on that later.) Place your packed bug-out bag(s), as well as whatever firearms, etc. you'll be carrying inside the marked off area. If you don't have packed bug-out bags, use several small suitcases or whatever else might approximate the size of a fully loaded backpack. Now put down your pads and bags and everyone grab a bunk. . . . Oh, oh! And bear in mind, that's allowing a 6" buffer. A 12" buffer would probably be more appropriate.

You'll now have a good idea of what size tent you're going to need.

Survival tent use ratings

Tent use ratings are based on an average and are designated as three season or four season use, which means a three season tent (on average) can be used for everything except winter camping, and a four season tent can be used for (most) winter camping. The differences between the two are usually the number of poles used to support the weight of snow, to provide additional stability in higher winds, perhaps a heavier weight tent fabric for the four season tent, or the way in which the tent is sewn together.

However, the area you live in or where you intend to use your survival tent has a lot to do with your seasonal choice. If you live in south Florida, you don't need a four season tent, but at the same time choosing one won't be a drawback. By the same token, a quality three season tent may work reasonably well as a winter tent, providing the winter weather you'll encounter isn't extreme, and if precautions are taken to remove snow from the fly.

In a nutshell, all quality four season tents will work as three season tents, and some quality three season tents will work as a four season tent. It all depends upon where you live and the weather conditions you're likely to encounter. A good four season tent can cost substantially more than a good three season tent.

Construction materials

The construction materials list used in the manufacture of today's tents might as well be written in an alien language. 75D this, 210D that, 185T, poly taffeta, Oxford cloth, aircraft aluminum, 7000 series aluminum, DAC aluminum, rip-stop, polyurethane etc. And the sizes (of course) use the metric system.

What do those terms mean? Are they relevant? If the tent in question is made by a reputable manufacturer, the short answer is no. The information is basically irrelevant. None of those terms mean much in the grand scheme of things. It comes down to whether the manufacturer has a good reputation and won't jeopardize that reputation by using inferior products in the construction of the tent.

For those of you who just have to know what some of those hieroglyphics mean, here's a simplified explanation of the most relevant ones.

DENIER: Most tents, as well as other products made from nylon, have sub-categories, like taffeta etc. The fabric description for a tent will be something like 75D. The D after the number is a denier, which is a *weight per unit length measurement*. A women's pair of nylons is about 10 denier, which in English translates into, the lower the number, the finer the material. The higher the number, the courser (and therefore tougher) the material will be. Therefore, a tent made from 75D nylon, is tougher than a 10D pair of women's nylons. A tent fabric made from 100D nylon would be tougher than the same tent constructed of 75D nylon.

185T: When you see a number like this, the T after the number is the diameter of the thread used when sewing the tent together.

AIRCRAFT ALUMINUM: There's no such thing as aircraft aluminum. Different types of aluminum are used in aircraft, which means that any aluminum used in the construction of an aircraft is, by definition, aircraft aluminum. It's a marketing term. However, any tent stating the poles of the tent are constructed from aircraft aluminum, 7000 series, 6061 etc. is undoubtedly a good grade of aluminum.

RIPSTOP: Is a term denoting an extra stitch taken every 1/4" to prevent the stitch from unraveling and causing the tent to tear or rip.

POLYURETHANE COATING: Is a type of plastic put on nylon to make it waterproof.

How to select a survival tent

Selecting a survival tent isn't quite the same as picking a tent that will be used for an occasional camping trip into the woods, your back yard, or at the local campground.

While the requisites for a recreational tent and a survival tent are similar, there's no margin for error when choosing the survival tent. If you're involved in a survival situation, you can't pack up and go home because your tent leaks, is too small, isn't stable, or for any other reason your tent "isn't." Therefore, it's imperative an informed decision is made prior to purchasing a tent that you'll to be depending on for adequate shelter and protection during a survival situation.

Before we take a look at the features the survival tent should have, you should be aware there are a lot of tents on the market masquerading as survival tents.

Since the term *survival* is simply a name, who determines what constitutes a survival tent? Is a $500 survival tent that much better than a $300 survival tent of the same size? That's a good question, and I'll answer it this way. If you compare the features, construction materials, and methods used in the construction of the two tents and they're identical, or even close, then someone is making a hell of a lot of money; or not enough, as the case may be. However, the difference between the $100 tent and the $300 tent is probably the difference between night and day.

Do you really think a manufacturer can create, market, store, ship and sell a quality survival tent for $100 that will compare favorably to the features and quality in the same size $300 tent? As a general rule, the answer is a resounding no! As most of you know, you get what you pay for, and that statement is especially accurate when it comes to tents. Is the difference between the two tents worth $200?

That depends. While the $100 tent may work well in calm, clear, warm weather, and may be durable enough to withstand some degree of abuse, (which is going to happen to any tent regardless of the price, or your efforts to prevent it,) the real question is, will it be able to withstand (perhaps) daily pitching, packing and unpacking, severe thunderstorms with high winds, monsoon rains, hail, wet heavy snow, and other severe weather events? Can it be zipped and unzipped thousands of times, and will the guy loops hold up? Is the floor tough enough to withstand constant abuse and foot traffic? Will the poles hold up or break?

The list goes on. I don't know about you, but if I'm betting my life on the effectiveness of a survival tent, my money's going to be on the $300 tent every time. In the end, however, it's the consumer who decides what constitutes a survival tent.

By the way, (depending on the size) you don't have to spend $300 to find a good survival tent. But, since a survival tent may end up as one of your more important survival purchases, you should buy the best survival tent you can afford.

These are the features to look for when selecting a survival tent.

FREE STANDING: Free standing means you can set the tent up (in your living room if you like) and it will stand by itself without stakes or guy-lines. A free standing tent will allow you (with some assistance) to pick-up the erected tent and move it to another location without taking it down. After you've moved the tent, it can be re-staked and re-guyed. Free standing tents aren't generally practical in tents over four or five person sizes.

TENT POLES: While a survival tent with fiberglass poles works just fine, fiberglass poles aren't as effective as aluminum poles for a couple of reasons. Fiberglass poles are more fragile than aluminum and are much more likely to break. In addition, they weigh quite a bit more. An aluminum pole may bend or even break, but they're much stronger than fiberglass and can be re-bent or repaired (to a degree) in the field. In addition, aluminum poles will decrease the overall weight of the tent. Aluminum poles are generally attached to the tent by a series of clips, while most fiberglass poles slide thru a series of sleeves. Pole attachment points *must* be sewn onto the tent, not glued or taped on.

SHOCK-CORDED POLES: Shock-corded poles are aluminum poles that have elastic cords running through them that bind them together as a foldable-unit. Shock-corded poles allow the packed tent to be compact and allows for simple, fast set-up.

FULL COVER RAIN-FLY: A survival tent is only going to be as good as the rain-fly that protects it. Avoid tents that have a 1/2 cover rain-fly or have a rain-fly cap over the very top of the tent. They're worthless.

A full cover waterproof rain-fly will protect every inch of the tent, giving it complete protection from rain. Consider a full-cover rain-fly to be an absolute necessity for a survival tent.

TUB "STYLE" FLOOR: A tub floor means the floor extends four inches or more up the sidewalls of the tent. Make sure the tent floor material is made from oxford cloth or similar tough material and that it's *waterproof.* (Not water-repellent.)

RIPSTOP NYLON WITH DOUBLE STITCHING AND FOLDED SEAMS: Rip-stop nylon has an extra stitch every quarter inch so the material can't rip. Double-stitching creates a much stronger and more leak-proof tent. The seams should overlap and be factory taped.

GUY LINES: If the tent you're looking at has guy line loops attached to the tent with glue, or tape, pass. The loops *must* be sewn onto the tent. In addition, make certain there are enough loops on both the tent and the fly to adequately stake-out the tent and to keep it taunt. Depending on the size of the tent there should be one or more loops on the sides, one on each corner, and perhaps one at the front and back.

STAKE-OUT LOOPS: Stake-out loops take a lot of abuse. They have to be heavy-duty and large enough to accept the head of a large metal stake. Stake-out loops that are taped or glued onto the tent won't last long. Make certain the stake-out loops are also sewn onto the tent.

ADEQUATE VENTING: In addition to the door(s) and window(s) there has to be at least one vent inside the tent, preferably a large one in the roof. If the tent's large, there should be additional vents. Adequate air-flow and venting is necessary to avoid condensation inside the tent. A tent with inadequate air-flow isn't a comfortable tent to sleep in, and waking up to discover everything in the tent's damp and clammy isn't a fun way to start the day.

NETTING: All windows, doors, and vents have to be covered with *no-see-um* netting, not mosquito netting. This is an *absolute requirement*. If the tent has mosquito netting, pass.

ZIPPERS: Zippers should be self repairing, 2-way heavy-duty nylon. The preferred size is #10 for the doors and windows. Minimum size should be #8.

VESTIBULES: A vestibule is not an absolute necessity for a survival tent, but, boy, do they make a difference. An attached vestibule(s) will allow you to store some (or all) of your gear, muddy footwear, wet clothing, and depending on the configuration, will allow you to cook in inclement weather. Some vestibules can also be used (in fair weather) as a screen room or for additional sleeping space. A vestibule may, or may not, have an attached floor. Some tents have vestibules at both the front and the rear.

DOORS AND WINDOWS: Depending on the size of the tent, there should be a front and a rear entry with at least one window on each side. As mentioned earlier, the zippers should be heavy duty and self-repairing 2-way, (meaning you can zip them up or down) and there should be a storm flap covering them. Door zippers are used a lot, so pay particular attention to the zipper on the door.

TENT FABRIC: Almost every reputable tent manufacture will use a tent fabric of the proper quality that allows air to flow through the fabric. The tent fabric itself may also be water-repellent, not waterproof. The large, cheap family-style tents sold at discount stores won't provide adequate protection from rain, especially if that rain is wind-driven and is falling anything other than vertically. Rain *will* get inside those tents! It's that simple.

As mentioned earlier, the fly provides the waterproofing necessary to keep the inside of the tent dry. There's a huge difference between a reputable manufacturer and a reputable retailer. While both are in business to make money, the reputable manufacturer of high quality tents generally doesn't make inferior, polyester-cotton blend, or water-repellent poplin tents with equally inferior tent hardware and features. For the most part, the tents sold at large discount stores (you know who they are) don't qualify as a survival tent. I've tried them; part of the learning process. Save your money.

COLOR: A tent that blends in with the environment, (IE: green, tan, etc.) makes it difficult for enemy eyes to see it, but it also makes it more difficult for you to locate the tent after a hard day's work in the woods. On the other hand, a dark colored tent is warmer in colder weather, while a lighter colored tent will be cooler in warmer weather. For the most part, tent color's a matter of personal preference.

PACKED WEIGHT AND PACKED SIZE: The advertised weight is normally the total packed weight of the tent and should include the weight of the stakes, guy-lines, and carry bag if all of them are included in the price, or it may just be the weight of the tent itself. If you're going to buy a tent for a bug-out bag, make sure you know exactly what the packed weight and the packed size of the tent is, to the ounce and to the half inch. The weight and size of the tent is a *very important* consideration if you're going to strap that tent to a backpack. Obviously, the lighter, the better. You may also decide a larger tent would be ideal for use as a base camp. If you have a way to carry it, a base camp tent is ideal for daytime activities, group meetings etc. and frees up smaller tents for use as sleeping quarters.

Tent selection pointers

1. Attempt to determine how you're going to use the tent, how many people will be using the tent, how big those people are, and under what conditions the tent might be used.
2. Make a list of the features you deem necessary.
3. Determine the size, and maximum weight of the survival tent you can carry and use.
4. Go shopping. You may have to make a compromise on some of the features, but the chances of finding a survival tent that meets, or even exceeds your criteria is actually pretty good.

One last thing. Depending upon where you purchase the tent, you'll almost certainly encounter the following:

FROM THE INTERNET: Most e-tailers use the tent write-up provided by the manufacturer. Those listings may lack some of the information you require. An e-mail or phone call might provide you with the information you seek. However, since you can't touch the tent, the only input you're going to receive is through that write-up, e-mail, or phone call. Good Internet retailers take the time to check the products out themselves, and, if necessary, do their own write-up. Unfortunately, the vast majority have zero product knowledge other than the description given on the website.

FROM A BRICK AND MORTAR STORE: The majority of sales people, and that includes the "tent expert" at the local sporting goods store, has probably never camped a day in his or her life. Yet in an effort to sell you something other than what you want, they're likely to tell you "that" doesn't really matter. But you now know "it" does matter. Arm yourself before you go in. Know exactly what you want, and ask questions. You'll know soon enough if the sales clerk knows what he/she is talking about. If they don't, you may want to shop elsewhere.

Using your survival tent effectively

Now that you know how to select a good survival tent, it's time for some tips on using it and what accessories you'll find useful.

Before you set up your survival tent for the first time, purchase a roll of seam tape, a tube or two of seam-seal, and a floor saver that fits your tent. If the tent came with plastic stakes, throw them away and buy some good steel or aluminum tent stakes.

As soon as you unpack your tent, check to ensure all the parts are enclosed and familiarize yourself with the instructions. A set-up area in the yard is preferable, but if necessary a free-standing tent can be set up in an area of your home. If outside, put down the floor saver and set up the tent. During set-up, check the ends of the pole sleeves (if any) for tears or frayed edges and check the clips and/or snaps to ensure they function properly. The initial set-up will probably take a bit longer, but once you're familiar with how to set-up a quality tent, you can erect it in a matter of minutes. Leave the fly off for now.

Even though the seams on most good tents are factory taped for waterproofing, you know how hard it is to find good help these days. Re-tape all of the seams in your tent. If the fly failed (for any reason) or if you had it off and a sudden storm cropped up, the needle holes created when the tent was sewn together will allow water to run into the tent. The tent itself, although water repellent, will leak like a sieve through those needle holes if they're not sealed. Seal the needle holes with seam-sealer. Seal them once on the inside of the seam, then again from the outside. Put the fly on the tent. If the fly has a seam, re-tape it.

Next, check the function of the zippers, ties, gear-lofts, windows, vestibules etc. Stake the tent and the fly down, or guy out as necessary. Make sure you inspect all of the loops for tears. Button the tent up.

Turn on the hose and soak the tent, using a setting that might approximate horizontal wind driven rain. Five to ten minutes should be sufficient. Inspect for leaks. There shouldn't be any water inside the tent. None, nada, zilch. If there is, find the source and seal it. Your tent is now operational and is as water-proof as it's ever going to be.

You should actually use the tent as soon as possible. You can simply leave it pitched and sleep in it that night or go on a short camping trip ASAP.

There's nothing like familiarity. When you become totally used to setting up your tent, you'll be able to pitch it quickly in the dark or in a rainstorm,

When re-packing the tent, make sure it's clean and, if at all possible, ensure it's totally dry, as in *not wet*! If you're unable to dry the tent completely prior to packing it, unpack it and dry it the first chance you get. Tents don't require a lot of maintenance. Just keep them clean, dry, and repair any areas that need to be repaired.

When you're actually using the tent, try not to let any of your gear touch the walls of the tent, which is a lot easier said than done. In high humidity, condensation will form where-ever item X and tent wall meet due to the temperature difference between the outside air, and the air inside the tent. Clammy is *not* good. If you're going afield during the day, *pile your gear in the center of the tent away from the tent walls.*

Some tent do's and don'ts

Do clean the area where you intend to pitch the tent. Remove as much brush, twigs, branches, rocks etc. as possible prior to putting down the floor saver. Always use a floor saver. It will protect the floor of the tent.

Do keep the *entire* floor saver under the floor of the tent. If the floor saver sticks out (even a little), rain will puddle between the floor saver and the floor of the tent. Not good.

Do inspect your survival tent periodically for rips, scuffs, and tears. Pay particular attention to the loops and the pole attachment points. Repair immediately, if necessary.

Do make up a small tent repair kit consisting of a sewing kit with heavy needles and heavy nylon thread, lighter thread, seam-seal, seam-tape, and a roll of duct tape. If a pole breaks, you can provide a quick fix by placing a brace between the break in the pole and wrapping the entire area with duct tape.

Don't pitch your tent under a tree that's sapping or that's a roost for birds.

Don't pitch your tent too close to a campfire. Don't smoke in the tent, and if you use candles, make sure they're in an enclosure such as a candle lantern.

There's no such thing as the perfect tent, which means there's no such thing as the perfect survival tent. But you can get close. A good survival tent in conjunction with a little common sense will take you a long way down survival road.

Build a medical kit

Go online and look at the prices being charged for so-called survival medical kits. It's appalling. Annoying, too. The supplies that make up those medical kits wouldn't provide adequate first aid for a Little League baseball team, let alone provide the necessary medical requirements for your family during a true national catastrophe. Not only that, but you're being charged about a buck for an inferior band-aid made in China.

You don't have to settle for the convenience of purchasing overpriced and inadequate medical supplies. You can build your own first class first aid medical kit and save a bundle in the process.

To begin with, let's ascertain what a survival medical kit should be able to do. Not as simple as it sounds actually, and like everything else, one man‘s medical kit is another man‘s basic first aid supply. The reason? Different people with different levels of expertise will want different items in their kit. A doctor, for example, will want a medical kit that can provide a higher level of care than a layman, simply because of the doctor‘s knowledge and skill. Regardless, the first order of business for a medical kit is to provide the basic requirements of first aid; i.e.: Treat scrapes, cuts, bruises, burns etc.

Unfortunately a medical kit, and more specifically a survival medical kit, seldom receives the attention it deserves.

"Let's see, some band-aids, couple of pads, some antibiotic ointment, a roll of tape and uhh, . . . some Tylenol. Yeah, that should do it!"

Man I know people who need those things after a night out. We're talking about a *survival medical kit* here, not a remedy for last night's festivities.

At any rate, to be effective, the medical kit has to be built upon a solid foundation. So before we begin selecting items let's answer some questions.

1. What's your particular level of medical skill and/or what are you willing to do to increase your knowledge?
2. What level of care do you want the medical kit to be able to provide?
3. How many people will the medical kit be supporting? What are their ages, and what is their general health?
4. Will the medical kit be used in a bug-out bag, or will it be packed for a permanent location? In other words, how big can the medical kit be?
5. Might the area in which you live, or where your safe area is located, require any special items such as a snake bite kit?
6. Do any members of your family (or group) require special medical care or are they likely to require specialized care or medication in the future?
7. This is the hardest part. How often will members of your family be injured and or require medical attention? How serious are those injuries likely to be, and/or how often are they likely to get sick?

The answer to question one could be anywhere from zero to brain surgeon, and from "the sight of blood makes me faint" to "whatever it takes, short of becoming a brain surgeon." By answering question one, we're simultaneously answering question two. Let's create three medical kit levels. You choose the one appropriate for you.

The answers to questions three, four, five and six, are all self-explanatory and will vary from person to person or group to group. Question seven can be answered this way.

Common sense will tell you that people who are unaccustomed to continuous hard work to survive, and who may have to walk miles every day under adverse conditions and over treacherous terrain are going to be injured *much more often* than when they were sitting around watching the boob-tube. The chores of cutting wood, pitching and un-pitching a tent, planting and tending a garden (and on, and on) is going to produce a slew of minor injuries in the form of blisters, scrapes, bumps, bruises, and cuts. In addition, you can pretty much count on pulled muscles, strains, sprains, and maybe broken bones with alarming frequency, at least initially.

As for illnesses, the situation will definitely open the door to a host of illnesses you seldom, if ever, had to concern yourself with BTC. (See Infectious diseases under National Natural Disasters)

Let's create three medical kit levels.

LEVEL 1 - Well beyond first aid (which doesn't take much) but that stops short of being able to treat critical injuries and illnesses. Includes simple diagnostic tools.

LEVEL 2 - A kit capable of treating all minor injuries and most major injuries and trauma, as well as some of the more common illnesses. Includes diagnostic as well as simple surgical tools.

LEVEL 3 - A kit capable of treating almost any major injury, including surgical procedures, most serious illnesses, and common dental procedures. Includes diagnostic and surgical tools.

Logic dictates we begin building the medical kit with the "bag." If the medical kit's going into a bug-out bag, the container(s) should be soft-sided, since a rigid container will make packing the bug-out bag more difficult and take up too much room. You might also decide to break the kit into sections to facilitate packing and to provide easy access to those items you're likely to use more frequently, such as band-aids.

Place the medical kit(s) in freezer bags or wrap them in plastic to ensure waterproofing. If the medical kit is being prepared for a permanent location, the container can be just about anything, but bear in mind you still need a medical kit for your safe-area bug-out bag.

The size of the medical kit will be determined by what you to put into it, thus the items you select from the "list" may have to be adjusted to accommodate the size of the container.

The following list won't include those specialized items or medications you or your family may currently require, or that you project may become necessary in the future. It also won't take into account your level of medical expertise. Finally, the quantities of any item will be determined by the amount of people the medical kit will be servicing.

Almost all of these items can be purchased at any good pharmacy. Some, such as a field surgical kit, may require shopping at a medical supply store or online. When purchasing diagnostic tools, stay away (if possible) from those requiring batteries. While they're convenient, they won't do you any good if (and when) the batteries die, or if the device gets wet or damaged.

The bottom line is, your medical kit will be vastly superior to a basic first aid kit and will probably be cheaper too.

The first item for your medical kit should be a good book on first aid. Remember, although you may have expertise and know a lot about treating injuries etc., you might not be in the picture. The medical kit will have to be able to be used by everyone, even those with zero knowledge. Therefore, books on first aid, surgical procedures, and information on how to treat illnesses are essential.

Bug-out bag medical kit list

Container
Medical books (including dental procedures)
Blood pressure cuff and stethoscope
Oral thermometer and anal thermometer (mouth injuries may preclude using an oral thermometer)
Scissors
Tweezers
Small field surgical kit with hemostats
Needles (several sizes)
Safety pins
Nail clippers
Eye patch
Surgical masks
Surgical gloves
Compression (Ace) bandage
Arm sling Strap
Hot water bottle
Matches or bic lighter (for sterilization of needles)
Tongue depressors
Cotton balls
Sterile eye wash
Disposable razor (shaving hair from around wounds)
Kling bandages
Sterile gauze dressings (several sizes)
Waterproof band-aids (several different sizes)
Plastic Band-aid sutures (two different sizes)
Surgical thread (sutures)

Surgical or medical tape
Isopropyl alcohol
Peroxide
Neosporin (or equivalent)
Vaseline
Q-tips (cotton swabs)
Pain and fever reducers (Ibuprofen, acetaminophen etc.)
Aspirin
Antacids
Antibiotics (Penicillin if nothing else)
Throat lozenges (or small jar of honey)
Toothache medication
Calamine lotion
Aloe
Other over-the-counter products as you deem necessary

For safe area locations, or if it will fit in your bug-out bag, you may wish to add.

Medical library
More of everything on the list
Otoscope
Several different types of splints
Advanced surgical kit
Anesthesia (Ether – – BE CAREFUL)
Various medications
Back up for diagnostic instruments
Snake bite venom kit

CHAPTER 16

WHEN THE SMOKE CLEARS

A CATASTROPHE OF THIS MAGNITUDE WILL be like a story. It'll have a beginning, a body, and an ending. This epic won't be any different from all of the others down through antiquity. It'll begin, it'll reach a peak, it'll begin to subside, and it'll end. Your goal is to navigate the obstacles and challenges that you'll be facing to emerge safe, sound, and secure when the smoke finally clears.

We have an idea of what might happen in the early stages ATC begins, and we can assume some sort of stability or routine will take place within a reasonable amount of time following the inception of the chaos. Defining the end, however, is likely to be considerably more difficult to figure out. When does the end arrive, and how will you be able to recognize it? What shape will it take?

From a standpoint of the status quo there may never be an end in our lifetime. Things will never be as they were before. They may be better, they may be worse, they'll definitely be different, but they'll never, ever be the same again.

I think you can define the "end" as a point in time when you no longer have to maintain a constant vigil, when you can think in terms of rebuilding, and of a future. It's not possible for us to determine how much time must pass to reach that point, except to say it'll probably be reached in different areas at different times and that there'll likely be occasional and temporary relapses. The actual timeline could be anything from months to a generation or even longer.

In addition, if the country splinters into a series of individual settlements, the likelihood of every governed locality adopting the same set of rules or laws is remote at best, which means resurrection of the nation may not occur for decades, if ever.

That's not a pretty picture, and, of course, it's one none of us want to see painted, but from a logical perspective, we'll all be better of preparing for a worst-case scenario and not have it happen than to stick our heads in the sand and suffer the consequences if it does.

How many potential endings are there to an event of this magnitude? A definitive answer to that question is difficult to determine too, but we can make an educated guess.

The end is likely to come down to good vs. evil, and good will win, which shouldn't really surprise anyone, since history tells us that's what happens every time. Good vs. evil is happening even as we speak, although most people prefer to call it something other than what it is.

The everyday citizens of America, you and I, have been uninvolved and have been sleeping on watch for too long, and it's our own fault the country's in the shape it's in. We've allowed those in the Federal Government to lead us down a pathway toward ruin because we've sat quietly by while an active left-wing liberal community and an increasingly moderate Republican Party has dictated to us what our country is going to be. We've trusted our elected officials to do the right thing, the honorable thing, the constitutionally correct thing, and to do what's best for the United States of America. It hasn't happened.

Although it appears a significant portion of the population is alert to what needs to be done and has gotten involved, it may be too late to stop the slide into the abyss. Unless something dramatic occurs to impede that slide, I believe we'll be facing that catastrophe, and be on our own in America, soon enough. It could be tomorrow, two years down the line, or even a decade from now. Regardless of the timeframe, the conditions in the United States can't remain where they are for any length of time without something catastrophic taking place. You don't have to be a Rhodes Scholar to figure that out.

The words of our Constitution, written by our Founding Fathers are, to many currently in power, not applicable to today's society, because the men who wrote that incredible document were little more than ignorant peasants, and the words of our Constitution miraculously don't mean now what they meant then.

If you're comfortable being a modern day ignorant serf, and no longer wish to live under the protective umbrella of the Constitution, by all means do nothing, see nothing, hear nothing, and say nothing.

The rest of us are getting ready to survive what may be coming our way.

LEGENDARY PHOENIX

The period following the *Black Winter* of 2012, when the United States Government collapsed, and the spring of 2016, when the new United States Government formed in Chicago, was a period of unparalleled chaos, and violence around the world. It was a time of war between good and evil, of absolute depression and of total anarchy.

The greatest civilization the world had ever known imploded due to the overwhelming size, weight, and ineptitude of its government. Like dominos, the rest of the world followed suit.

During that bleak three year period, Daniel Clark, the man referred to as the second Father of our Country, emerged to lead America and humanity back from the brink of extinction and re-established the United States to its position as the leader of the free world.

Daniel Clark was appointed acting President of the United States by the Coalition of Regional Governors in May of 2016. He served in that capacity until January 20, 2018, when Randal Robert took the oath as the 45th President of the United States.

Twenty years after his death in 2046, President Clark's daughter Jody discovered his personal journal, written during the Black Winter, in an old trunk, in the basement of his family home in Eagle River, WI.

The following are *selected excerpts* from that journal.

AUG 5, 2012

The dollar has collapsed. It's virtually worthless. Riots are breaking out everywhere. We're in bad shape, to say the least.

OCT 10, 2012

The situation here in the North Woods is bad but compared to some areas of the country we have it pretty easy. At least we have food, water, and an entire forest to burn to keep warm. I try to follow what's going on with the shortwave. To say things are bad would be an understatement.

NOV 15, 2012

That's it. The government collapsed. Washington and New York disappeared in nuclear fireballs. Damn terrorists! What in the hell have those morons in Congress been thinking the past few years.

NOV 19 2012

The entire world's gone nuts. Pakistan and India nuked each other, and Iran tried to take out Israel. The Israelis' blew them off the map. The entire world's at war, but it's not like a World War, it's just senseless violence. From what I can tell, there's anarchy nationwide. People are killing each other by the thousands for food. Even for a band-aid for crying out loud. Nothing from the National Guard or the Military.

DEC 20 2012

Almost Christmas. Gangs have pretty much taken over the country. Apparently the military has been disbanded. Not sure.

JAN 25 2013

Well at least 2012 didn't happen. Not that it matters much. Things have quieted down here in the North. Probably because of the cold. The Southern States are still full of violence. Lots of fallout hitting a lot of people, too. We've been lucky here. None yet.

JUNE 16 2013

Heard that some military units are functioning again, but don't know if it's true.

AUG 31 2013

It's been almost a year now. Looks as though the worst may be over. At least as far as the violence goes. Some military units are definitely operational in some areas, but it's all unofficial. As far as I can tell, the rest of the world is still in chaos. The entire Middle East ganged up on Israel. Not sure of the outcome there. Still lots of fallout circling the globe. Don't know why, but I keep wondering about Bill Chambers. He was a good man. Hope he and Heather and the two girls made it.

MAY 24 2014

Didn't really want it, but I was elected governor for this region. Whatever that means. Just make some sensible decisions, I suppose.

AUG 20 2015

Order of sorts has been restored to parts of the country. It's reasonably safe around here now. In fact, it's possible to go all the way to Milwaukee without too much trouble.

NOV 6 2015

Still pockets of violence around the country, but they're pretty isolated. Barter and trade are going bananas. It's almost like being transported back in time. The world situation is a lot better now, too. At least they're not bombing each other anymore. The Middle East is pretty much wiped out, but I think

Israel survived. With the exception of the nukes in DC and NYC, Europe has fared far worse than we have. Not too certain about China and the Far East, though. I know there were major riots taking place in China, and N. Korea nuked S. Korea and Japan.

NOV 25 2015

Thanksgiving already! I've had a lot of time to think about what went wrong and how this whole thing could have been averted. It would have been easy to do, too. All we had to do was to follow the blueprint of the Constitution to the letter. That's it. Simple as it sounds.

DEC 29 2015

China's still there, but they've apparently replaced their leaders with regular people. There's going to be a meeting of the Regional Governors in Chicago in a couple of weeks. I'm definitely going to go. I have something I want to say. Should be interesting.

The following are the final words of the speech given by Daniel Clark at the meeting of Regional Governors in Chicago, IL on Jan 19, 2016

"You can argue about the type of government we should adopt until the end of time. As far as I'm concerned there's nothing to discuss. I *insist* that the *only* form of government that can *ever* be considered for the rebuilding of this country be based upon the Constitution of the United States of America.

I also *demand* that from this day forward, the Constitution will be interpreted to mean *exactly* what it says, and that there will never again be an interpretation by anyone, at any time, that would conflict with the intent, nor distort the meaning of those words.

I will also remind each of you that the United States of America was never a democracy, it was, and is, a republic based on democratic principles. Furthermore, this once great country will, like the legendary Phoenix, rise from the ashes of her destruction.

When she does, it's imperative that every member of Congress, every member of state government, every local official, and every citizen of this Nation understand and affirm that this time around it will not, nor can it ever again be, we the Congress or I the President, but that it has always been, and will forevermore be , *WE THE PEOPLE, AND IN GOD WE TRUST!*

FINAL THOUGHTS

I hope this book has given you insight into what it might take to survive a major catastrophe, as well as what that catastrophe might consist of.

I also hope that after reading my thoughts and suggestions you can come up with some ideas that will work better for you than those I mentioned. No one's going to view every situation from the same perspective, apply the same type of logic, or respond in the same manner. Again, one size never has and never will fit all.

Do I truly believe something catastrophic is on the horizon? Unfortunately, considering the seemingly endless possibilities for something to go dramatically wrong, I think it's more likely to happen than not.

In any event, if the catastrophe does happen, I'm positive the plan I've developed will provide my family with an outstanding chance of surviving. I hope within a short period you'll have that same level of confidence.

GOOD LUCK!

APPENDIX

Recommended books

1. Square Foot Gardening by Mel Bartholomew
From Cool Springs Press or visit www.coolspringspress.net
ISBN 13-978-1-59186-202-4

2. Emergency War Surgery (A NATO handbook) by Desert Publications
ISBN 0-87947-410-6

3 Indian Crafts and Skills by David R. Montgomery
From Horizon Publishers
ISBN 0-88290-274-1

4 Survival Skills of the North American Indians by Peter Goodchild
ISBN 1556523459

5. Be Expert with Map & Compass by Bjorn Kjellstrom
ISBN 9780020292654

6. Eat the Weeds by Ben Charles Harris
ISBN 0879836261

7. Back to Basics (a Reader's Digest book)
ISBN 0-89677-086-5

8. Alaskan Sourdough Cooking from Arctic Circle Enterprises LLC
   Alaska Jacks 1-888-660-2257
   ISBN 12:978-1-56944-201-2

9 Putting Food By: Hertzberg, Greene & Vaughan
   ISBN: 9780452296220

10. Countryside Magazine & Small Livestock Journal
   www.countrysidemag.com
   (Not a book, but a monthly magazine. I highly recommend it)

There are so many excellent books on so many different subjects that it would be impossible to list them all. You could spend the next twenty years reading one a week and never scratch the surface. Make a list of the categories you want to check out, make your selections and visit the local library, bookstore, or Amazon.

Hard to locate items-seeds & e-tailers

Lehmans www.lehmans.com or call 1-888-438-5346 Lehmans sells turn of the century tools and supplies including hanging dehydrators, corn shellers etc. (You can even get a porcelain chamber pot)

Seed Savers Exchange www.Seedsavers.org

Survival Seed Bank www.survivalseedbank.com

Burpee Seeds www.burpee.com

The National Survival Center www.nationalsurvivalcenter.com Provides outstanding survival information, tips, techniques, and an explanation of why a certain product is required, how best to use it, and in most cases gives a product rating. The site also carries survival foods, genuine heirloom seeds, and outstanding survival products at excellent prices.

e-military manuals www.emilitarymanuals.com Offers the latest versions of every military manual in use today, including outstanding army survival manuals, as well as field surgery and medical manuals. Everything is available in both book and CD form.

CPSIA information can be obtained at www.ICGtesting.com
Printed in the USA
242586LV00001B/8/P